THE
HISTORY and CULTURE of ANCIENT WESTERN ASIA and EGYPT

A. Bernard Knapp

Department of Anthropology
University of Sydney

The Dorsey Press
Chicago, Illinois 60604

Cover Photo: The Granger Collection, N.Y.

© THE DORSEY PRESS, 1988

Acquisitions editor: *David Follmer*
Project editor: *Mary Lou Murphy*
Production manager: *Charles J. Hess*
Designer: *Michael Warrell*
Cartographer: *Mapping Specialists*
Compositor: *Carlisle Communications, Ltd.*
Typeface: *10/12 Palatino*
Printer: *R. R. Donnelley & Sons Company*

ISBN 0-256-05698 (hardbound)
ISBN 0-256-06217-X (paperbound)

Library of Congress Catalog Card No. 87–72399

Printed in the United States of America

1 2 3 4 5 6 7 8 9 0 DO 5 4 3 2 1 0 9 8

To the memory of Professors T. T. Duke and Robert McNeil
University of Akron
and
For Professors Anne D. Kilmer and Wolfgang Heimpel
University of California, Berkeley

MILLENNIUM BC / COUNTRY	9000-8000	8000-7000	7000-6000	6000-5000	5000-4000	4000-3000
MESOPOTAMIA AND IRAN	EPIPALEOLITHIC *Advanced hunter-gatherers* Asiab (Iran) Karim Shahir Zawi Shemi *Sheep herding in Zagros?*	NEOLITHIC *Small agricultural settlements* Ali Kosh (Iran) Ganj Dareh (Iran)	NEOLITHIC *Spread of farming in Zagros* Jarmo Sarab (Iran) Guran (Iran)	Rained agriculture and pottery (NORTH MESOPOTAMIA) Hassuna, Halaf *Irrigation farming* (CENTRAL MESOPOTAMIA) Baghouz, Samarra, Choga Mami, Matarah, Tell es-Sawwan *Specialized production* Umm Dabaghiyah	Agricultural Settlements (SOUTH MESOPOTAMIA) Eridu Ubaid	*Urban beginnings* *Ceremonial architecture* *Long-distance trade* Eridu, Uruk, Khafaje, Gawra, Brak, Nineveh *Writing* Uruk, Jemdet Nasr, SUMERIANS
EGYPT	UPPER PALEOLITHIC	UPPER PALEOLITHIC	UPPER PALEOLITHIC	UPPER PALEOLITHIC Fayyum A	NEOLITHIC *Early farming villages* Fayyum El-Badari Merimda	NEOLITHIC (PREDYNASTIC) *Irrigation agriculture* *Decorated pottery/palettes* El-Amra, Naqada (early) *Urban centers ??* El-Gizeh, Naqada *Writing*
SYRIA-PALESTINE	EPIPALEOLITHIC *Earliest settled villages* Ain Mallaha Beidha Jericho	NEOLITHIC (PPNA) *Walled community* Jericho *Earliest use of pottery* Mureybet *Small agricultural settlements* Beidha Tell Abu Hureyra Mureybet	NEOLITHIC (PPNB) *Craft specialization* Beidha *Increasing use of pottery* Ramad Tell Abu Hureyra	NEOLITHIC (PNA) *Desiccation and widespread settlement abandonment* Continuity at: Jericho Munhata	NEOLITHIC (PNB) *Settlement on Mediterranean coast and in northern Levant* Byblos Ramad Ras Shamra	CHALCOLITHIC *Walled urban center* *Long-distance trade* Habuba Kabira
ANATOLIA	UPPER PALEOLITHIC	NEOLITHIC *Small agricultural settlements* Çayönü *Early use of metals*	NEOLITHIC *Early village sites* Çatal Hüyük Hacilar *Obsidian production/trade* *Wall paintings and molded relief sculpture* Çatal Hüyük	NEOLITHIC *Early village sites* Can Hassan III Hacilar	NEOLITHIC Beycesultan Can Hassan	NEOLITHIC Kum Tepe (Troad)
AEGEAN AND CYPRUS	UPPER PALEOLITHIC (AEGEAN) *Sea travel and resource exploitation* Franchthi Cave Melos (Cyclades)	EPIPALEOLITHIC	EPIPALEOLITHIC *First island settlement* Crete Cyprus ?	EARLY NEOLITHIC (AEGEAN) *Early village sites* Nea Nikomedeia, Franchthi Cave, Knossos (Crete) ACERAMIC NEOLITHIC (CYPRUS) Khirokitia Tenta Cape Andreas Kastros	MIDDLE/LATE NEOLITHIC *Large Aegean Islands settled* Euboea, Chios, Rhodes, Samos *Occupation gap* *(Failed colonization?)* Dhali Agridi	FINAL NEOLITHIC Kea Lemnos Knossos Phaistos (Crete) CERAMIC NEOLITHIC Ayios Epiktitos Vrysi Sotira Teppes

MILLENNIUM BC / COUNTRY	3000-2500	2500-2000	2000-1500	1500-1000	1000-500	500-0
			MIDDLE BRONZE AGE			IRON AGE
MESOPOTAMIA AND IRAN	EARLY BRONZE AGE Use of bronze tools/weapons SUMERIAN CITY STATES Temple Elites Palatial Power land ownership Widespread use of writing Eridu, Kish, Lagash, Nippur, Ur, Uruk	(2350-2200) AKKADIAN NATION STATE Secular power and private land ownership Agade (Akkad) Ur, Kish (2112-2004) UR III DYNASTY (Neo-Sumerian) State ownership of land Ur, Umma, Selluah-Dagan	EARLY OLD BABYLONIAN Isin, Larsa OLD ASSYRIAN Anatolian trading colonies Assur, Kanesh OLD BABYLONIAN Shamshi-Adad and Hammurapi Assur, Shubat-Enlil, Babylon, Mari	KASSITE DYNASTY (1500-1150) Trade/diplomacy (Amarna Letters) Dur Kurigalzu HURRIANS (Mitanni) Northwest Mesopotamia MIDDLE ASSYRIAN STATE	NEO-ASSYRIAN EMPIRE (900-626) SARGONID DYNASTY Assur, Dur-Sharruken, Khalu, Nineveh NEO-BABYLONIAN STATE (626-539) CHALDEAN DYNASTY Babylon	PERSIAN EMPIRE (539-330) ACHAEMENID DYNASTY Ecbatana, Susa, Pasargadae, Persepolis Imperial Rule Zoroastrianism War with Macedon and Alexander the Great
EGYPT	DYNASTIES 1-2 (2900-2650) PHARAONIC STATE King Menes Hieroglyphic writing Abydos, Saqqara	DYNASTIES 3-6 (2650-2180) OLD KINGDOM Step pyramid of Djoser Saqqara Great pyramids (Khufu, Khafre, Menkaure) Giza Worship of Re Heliopolis	DYNASTIES 7-11 (2180-2050) 1ST INTERMEDIATE Memphis Herakleopolis DYNASTY 12 (2050-1800) MIDDLE KINGDOM Thebes DYNASTIES 13-17 (1800-1570) 2ND INTERMEDIATE Memphis, Itj-towy (1700-1570) DYNASTIES 15-17 Hyksos era Avaris	DYNASTIES 18-20 (1570-1080) NEW KINGDOM Thebes, Eastern Delta Egyptian State in Levant Amarna Period: Tell el-Amarna Ramesside Era: Abu Simbel	DYNASTIES 21-25 (1080-712) 3RD INTERMEDIATE Nubians Thebes	DYNASTIES 25-31 (712-322) LATE PERIOD Nubians and All Egypt (Dyn 25) Saitic Dynasty (Dyn 26) Persian Dynasty (Dyn 27) Libyan Dynasty (Dyns 28-30) Persian Dynasty (Dyn 31) GRAECO-ROMAN (322-)
SYRIA-PALESTINE	EARLY BRONZE AGE Urban Centers (Palestine) Ai Arad Beth-Shan Megiddo	EARLY BRONZE AGE Urbanism, Literacy, Commerce (Syria) Ebla Mari	MIDDLE BRONZE AGE Strong Fortified Cities (Palestine) Aphek Hazor Megiddo Palaces and Emporia (Syria) Alalakh, Ebla, Mari, Yamkhad, Qatna HURRIANS Jezirah	LATE BRONZE AGE (1500-1200) INTERNATIONAL ERA (Amarna Letters) Hapiru-Hebrew Mediterranean trade ports Beyrus, Byblos, Ugarit, Tyre Alphabetic origins Peoples of the sea	IRON AGE (1200-539) Mediterranean trade PHOENICIANS: Sidon Syre Byblos HEBREWS: Jerusalem United Monarchy Kingdoms of Israel and Judah Old Testament Babylonian captivity	PERSIAN RULE
ANATOLIA	EARLY BRONZE AGE Troy	EARLY BRONZE AGE Troy	MIDDLE BRONZE AGE OLD ASSYRIAN COLONIES Kârum Kanesh HITTITE OLD KINGDOM INDO-EUROPEANS Hattusha	LATE BRONZE AGE (1500-1200) HITTITE NEW KINGDOM Agriculture and metallurgy Expansion into Syria Hattusha Western Anatolia AHHIJAWA (ACHAEANS?) Arzawa	IRON AGE NEO-HITTITE STATES Carchemish URARTU Tushpa (Van)	PERSIAN RULE
AEGEAN AND CYPRUS	EARLY BRONZE AGE (Aegean) Urban Centers Lerna Tiryns Crete Cyclades CHALCOLITHIC (Cyprus) Erimi	EARLY BRONZE AGE (Aegean) Development toward palatial centers Knossos EARLY BRONZE AGE (Cyprus) Philia Sotira Kaminoudhia	MIDDLE BRONZE MINOAN First palaces-commerce Knossos, Mallia, Phaistos GREECE: MIDDLE HELLADIC Shaft graves Mycenae CYPRUS: MID-LATE CYPRIOT Urbanism-metallurgy Enkomi	LATE MINOAN NEW PALACE PERIOD Minoan settlements abroad Knossos, Phaistos, Mallia, Zakro, Khania LATE HELLADIC Mycenaean palaces-commerce Mycenae, Pylos, Tiryns LATE CYPRIOT I-III Commercial centers-trade Enkomi, Kition, Hala Sultan Tekke, Ayios Dhimitrios	SEA PEOPLES → (S E A P E O P L E S)	

PREFACE

The study of the past takes a variety of forms and involves many different disciplines. Although scientists, humanists, and social scientists share common goals of understanding and interpreting the past, each discipline pursues its goal by adopting specific methodological and theoretical guidelines. Indeed, even within particular disciplines, the study of the past assumes unique forms as individual scholars apply the fruits of their training, teaching, and research labors to the task at hand.

This book is no exception. Training in Classical and Near Eastern languages and civilizations came as part and parcel of a mainly historical bundle. Research brought me increasingly into contact with the world of archaeology, a profession I currently call my own. The archaeology I practice, however, invokes both traditional and more theoretical muses to study the past. On the more purely theoretical side, I follow economic and anthropological trends in archaeology, specifically studying the evolution of complex societies and the intricate systems of trade that characterize those (and often simpler) societies. Those who would study and attempt to interpret the human past must use every means available in that endeavor. That holistic approach should be apparent in these pages, even if a traditional stance looms largest.

In contrast to most books in this general field, I have adopted a more specifically social and economic perspective; yet the presentation lies within the traditional confines of political history. From a modern or even medieval historian's viewpoint, this history will seem woefully incomplete. We catch only split-second glimpses of a 10,000-year-long parade of events and recurrent processes. One important aim of this textbook is to return repeatedly to those recurrent themes and to weave them into the political history of events.

I have tried to incorporate as much relevant recent research as possible. Undoubtedly this will still not satisfy everybody; some will find that specific eras or areas have received too much attention, others that they have received too little. The multifaceted nature of our discipline makes such opinions inevitable. I find this to be the sign of a healthy, evolving field of study. In the end, I shall be satisfied if I have been able to convey a reliable and comprehensive sense of pattern, process, and event—the "stuff" of archaeology and ancient history—to readers of this book.

A. BERNARD KNAPP
SYDNEY, AUSTRALIA

ACKNOWLEDGMENTS

Over the course of the seven years it took to write this book and during the ten years of teaching the course material upon which the book is based, I have relied on the expertise and advice of many colleagues and friends. I am most deeply indebted to my former teachers and colleagues in the Department of Near Eastern Studies at the University of California at Berkeley, especially Wolfgang Heimpel and Anne D. Kilmer. Others, in alphabetical order, include Guitty Azarpay, David Larkin, Leonard Lesko (now at Brown University), Jacob Milgrom, W. J. Murnane (now at UCLA), and Ruggero Stefanini. James D. Muhly (University of Pennsylvania), Jack Sasson (University of North Carolina, Chapel Hill), and Paul Zimansky (Boston University) read earlier versions of the entire manuscript and made numerous helpful suggestions. John F. Cherry (Cambridge University), Denise Schmandt-Besserat (University of Texas, Austin), and Michael Weiskopf (then at Berkeley) provided valuable critiques of specific sections in the book. I am pleased to acknowledge Alan Dobel's original work and ideas, upon which Chart 4–1 is based. To all of them and to a seemingly endless chain of nameless referees, I express my sincere thanks; to those I've inadvertently omitted, I apologize. The quality of this book reflects their collected wisdom; its shortcomings reflect upon the author alone.

I am also particularly indebted to three friends at Berkeley— Jeffrey Barash, Scott Handelman, and Gary Rasnick—who took the time to read the entire manuscript and to provide detailed comments on style, sequence, and logic. Only at Berkeley could one find literate, capable, and intellectually critical people in such abundance, so generous with their time, so steadfast in their support.

On the purely administrative and technical side, I wish to express my thanks first of all to Betsy Taylor and the entire staff of the Near Eastern Studies Department at the University of California at Berkeley for support and all sorts of clerical assistance over the years 1973–1983. Secondly, to Madeline Anderson and the excellent teaching assistants at Berkeley's Quantitative Anthropology Laboratory, I owe my first introduction to word processing, which made it so much easier to produce all those revisions. I should also like to thank Leah McKenzie (Department of Archaeology, University of Sydney) for her help in preparing the Glossary. To David Phipps at the University of Sydney's Computing Centre, I am grateful for the transfer of all my EBCDIC files from magnetic tape to an MS–DOS readable format on floppy disks. Lastly, I wish to thank all the people from Dorsey Press involved in this publication, particularly Mary Lou Murphy (Project Editor), and David Follmer (Publisher) who strongly supported the concept of this textbook from the outset, and who came to my rescue in the well-nigh impossible task of obtaining the figures and permissions for it.

On the personal side, I acknowledge the support of a long list of friends in Berkeley who never questioned my long work hours and erratic behavior. To my mother and aunt, I shall always be grateful for support: family, financial, and otherwise. To my wife Christina Sumner, I am particularly grateful for encouragement when the possibilities of publication seemed so remote, the future so unclear. She has supported this work in its final stages and helped with its original artwork.

Finally I must single out Professor Erich Gruen, Department of History, University of California at Berkeley, without whose constant encouragement, criticism, and excellent critical advice this book would never have been possible. Erich Gruen first invited me to write a section on ancient Near Eastern history for quite another project in 1979, and he devotedly read and critiqued all subsequent versions except the final one. His commitment to the project was unwavering, his time given freely. I sincerely hope he finds the ultimate result worthwhile.

A.B.K.

CONTENTS

xi

C H A P T E R

III

THE THIRD MILLENNIUM B.C.: DIVERSITY OF DOMINION 61

C H A P T E R

IV

THE SECOND MILLENNIUM B.C.: THE ERA OF INTERNATIONALISM 135

C H A P T E R

V

THE FIRST MILLENNIUM B.C.: THE PASSAGE TO EMPIRE 218

C H A P T E R

VI

EPILOGUE: VESTIGES OF ANCIENT WESTERN ASIA AND EGYPT 268

LIST OF MAPS

ABOUT THE AUTHOR

A. Bernard Knapp holds a Fulbright Senior Research and Lecturing Fellowship in Cyprus, and recently was a fellow in Archaeology at the University of Sydney. He is the author of numerous articles on social aspects of Bronze Age societies. Dr. Knapp received his masters and doctoral degrees in Ancient History and Mediterranean Archaeology from the University of California at Berkeley.

I

THE STUDY OF
THE PAST

Human history—what is it? When did it begin? And where? There is only one human past, but there are many different ways to study it. History, archaeology, anthropology, sociology, psychology: each discipline would analyze the human past with different methods and techniques. Such diversity enriches the study of human history; it is also very appropriate. Consciousness of the past is not only characteristic of human beings, it is also unique to our species, **Homo sapiens sapiens** (literally, wise, wise man, a term used to distinguish modern human beings from their forebears). Without the past to set the stage, the present remains but an empty scene. To understand our contemporary existence, to discover the experiences and achievements that have formed our attitudes, above all to gain a sensitive appreciation of the general forces, specific events, and personalities—great and small—that have shaped our identity: these are compelling reasons to study human history.

To study history, we must define history, specifically the brand of history that is our particular concern. Since this book commences in what is commonly known as the **prehistoric pe-**

1

riod, it is necessary first to clarify that history is distinguished from prehistory by written records, documents that deal on some level with human consciousness and the collective human past. The historian's chief interest lies in the causes and motivations that lay behind human actions as these actions may be traced—however tenuously—in written records. Generally speaking, then, history attempts to interpret and explain human actions during specific time periods by analyzing the written remains of that period.

Human history is often exceedingly difficult to reconstruct. The historian must possess the objectivity of a scientist and the subjectivity of a humanist. Like a scientist, the historian needs to set rigorous standards in judging evidence, framing hypotheses, and testing conclusions. Like a humanist, the historian must be able to examine critically the implications of human relationships and the vagaries of human character. Since each historian's insight will therefore be personal and somewhat subjective, the past is observed from many different viewpoints. Given such variability in interpretation, what sort of standards do historians set to re-create the past?

Historical research tends to focus on individual events rather than generalized propositions: on the Trojan War rather than the nature of war, on Egyptian kingship rather than the nature of the state. Yet the broader view often provides very useful insight into the particular situation. Historical sources are often scarce, especially so as we move further back in time. "Facts" derived from historical sources may be completely unrelated or intricately interrelated. One task of the historian is to combine or separate these ambiguous facts, to question them in imaginative ways, and to establish their relationship to unique events or groups of events. The historian must incorporate this maze of details into an intelligible scenario that takes into account other factors critical in recreating the past: environment, climate, technology, and culture. Skillful and inspired reconstructions of the human past are a challenge to the historian and an inspiration—as well as a necessity—to the student of history.

Since interpretation of historical sources is always difficult, reexamination and reinterpretation of historical "facts" are perennially in progress. The face of history as a discipline is ever-changing. Each era studies the past anew in light of its own attitudes and experiences. Economic motives inspire the historians of one generation; psychological and social factors condition the interpretations of the next. The veracity and worth of these changing approaches can only be measured by the extent to which they allow historians cumulatively to move toward a better understanding of the past, to create a bridge between past and present.

If the task of the historian is difficult, that of the ancient historian is doubly so. The fabric of ancient history is woven by two craftspeople: the historian and the archaeologist. Historians, on the one hand, work chiefly with written records of various sorts. Archaeologists, on the other, work more frequently with the material record: artifacts and architecture, stones and bones. Those who would study certain periods and aspects of the ancient world must master both disciplines.

As in the field of history, each new generation of archaeologists redefines its attitude to fieldwork and interpretation. As archaeological excavations produce new evidence, so archaeological research provides new interpretations. Whereas in the first part of the twentieth century, archaeology devoted itself almost exclusively to the description and chronological classification of finds, current approaches lean heavily toward ecological, environmental, and social explanations—a reflection of prevailing attitudes in contemporary society. Fertile ideas, and ever-changing and refined methods allow archaeologists to feel more assured of their cultural and historical interpretations. Archaeology today is a very exciting discipline indeed.

How do historians go about the study of the past? Virtually all cultural materials, prehistoric or historic, derive from archaeological investigation and excavation. Every archaeological site must be treated as if it were a document. Like written records, archaeological data must be deciphered, classified, translated, and interpreted before they become useful to the historian. Some of the most dramatic cultural and technological developments in human history—agriculture and animal domestication, control and use of fire, metallurgy, use of the wheel, urbanization—took place in a prehistoric setting. To understand these developments, historians must make the mute archaeological record speak. The methods and recovery techniques of prehistoric archaeology inspire confidence in realizing this objective. New attitudes have brought archaeology face-to-face with the contemporary social sciences (anthropology, geography, sociology), and the resultant interdisciplinary relationship has been warm and productive.

The human past can only be examined and interpreted through its remnants: literary records of all sorts (histories, myths, poetry, drama, liturgies, orations); documents of every type (inscriptions on stone and bronze, clay tablets, coins, papyrus); and material remains (buildings, pottery, frescoes, sculpture, weapons, stone and metal tools, plant and skeletal survivals).

While remnants of the past are considerable in variety, their actual preservation is often poor, and their number is always scant compared to what existed in the living culture. Gaps in our knowledge are consequently always large. The ancient historian or prehistorian has to wring dry every imaginable source of information: determining trade routes on the basis of unearthed bits of pottery, metal, or stone; speculating on ideology and religious beliefs from "fertility" figurines, architectural remains, or painted symbols and designs on various objects; piecing together early bureaucracies by inspecting fragmentary clay tablets or papyrus rolls; reconstructing public policy by analyzing law codes or regal proclamations carved on stone monuments or inked on papyrus.

Such are the tasks and techniques of the ancient historian. But why study ancient history in the first place? If the aim is to discover and understand ourselves in light of the past, to build a bridge between past and present, may it not be that the societies of ancient Western Asia—Egypt, Mesopotamia, and the lands of the eastern Mediterranean—are too remote to cast light on contemporary society or on a more enlightened path to a humane future?

Remoteness in time can be deceptive. Certainly the temporal distance between ourselves and our ancient Mediterranean and Western Asiatic forebears allows a sense of detachment important in historical analysis. Yet it must be remembered that the history of ancient Western Asia is half of all recorded history, about 2,500 years. Furthermore, remoteness takes on an entirely different dimension when we recall that our own western culture is rooted in the cultures of the ancient Mediterranean and ancient Western Asia. These were our ancestors who first came to grips with the challenges posed by the complexities of agriculture and urban living, who developed the basic social and economic institutions, moral constructs, political structures, and ways of thinking that shaped Western civilization as we know it today. To be truly rational, thinking human beings (Homo sapiens), to better understand the past and prepare for the future, we can only benefit by studying the past, both remote and recent.

Studying the past, however, must not be construed solely as a way of focusing attitudes on the present. Differences between prehistoric and historic cultures provide interesting and challenging areas of study in their own right. Comparisons may be enlightening but inferences based on them hazardous: the social and moral degeneration that biblical writers cited as cause for the fall of Babylon does not necessarily mean that similar behavior—at least as envisioned in the eyes of modern-day prophets—will necessarily lead to the decline of Western civilization. Much more meaningful is the realization that different cultures in different eras find different solutions to similar problems. History cannot change the past nor prophesy the future; rarely does it seem to have a noticeable impact on the present.

This book offers an introduction to the ancient world. It does not pretend to cover all relevant subjects nor to treat any of them in the detail they deserve. The survey encompasses a broad spectrum: from prehistoric times to the death of Alexander the Great in Babylon; from western Asia and Egypt through the eastern Mediterranean to the borders of Greece.

The story of Western culture is followed from its beginnings: settlement and domestication in Western Asia, the emergence of agricultural society, the turn to urbanization, the cities and nation-states of Mesopotamia, the imposing kingdoms of Egypt, the complex rivalries of peoples and states that dominated the history of Syria-Palestine and Anatolia, the imperial powers of

Assyria and Persia, the roots of Greek culture, and the vast expansion of Hellenic civilization through the conquests of Alexander the Great.

One important goal of the book is to view this long and rich period of human history through a variety of lenses. Another aim is to strike a balance between a purely chronological narrative and cultural history. Political and military events form a framework for discussion. The investigation of attitudes and institutions paves the way to an understanding of ancient social, economic, and behavioral patterns.

The book endeavors to discern how past cultural achievements—art, literature, religion, and science—arise from and reflect historical circumstances. Concentration on certain themes helps to give structure and meaning to developments traced over many centuries. The book also emphasizes important tensions in order to gain a deeper appreciation of the forces at work in ancient Western Asia: the tension between unity and diversity, between settled agriculturalists and migratory pastoralists, between local particularism and national identity, between public authority and private enterprise, between conservatism and innovation. The stresses were never fully resolved. For that very reason, they underscore the dynamism and vitality that characterize the societies of ancient Western Asia.

A NOTE ON CHRONOLOGY

Absolute time and the sequence of known events form the heartbeat of any historical re-creation. In the modern world, we are accustomed to accurate time, exactly datable events, and reasonably precise temporal predictions (work routines, bus schedules, doctor's appointments). The past cannot be dated in such an accurate manner; as a general rule, dating becomes progressively more difficult as we move further back in time. Certainly historians aspire to know the exact years that an Egyptian pharaoh ruled or at least the approximate date that a Babylonian king died. But written records that preserve a king's name, describe a specific battle, or recount some other exactly datable occurrence are rare. When such data do not exist, we cannot have **absolute dating** (exact dating); it can only be **relative dating**.

Relative dates are frequently based on *stratified* archaeological materials that have a sequential aspect. By **stratification**, we mean that pottery, figurines, metal or stone tools, and other materials found in the lowest part of an archaeological excavation are sequentially and relatively earlier in time than material that has accumulated above them.

For much of the prehistoric era, relative dating is the rule. Absolute dates for prehistoric material are based on **radiocarbon dating** determinations, precise chemical measurements of ratios of carbon isotopes that help to determine the "exact" time that particular carbon-containing organisms (charcoal, bone, shell, etc.) died. The specific archaeological level from which the radiocarbon-analyzed material was recovered may thus be given an approximate absolute date—approximate because the computation provides a statistical factor ($\pm$ x number of years) that can be quite high.

Recent use of **dendrochronology** for **calibration** of radiocarbon-derived dates suggests that they deviate increasingly from actual calendar dates, from an error of about 200 years at 1000 B.C. up to an error of about 900 years at 5,000 radiocarbon years B.C. Therefore, a radiocarbon date of 1000 B.C. should be calibrated to about 1200 B.C., and a date of 5000 B.C. to about 5900 B.C. Although **calibration curves** are designed to bring radiocarbon dates into line with actual dates, the limits of these curves currently do not extend earlier than about 5200 B.C. As is customary in the archaeology of ancient western Asia, dates for the prehistoric period provided in this book are uncalibrated, and thus too "young," occasionally by a wide measure.

For the **historical period**, there exist long lists of actual year names, king lists, historical chronicles, building inscriptions, and other written records—often based on astronomical observations—that allow "absolute" dating. Yet it must be borne in mind that for much of ancient western Asiatic and Egyptian history, accurate dates B.C. are hard to come by; sources frequently seem to be in conflict with one another. Following the general axiom noted above, the most recent dates have proved to be the more accurate and have a lower margin of error.

In Mesopotamia, the *limmu* lists, named after an annually appointed official of the Neo-Assyrian period (first millennium

B.C.), allow us to date events back to 910 B.C. Earlier Assyrian and Babylonian king lists make it possible to date particular events or more general epochs within a margin of about ten years. Absolute dating in Syria-Palestine, Anatolia, Cyprus, and Iran requires synchronizations with episodes in Babylonia, Assyria, or Egypt, where more secure chronologies have been established.

The Babylonian "Venus tablets," which record the planetary movements of Venus, provide astronomical dates for the era prior to 1450 B.C. Unfortunately these tablets offer a series of possible dates rather than an agreed-upon single date. Observations of Venus are only possible once every sixty-four years, but scholars still dispute which of three possible Venus cycles these tablets refer to. Consequently three separate chronologies exist for Babylonia during the second **millennium** B.C.: the high, middle, and low chronologies (the latter finds few supporters). Although the internal and relative chronology of Babylonia has been reasonably well worked out on the basis of year names, it remains difficult to pinpoint relative events to a secure, absolute dating system. This book uses the middle chronology, which dates the reign of Ḥammurapi of Babylon (First Dynasty) as 1792–1750 B.C. While the middle chronology is indisputably the most commonly accepted and frequently used, it reflects only a compromise solution to a very complex problem. For the purposes of this book, it is much more important to consider the relative sequence and sociohistorical significance of events rather than to contemplate and debate endlessly about exactly when they occurred.

Relative dating is well established from the sixteenth century B.C. all the way back to the twenty-fourth century B.C. (the reign of Sargon and the Akkadian dynasty). There exist, however, two "historical" gaps of unknown duration during these 800 years. The first occurred about 2200 B.C., the second about 1600 B.C. Even though documents record the succession of kings and the length of their reigns, incidents and eras remain unanchored in "absolute" time. In Mesopotamia, only approximate dates are possible before 2400 B.C.: time estimations are made on the basis of purely archaeological evidence, from **palaeographic** data (namely the evolution of the **cuneiform** script in its earliest stages), and by a few (too "young") radiocarbon dates.

In Egypt, absolute dates for the prehistoric period are plagued by the same radiocarbon dating problems that exist in Mesopotamia. During the historic era, after about 3000 B.C., written sources for dating are similar to those found in Mesopotamia: king lists, royal annals, and biographic treatises. In addition there exists a history of Egypt, written in Greek during the third century B.C. by an Egyptian priest (Manetho), most likely compiled from some of the very lists that modern scholars use to reconstruct ancient Egyptian chronology. As in Mesopotamia, the earlier the time period under consideration, the less confidence is placed upon absolute dates. On the whole, the era from about 330 B.C. (where our survey of Egypt ends) back to 945 B.C., is reliably dated on the basis of astronomical observations, synchronisms, and some historically well-dated reigns.

From approximately 1050 back to 1550 B.C., two chronologies—a high and a low chronology—have been postulated on the basis of astronomical observations of the star Sothis (Egyptian *Sepedet*, our *Sirius*). Noting the precise moment that this star appeared was critically important to the ancient Egyptians: their agricultural year dated from the inception of the annual rise of the River Nile (caused by melting snows in the highlands far to the south), an event that more or less coincided with the heliacal (predawn) rising of Sothis on the horizon. The reason for two chronologies is that scholars cannot agree whether these ancient observations took place in the north, near Memphis (high chronology), or in the south, near Thebes (low chronology). At this stage, the dispute cannot be settled finally; and in any case, the internal dating of some pharaohs' reigns is complicated by the possibility of overlap (coregency). Nonetheless, the margin of error for the period 1550–1050 B.C. is only a matter of 10–20 years, much less than the discrepancy in Mesopotamia (up to 120 years).

A Sothic date also exists for a pharaoh who ruled during the nineteenth century B.C. (Sesostris III). Working backwards from that time, however, dating becomes increasingly uncertain, and again there are no fixed points upon which to hang a well-

known, "relatively" dated sequence of events. As in Mesopotamia, archaeology, palaeography, artistic style, and radiocarbon
determinations provide at best a broad range of possibilities.

People who dwelt in the lands of ancient western Asia and
Egypt had little sense of history as we understand it today. Royal
annals and king lists existed to glorify rulers or to demonstrate
legitimacy and continuity of rule; year dates were bureaucratic
records pure and simple. Only by linking these records to what
might be called neutral events, the observance and registry of
certain planets, is it possible to provide absolute calendar dates
B.C. Real difficulty accompanies any attempt to synchronize specific happenings in diverse areas, especially in Syria-Palestine,
Cyprus, or Iran, where finds of written records are few and far
between. Given this situation, the ancient historian can only
offer what seems to be a plausible reconstruction of events,
founded on painstaking and detailed research into a variety of
currently available material. Such scenarios must be regarded as
tentative; of necessity, they will shift and readjust as more archaeological data and written evidence accumulate.

II

THE RISE TO CIVILIZATION: 9000–3000 B.C.

Between about 9000 B.C. and the beginning of the Christian era, the world's earliest known civilizations arose and matured in the Near East. The area known collectively as the ancient Near East is also referred to separately as ancient western Asia and Egypt. Ancient western Asia, as used in this book, comprises the area bounded by the modern countries of Cyprus, Syria, Lebanon, Israel, Jordan, Turkey, Soviet Armenia and Georgia, Iraq, Iran, and parts of Saudi Arabia. The earliest permanent settlements appeared during the period from about 9000 B.C. to 6000 B.C., accompanied or followed by the **domestication** of plants and animals. Over the next two millennia, the practice of **rain-fed agriculture** spread, and simple irrigation techniques were developed in both Mesopotamia and Egypt. The first cities arose between approximately 4000 and 3000 B.C., in response to the pressures of population growth, the social and organizational requirements of irrigated agriculture, and the demands of complex trading systems. The advent of writing, shortly before 3000 B.C., roughly coincided with the growth and spread of city life.

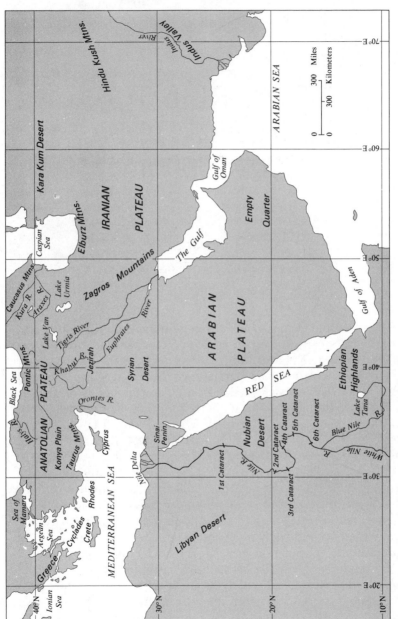

Map 2-1 Geographic Features of the Middle East

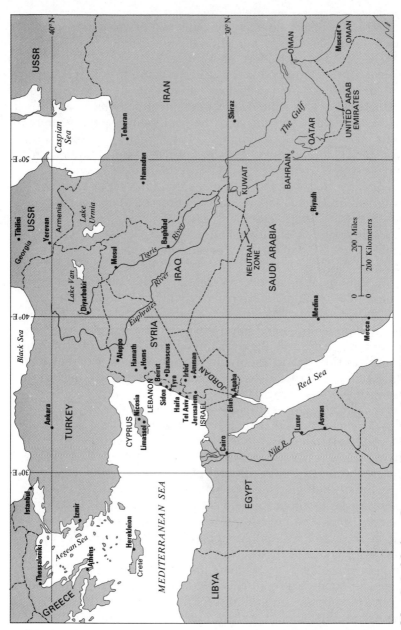

Map 2-2 Modern Countries/Capitals of the Middle East

Most historians agree on four minimal prerequisites for civilization: subsistence by agriculture, the existence of cities, advanced social organization, and the use of writing. But there were no predetermined steps leading to these achievements, and the path of human history rarely exhibits uniformity or predictability. The sequence of permanent settlement and domestication, urbanization, and the evolution of writing represents merely a developmental pattern, not a blueprint. Nomadism, for example, may be regarded as an economic response to the specialized needs of settled villagers who maintained large flocks of sheep or goats. And the earliest advances in agriculture and social organization proceeded not only slowly but unevenly. Large settlements such as Jericho in Palestine or Çatal Hüyük in Turkey, for instance, whose good-sized buildings testify to their complex social organization, never made use of writing.

Variations in environment—land, climate, and resources—profoundly conditioned the rise to civilization in the Near East. In different regions, the distinct combinations of features offered different possibilities and imposed different restrictions on their inhabitants. Above all, the rivers of the Near East enabled people to live, to thrive, and eventually to pursue new activities less strictly associated with the production of food and other basic necessities. Rivers provided for irrigation, transportation, and—perhaps most significant of all—communication.

The civilizations that arose in the Tigris-Euphrates River valley of Mesopotamia and in the Nile River valley of Egypt dominated cultural developments in the ancient Near East. These rivers built up extensive **alluvial plains**, forming the fertile environments that nourished the world's earliest high cultures. By contrast, the rivers of the two other distinct regions of ancient western Asia—the **Levant** (Syria and Palestine) on the eastern Mediterranean coast and Anatolia or Asia Minor (modern Turkey)—did not lend themselves to transport or to construction and use of canals. Nor was there need for irrigation: rainfall was adequate for agriculture. This circumstance had profound but ultimately different implications for the two regions. As we trace the rise to civilization, we shall thus be looking extensively and comparatively at the physical features of the lands of ancient western Asia and Egypt.

PERMANENT SETTLEMENT AND DOMESTICATION

Throughout virtually the entire span of time that human beings have existed on earth, they lived as roving bands, migrating from one campsite or cave to another, hunting and gathering their food and other necessities. The tools used by these hunter-gatherers were made primarily of stone, less often of wood or other perishable materials. The long period of rudimentary developments in stone tool technology is therefore known as the **Paleolithic** (Old Stone) Age, about 700,000 to 20,000–10,000 years ago. People may have intermittently supplemented hunting and gathering by selecting certain strains of plants and breeding certain animals. Yet the basic hunting-gathering economy prevailed in the Near East until roughly 10,000 B.C., when attempts at plant domestication and animal raising began to crystallize and to alter the course of human history.

Refinements in stone tool manufacture occurred throughout the Paleolithic period. By 10,000–9000 B.C., archaeological evidence implies a gradual change in food-procuring methods from intensive hunting and gathering to the earliest domestication of plants and animals. Changing human needs and the new methods of **food production** were accompanied by a new tool kit; the era from about 9000 B.C. to 3000 B.C. has thus been termed the **Neolithic** (New Stone) Age. The first permanent settlements appear at or just before this time in the archaeological record.

The adoption of a sedentary (settled) food-producing mode of existence was one of humanity's most daring steps. Noted archaeologist V. Gordon Childe drew attention to its momentous significance by calling this change the "Agricultural Revolution." Although it is now regarded more as a gradual transformation than a revolution, the changes it wrought—loss of mobility, population growth, and the accumulation of goods—had massive implications for subsequent stages in the rise to civilization.

The transformation from hunting and gathering to settled agriculture was not linear, nor did it follow a consistent pattern throughout ancient western Asia. The people who dwelt in these early communities were not dependent exclusively on agriculture; most sites show evidence of a mixed economy based on hunting and gathering, herding of goats and sheep, fishing, and cultivation of wheat and barley. Some sedentary villages were established even before domestication had been achieved. The substantial walled community at Jericho between about 8000 and 7000 B.C., for example, still subsisted chiefly on hunting and intensive gathering of wild grains.

We may never be certain what first led people to settle down. It is difficult to speak authoritatively from our remote perspective of 10,000 years, and investigations of Near Eastern cultural developments before the historical period—that is, before the advent of writing around 3000 B.C.—must depend entirely on material evidence: bones, seeds, pottery, implements, weapons, art, and architecture. Archaeologists have speculated extensively on the reasons for this transformation to settled agriculture. They have offered climatic, environmental, technological, and demographic explanations. Population pressure, for example, is one theory that currently enjoys widespread support. The basic premise is that increases in population necessitated new methods of obtaining food, namely the deliberate planting of cereal grasses rather than the periodic collection of various wild food sources. And once people began to sow their crops, inevitably they had to remain in the vicinity of the crops in order to tend and raise them. Such proposals, of course, are necessarily speculative. Whatever the case, we can be certain that a settled existence was not the culmination of an inevitable evolutionary process, nor was it based on any universal ideal. Sheep and goat **pastoralists**, it is worth noting, have continued their predominantly migratory patterns throughout much of the Near East for the past 8,000 years.

It appears unlikely that the earliest villages were occupied year-round by all their inhabitants. Some hunters and gatherers apparently found it convenient to return annually to the same site, perhaps to gather whatever food that locale could provide. Modern ethnographic evidence has demonstrated that some present-day herders are also part-time farmers or villagers; similarly the earliest settled peoples were probably part-time pastoralists and part-time cultivators.

If subsistence could be maintained in one locale, the tendency to migrate in search of food and other necessities may have diminished. Increasing reliance on certain grains and animals may also have had unforeseen consequences. The bulk and weight of the harvest or the size of the herd may have caused logistical problems for a transient population. Farmers would have been forced to remain in one place to nurture and protect their crops. Such simple matters were certainly instrumental in the development of permanent villages between 8000 and 6000 B.C.

In brief, then, the agricultural transformation witnessed the successful domestication of certain animals and plants, which ensured an adequate food supply for a population that was probably on the increase. A warmer and wetter climate after about 10,000 B.C. presumably increased wild food resources and thus allowed population to increase. Population pressure eventually may have led to certain cultural and technological improvements, namely to the development of implements used in harvesting and preparing foods and to the invention of storage facilities, such as bins for grain. All these factors, plus others, seem to have had very positive, interacting effects.

Reliance on domesticated plants and animals became an almost universal means of subsistence. Sedentary living became the norm, and the social organization that accompanied it became a primary force in organizing and integrating agricultural villages, in coordinating trade activities that began to develop about this time, and in making agriculture such an efficient and profitable pursuit that reversion to a hunting and gathering way of life became increasingly difficult and unlikely. Although bad harvests periodically forced a return to hunting and gathering, the village community was here to stay.

The Fertile Crescent

Sometime before 7000 B.C. plant and animal domestication took place throughout an area extending along the arc of the Taurus-Zagros mountains, from the eastern Mediterranean to southwestern Iran. This is, roughly speaking, the zone that Egyptologist James Henry Breasted (1865–1935) called the Fertile Crescent. Successful agriculture without irrigation requires a reliable annual rainfall of at least 8 inches (200 millimeters); otherwise, irrigation is a necessity. Map 2–4 shows this 8-inch rainfall

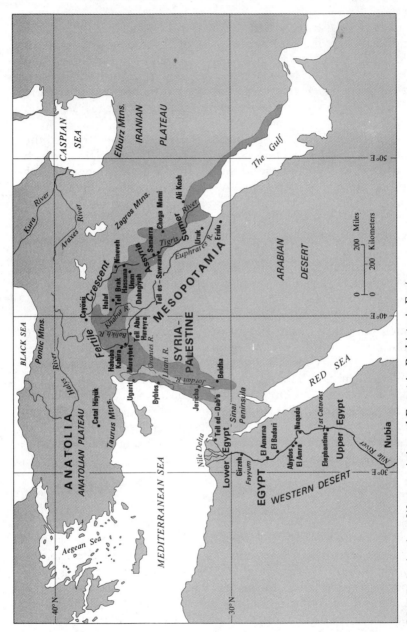

Map 2–3 Ancient Western Asia and Egypt in Prehistoric Era/
Neolithic Sites and Geographic Features

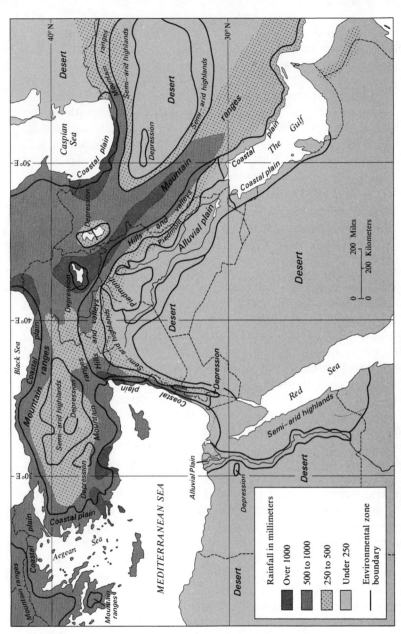

Map 2—4 Major Environmental Zones and Annual Precipitation

line, or **isohyet**, north of which the Syrian and Mesopotamian plains receive sufficient rainfall for rain-fed agriculture. South of the line, there is virtually never an average annual rainfall of 8 inches. It is certainly no accident that the arc of this rainfall line corresponds roughly to the arc of the Fertile Crescent.

Prominent among the small agricultural settlements in the Fertile Crescent during the eighth and seventh millennia B.C. were Jericho in Palestine and Beidha in Jordan, Mureybet and Tell Abu Hureyra in Syria, Ali Kosh in southwestern Iran, and Çayönü Tepesi in southeastern Anatolia. Domestication proceeded at different paces at these various sites. Certain species were probably domesticated independently and somewhat simultaneously at several different locales.

According to the once-popular "Oasis Theory" of V. Gordon Childe, a drastic change from a cold and dry to a hot and dry climate in the Near East at the end of the last ice age (about 18,000 B.P. ["before the present"]) forced hunter-gatherers and animals, as well as plants, to concentrate in well-watered oases and river valleys such of those of the Nile and the Tigris-Euphrates systems. The very proximity of plants and animals, so Childe believed, allowed humans to observe annual and behavioral cycles and subsequently stimulated people to adopt the agricultural techniques of plant and animal domestication. While this proximity of potentially domesticable plants and animals to people was an important prerequisite to agriculture, and while the changes introduced by agriculture were indeed vast, Childe was wrong in his belief that a climatic change forced people, plants, and animals to concentrate in the oases and river valleys.

Archaeological and climatological evidence demonstrates almost conclusively that plant and animal domestication began within the piedmont hills and valleys of the Taurus-Zagros arc. Domestication advanced as part of the favorable response to the improved climate and suitable environment and also in response to the beginnings of sedentary life with all the appropriate sociocultural and technological mechanisms (sickle blades, grinding stones, and other agricultural implements; more effective weapons, such as the bow and arrow; a much broader-based food supply including cereals, vegetables, hoofed animals, small mammals, and aquatic resources). Some of the wild progenitors

(Courtesy of the Joint Prehistoric Project, Universities of Chicago and Istanbul)

Aerial photograph of Çayönü Tepesi, an early agricultural settlement of the Neolithic Near East, in southeastern Turkey.

of the first domesticated plants and animals originated in these well-watered southern foothills of the Taurus and Zagros mountains that make up the northernmost part of Breasted's Fertile Crescent. Within these "hilly flanks," people subsisted on barley, emmer or einkorn wheat, lentils and other legumes, and animals such as cattle, pigs, sheep, and goats, all of which were eventually domesticated. Some of these same species still inhabit these foothills today.

The practice of agriculture and the raising of animals transformed the way people thought about their world. Herders replaced hunters, and most migratory pursuits were abandoned in favor of goods and property, the trappings of a sedentary way of life. Changes in community size and organization are reflected in the archaeological record, where we find new house forms and community layouts instead of haphazard placement of huts. The remarkable increase in communications and contact among these villages is exemplified by imported objects like **obsidian**,

(Courtesy of the Joint Prehistoric Project, Universities of Chicago and Istanbul)
The "hilly flanks" region in the foothills of the Taurus Mountains, southeastern Turkey.

a hard volcanic rock used to fashion stone implements. Obsidian was exchanged along an intricate trade network that stretched from the obsidian sources in central and eastern Anatolia to destinations as far afield as Beidha in Jordan and sites in the Deh Luran plain in southwestern Iran.

In a sense, Childe's revolutionary characterization of this period was correct: the transition to settled living resulted in a social and economic metamorphosis. The 2,000 or so years it took for people successfully to cultivate staple foods and to commence living permanently in a village setting seem but an instant in comparison to the more than 3 million years they survived by hunting and gathering. Over the next 2000 years, from about 6000 B.C. to 4000 B.C., improvements in techniques of cultivation and the earliest attempts at irrigation resulted in the spread of agriculture from the Taurus-Zagros foothills to the northern plains of Mesopotamia.

Mesopotamia: Between Two Rivers

The history and culture of Mesopotamia are intimately bound up with the ways and wanderings of its two great rivers, the Euphrates and the Tigris. Mesopotamia, in fact, means "between the rivers" and is used in both a cultural and geographical sense to delimit that strip of land within modern-day Syria and Iraq that lies between the Euphrates and the Tigris.

Both rivers originate in eastern Anatolia. South of the Taurus foothills, spanning the 250 miles that separate the Euphrates and Tigris, lies the district known today as the **Jezirah** (Arabic for island) (see Map 2–1). The Euphrates and its two left-bank tributaries flow through the Jezirah in valleys too narrow and too far below the level of the surrounding plain to be useful for irrigation. Since rainfall in this area is sparse and unpredictable, any farming would have been strictly limited to narrow strips of land on those valley floors. Yet in the northern, hilly flanks of the Jezirah, where rainfall is significantly higher and more predictable, some of the earliest experiments with agriculture were successfully carried out.

The unpredictable rainfall in the plains of northern Mesopotamia (the Jezirah in the west and Assyria in the east) meant that agriculture without rainfall was a hit-and-miss affair. Early farming in these regions was probably possible only where seasonal streams or accumulated surface water would permit small-scale irrigation. Most of this "island" is a **steppe** zone. Very dry in summer, the steppe is covered with grass in the spring and thus offers ideal conditions for pastoralism. Later, in the historical period, a major communications route traversed this natural corridor, connecting the upper Tigris River valley with northern Syria and the Mediterranean coast. The proliferation of **tells** (the mounds that contain the ruins of ancient settlements) in the northern, more fertile reaches of this zone testifies to its eventual commercial importance and large ancient population.

In their attempt to identify ancient cultures and to establish chronological relationships among them, archaeologists categorize similarities in specific types of tools, weapons, or structures and seek to place these materials in a relative sequence. Typically they name an ancient culture after the site where its

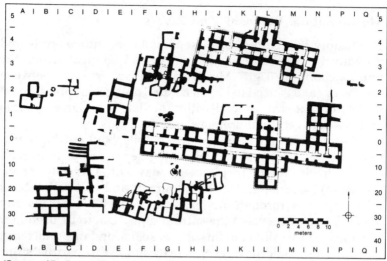

(Courtesy of Dr. Diana Halbaek, and the British School of Archaeology in Iraq)

Composite plan of structures at Umm Dabagiyah, northern Mesopotamia.

characteristic features and artifacts were first identified. Such sites have given their names to three distinct cultures that emerged during the spread of agriculture from the Taurus-Zagros foothills to Northern Mesopotamia: the Hassuna (about 6000–5000 B.C.), the Samarra (about 5500–5000 B.C.), and the Halaf (about 5500–4800 B.C.).

Although these north Mesopotamian cultures exhibit distinct criteria, according to which archaeologists classify them, certain general patterns may also be discerned. Their economies were primarily agricultural, and people lived in permanently established villages. Some Hassuna period sites, however, such as Umm Dabagiyah in the upper Tigris valley, still engaged in hunting. These villages were now occupied throughout the year. Although their actual size varied from site to site, an average village is thought to have had a population between 100 and 200 people. This modal village size seems to be very effective for agricultural pursuits; it has remained typical of Near Eastern farming villages to the present day.

The economic base of these villages became increasingly effective, or so it would seem on the basis of technological in-

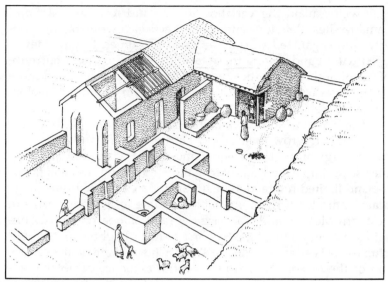

(Journal of Near Eastern Studies)

Isometric reconstruction of a house at Hassuna (Level 4).

novations in pottery (intricately painted, very thin-walled and well-made wares in new and distinctive shapes) and in architecture (more substantial structures that made use of external buttressing and durable, sun-dried **mudbricks**). The buildings ranged in type from large groups of structures attached to one another and often enclosing courtyards (Hassuna culture) to single, detached structures of varying sizes (Samarra and Halaf cultures). Both patterns vary from that of earlier villages, where each family had a house much like all others.

The nuclear family probably continued to be the basic social and economic unit in both early and well-developed villages. But the courtyard complex as well as the free-standing, varied-size houses signify new, distinctive changes in social complexity and community organization. Groups of families involved in some sort of specialized economic activity (for example, preparing and trading animal hides at Umm Dabagiyah) perhaps inhabited the structures clustered around a courtyard. Social stratification among families or individuals, as well as a ceremonial or religious function for some of the larger structures, may well explain the variation in size and form at Halaf and Samarra sites. Religious and ritual practices, ownership of property, and organized warfare are also presumed to have developed within and among these farming villages. The occurrence of many of these activities, it must be noted, is presumed more on the basis of archaeological theory than on extant archaeological evidence.

The Hassuna and Halaf cultures relied on rainfall, however precarious, to grow their crops. During the era of the Samarra culture, agricultural technique underwent a marked advance: the use of simple methods of irrigation, including seasonal flooding and limited redirection of streams. As evidence from Choga Mami indicates, irrigation enabled people to live and thrive in northern Mesopotamia, a marginal rainfall area previously unsettled by agriculturalists. Samarran sites—Baghouz on the Euphrates, Tell es-Sawwan on the Tigris, Choga Mami on the eastern rim of the Mesopotamian plain—offer evidence of notable advances in technological and organizational skill. The larger size of Samarran settlements, the material used in their construction (sun-dried mudbricks), and the earliest known adoption of defensive architecture in Mesopotamia reveal these people to have been highly advanced farmers. By virtue of their villages' location, on the lower foothills and plains of northern Mesopotamia, the Samarrans may also have played a role in the spread of agriculture to lowland Mesopotamia.

Lowland Mesopotamia: Productivity and hazards in the alluvial plain

Around 5000 B.C., the settled, agricultural way of life expanded south to the alluvial plain of the Euphrates and Tigris rivers. This was a move of enormous consequence. Southern Mesopotamia's alluvial lowlands were potentially far more fertile than the northern, upland zone. The region south of the 8-inch isohyet, however, lies in the distant shadow of the Levantine coastal mountains. These mountains catch almost all the rain that stems from Mediterranean weather patterns. The resulting, almost total lack of rainfall in the region meant that farming had to await

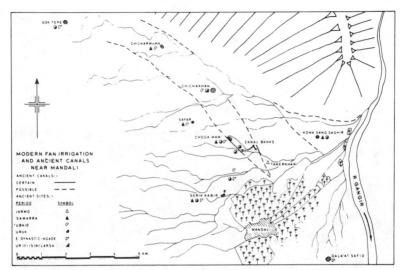

(Courtesy of Dr. Joan Oates)

Plan of early irrigation canals in Samarran period site of Choga Mami, northern Mesopotamia.

the development of irrigation. Prevailing climatic extremes (120°F. is common in the summer) intensified the region's dependence on irrigation. Access to water was thus crucial in the selection of settlement sites and in their subsequent development.

South of modern Baghdad, the riverbeds of the Euphrates and Tigris rise, as they did in antiquity. Both rivers still flow above the level of the plain and create lakes or swamps; occasionally they change their courses unpredictably. Today the ruins of great Mesopotamian river cities like Babylon, Ur, and Nippur are no longer even visible from the main channels of the rivers, eloquent testimony to the changeability of their courses.

The rivers' floods occur just before the spring harvest, when the agricultural cycle demands little moisture. Consequently, in antiquity, their waters had to be contained and the fields supplied with water only when farmers needed it. The earliest gravity-flow irrigation systems took advantage of natural topographical or environmental features: breaches were made in the embankments of the river or local floodwaters were redirected

(Courtesy of Professor W. J. Heimpel)
Water buffalo and modern village in the swamps of southern Iraq.

to the farmer's advantage. Even with such crude technology, irrigated agriculture yielded a dependable surplus of food.

Irrigation made the rich soil of southern Mesopotamia a veritable granary. Barley, more salt and heat resistant than wheat, became the main cereal crop in the south. Date palms provided not only a multipurpose food but also wood, fuel, and fiber. Sheep, though less hardy and less productive of milk than goats, adapted more readily to the hotter climate of the south; cattle proved very valuable both for milk and as beasts of burden. The dense swamps and thickets of southernmost Mesopotamia, meanwhile, provided sustenance in the form of dates, fish, and waterfowl, as well as a highly versatile substance: the reed. Used to make mats, baskets, and boats and as a building material for housing, reeds were later used to write on clay—a cultural innovation the significance of which can hardly be overestimated.

However bountiful the land, life in southern Mesopotamia was beset with perpetual hazards. The powerful streams that fed the Tigris produced seasonal fluctuations with potentially adverse effects on the spring harvest. Both rivers flow at a ca-

(Courtesy of Professor W. J. Heimpel)
Date palms in the swamps of southern Iraq.

pricious rate, and their sheer unpredictability posed a constant threat. Flash floods on the Tigris could strike without warning, destroying crops, livestock, and homes.

Devastating floods and torrential rains form a significant theme in Mesopotamian literature (the Gilgamesh epic and the Atraḫasis epic) as well as in the Hebrew Bible (the episode of Noah and the Ark). The ostensible purpose of floods in the Mesopotamian epics is to punish people for their iniquities or to impose a sort of divinely inspired control on overpopulation. Nonetheless, the way that the ancient authors described the annihilation of every living thing probably reflects the very real and frightening impact that these disasters made on people living in the alluvial plain.

Irrigation itself created other problems. The waters of both rivers contained a high proportion of dissolved salts, and irrigation hastened **salinization** of the soil. Inundated every year for centuries, the ground became encrusted with salt. Textual evidence from ancient Mesopotamia vividly describes the threat that salt posed to the harvest: when the groundwater reached the roots of the field crops, salinization and reduced yields were inevitable. Efficient natural drainage can neutralize the effects of salinization; but in southern Mesopotamia, the land was too flat, the soil too hard, and the rainfall too meager for good drainage.

Low water levels heralded still another kind of catastrophe: drought and famine. In Mesopotamian epics, historical texts, and omens, famine and drought are regarded, like floods, as divine retribution for human misdeeds. The reality behind these dire threats was a desert that stood perpetually poised to supplant fields of grain or palm groves whenever the rivers changed course or the canals silted up. Because of the unpredictability of its rivers, southern Mesopotamia virtually hovered between desert and swamp.

Egypt: The Nile as Provider

The Nile was the great unifying force in Egyptian history. Herodotus, the eminent fifth century B.C. Greek historian known as the Father of History, evidently traveled widely in Egypt and was well acquainted with its culture. Quoting Hecataeus, another Greek traveler, Herodotus called Egypt "the gift of the (Nile) River," a description often quoted approvingly by modern historians. The same sentiment is expressed in a Egyptian paean to the Nile:

> Hail to thee, O Nile, that issues from the earth
>   and comes to keep Egypt alive! . . .
> He that waters the meadows which Re created . . .
> He that makes to drink the desert . . .
> He who makes barley and brings emmer [wheat]
>   into being . . .
> He who brings grass into being for the cattle . . .
> He who makes every beloved tree to grow . . .
> O Nile, verdant art thou, who makest man and
>   cattle to live.[1]

The Nile was not only the source of Egypt's wealth but also the easiest route for transporting it. Ships with sails appear in the archaeological record as early as 3000 B.C.; even so, shipping may have developed earlier. Prevailing northerly winds pro-

(Marburg/Art Resource, NY)

Temples of Abu Simbel, reerected during construction of the Aswan High Dam, as seen from the Nile River.

vided a following breeze for boats traveling against the current and a headwind for those journeying downstream. The huge stone blocks employed in the construction of later, monumental structures—pyramids, temples, obelisks—were transported downstream by boat from Egypt's southern borders.

The Nile and the topography of the Nile valley jointly served a unifying function: ancient Egypt was a single land, uniform in its isolation from other lands. The narrow Nile valley restricted movement into and out of Egypt, and the high desert was, in effect, a defensive system. Virtually impenetrable in the west, two **wadis** (dry riverbeds) in the east provided limited access to the country from the Red Sea. **Cataracts** to the south prevented any fusion with the Sudan or the rest of Africa, though the products of black Africa did seep into the country near the first cataract.

Both Egypt and southern Mesopotamia depended fully on their rivers and on irrigation, but Egypt's environmental conditions were considerably more favorable for agriculture. The deeply cut channel of the Nile and its regular annual flood have contained the river on the same course for millennia; the sites of ancient Egypt, unlike those of Mesopotamia, are still visible from the Nile today. The Nile also lacks tributaries inside Egypt; Nile floods were thus more predictable than those of the Tigris and Euphrates, and they provided greater security for the Egyptian farmer. Furthermore, Egypt's late-summer flood had a beneficial effect on winter crops, while Mesopotamia's spring floods were unfavorable for the same yield. The annual inundation deposited over a very narrow strip on both sides of the Nile a fertile silt rich in minerals, a high-grade natural fertilizer for cultivation.

This natural irrigation process long supported human life and vegetation in the narrow valley of the Nile. When artificial irrigation was introduced in Egypt, probably by 3000 B.C. (at least a thousand years after its initial development in Mesopotamia), it was primarily to *control* the Nile's waters. The farmer's task was to divert the waters through canals into flood basins and then to retain the water in the basins until the soil had thoroughly absorbed it. The combination of fertile soil and irrigation enabled the Egyptian farmer to produce two crops a year in some areas.

Another beneficial factor for agriculture was Egypt's moderate, uniform climate. Summers were hot and winters temperate. There were no severe frosts to threaten crops. The entire year was comparatively dry, but the sparse rainfall was complemented by the Nile floods. Although annual rainfall in present-day Egypt is under 8 inches in the Nile delta and virtually nonexistent south of it, precipitation may have been slightly greater in the prehistoric period. If so, the additional rainfall would have provided sufficient vegetation to support early pastoralists in the Nile valley. Furthermore, salinization posed no problems in Egypt. Year after year, the earth was replenished with the rich black sediments of the Nile flood. With its favorable climate, annually renewed soil, virtually unceasing water supply, and the unremitting toil of its farmers, Egypt could supply a harvest of plenty for all its inhabitants.

The Nile still originates in Lake Victoria in equatorial Africa. At six points in its course, the river is interrupted by abrupt,

(© Roger Wood, London)
The Nile River at Beni Hassan, Upper Egypt.

irregular formations of rocks, usually called by their technical
name, cataracts. Other than these rapids, which would have
hindered boats, the entire course of the Nile was navigable.
Beyond the first (northernmost) cataract at Elephantine, the Nile
flows north without obstacle almost 750 miles to the Mediterranean. The valley north of this first cataract was the heartland
of ancient Egypt.

About 100 miles from the Mediterranean, the Nile enters its
Delta region, so called because the shape resembles the triangular Greek letter of that name. Within the delta, the ancient
Nile divided and flowed to the sea through seven different channels, only two of which remain today. Then as now, the delta
supported abundant wildlife and vegetation. Natural levees and
alluvial flats invited seasonal farming, grazing, and permanent
settlement. Only in the northernmost delta did salt flats, swamps,
and lagoons make habitation impractical.

The harborless coastline of the delta in the north, with its maze of irrigation canals and river channels, did not exactly encourage contact with the outside world. Yet migrating peoples, trade goods, and foreign influences did filter into the Nile valley at the northern corners of the delta, chiefly from the Mediterranean coastline of the Levant.

Since the Nile flowed north, the ancient Egyptians regarded southern Egypt to be upstream and northern Egypt downstream; hence a distinction was made between Upper (southern) and Lower (northern) Egypt. In ancient as well as modern times, the people of these two regions created distinctive cultures and even spoke different dialects. The long, narrow trough valley of Upper Egypt communicated closely with the Nile and with the stark desert cliffs that enclose it. By contrast, the broad expanding delta region north of modern Cairo stretched out flat in every direction. Agriculturally rich and commercially active, Lower Egypt looked outward toward the Mediterranean, Asia, and Europe. Upper Egypt, likewise very productive agriculturally, was oriented inward and south toward Africa.

The interaction between the ancient Egyptians and their environment influenced the choice of settlement sites, the development of irrigation, and agricultural land use patterns. Settlement in Egypt was virtually confined to the relatively narrow Nile River valley, either on levees flanking the river or in the low desert adjacent to the flood plain. Early hieroglyphs referring to *kemet* (the Black Land)—the flood plain with its black soil—and *deshret* (the Red Land, or desert) testify to the impact of their land's sharp contrasts on early Egyptians' vision and culture.

The Red Land was a frontier beyond which few Egyptians ventured. The term *deshret* was even written in Egyptian with a hieroglyph meaning foreign land. The distinction between the flood plain and the surrounding desert highlands was clear-cut: in the language of the ancient Egyptians, highlander was synonymous with foreigner, and "to descend" signified a homecoming from abroad.

Early farming villages did not appear in Egypt until about 5500 B.C., much later than in neighboring ancient western Asia. In northern Egypt, people who lived in the region of the Fayyum depression (once a major lake fed by the Nile) practiced crop raising, hunting, and fishing. The earliest of the southern Egyptian farming cultures, the Badarian of Middle Egypt (named for the site El-Badari), augmented its grain cultivation and stock breeding with hunting and fishing. Judging from the types of grain grown by these people, from their domestication of sheep and goats, and from the fact that equivalent developments occurred much earlier in the uplands of northern Mesopotamia, it appears that the concept and technology of agriculture originally spread to Egypt from western Asia.

By examining their burial practices, it is evident that the people of the Badarian culture were experienced artists and craftsmen. They fashioned ivory combs, handles, and figurines; clay statuettes (molded); cosmetic palettes worked from schist (an easily split, crystalline rock); beads coated with colored glaze. They had begun to experiment with metalworking and produced a few objects of cold-hammered, native copper. The increasing attention given to burials—the use of small wooden tombs in which the above objects as well as food were placed—heralds an early preoccupation with the dead, a trend that continued throughout 5,000 years of Egyptian culture. Later literature abounds with every sort of hymn, curse, prayer, and dedication to the deceased. The ancient tombs that pockmark the Egyptian landscape provide archaeological reality for these literary pictures.

By about 4000 B.C., the Badarian culture was succeeded by the Amratian (named for el-Amra in Upper Egypt and sometimes known as the Early Naqada). What little is known about this relatively short-lived and geographically circumscribed culture suggests some continuity of development with the Badarian. Artistic development continued apace as new pottery types developed and the very first decorated wares—painted naturalistic or geometric designs and incised decoration—appeared in Eqypt. Even through the working of copper was not as evident as stone tool manufacture, related mineral products such as malachite and galena were ground together on stone palettes. Such a practice indicates very early artistic activity (later Egyptian tomb painters were excellent craftsmen) as well as human adaptability (the likely use of these minerals to protect the eyes from the glaring rays of the sun). To judge from the clay figurines found in burials, men and women alike seem to have favored a variety of body ornamentation, including plumes in their hair. Of greater economic significance, the people of the Amratian culture seem to have been the earliest to exploit the natural possibilities of the irrigated Nile Valley.

The Levant and Anatolia

The topography of Mesopotamia and Eqypt shared an obvious focus: people were attracted to their great rivers, and culture developed along the river banks. Both Syria-Palestine and Anatolia lacked rivers as magnetic as the Tigris and Euphrates or as unifying as the Nile. The three rivers of Syria-Palestine (the Orontes, Litani, and Jordan) were impractical as transportation routes or as canals and served minimally, if at all, for irrigation. Anatolia's main river, the Halys (known today as the Kızıl Irmak), flowed chiefly through a steep-sided valley that seriously limited the river's usefulness for agriculture or irrigation.

The Levant

Though the Levant witnessed the development of sedentary villages and a food-producing economy as early as the rest of the Fertile Crescent (ninth–seventh millennia B.C.), subsequent advances there did not keep pace with those of Mesopotamia. Many southern Levantine settlements were abandoned around 6000 B.C., probably to escape the effects of desiccation. In any case, their populations moved toward the moister northern and coastal areas. What little is known of sixth and fifth millennium B.C. Levantine communities indicates an agricultural economy dependent on domesticated plants and animals.

The Levant lacked irrigation in ancient times, partly because it enjoyed sufficient rainfall for agriculture in the coastal areas and highlands and partly due to the absence of suitable rivers. The mountains of the Levant, however, like the rivers of Mesopotamia and Egypt, played a significant role in conditioning settlement and migratory patterns. When moisture-bearing winds off the Mediterranean encountered this formidable mountain barrier, they shed rain on the narrow coastal strip and also in the intermontane highlands.

The coastal plain is narrow in the north and is often broken by mountain spurs projecting into the sea. In the south, the plain broadens and slopes up to the fertile Galilean and Judean hills. The northern highlands in antiquity were thickly forested; they provided Mesopotamia and Egypt with wood from cypress, cedar, and pine trees for building. East of the mountain chain, a steppe zone gradually gives way to the barren wastes of the Arabian plateau, which separates the Levant from Mesopotamia. The approximately 400 miles of desert between the Levant and the Mesopotamian alluvium has always effectively impeded the movement of people, goods, and information. *prevented*

Anatolia

The heartland of Anatolia is virtually surrounded by mountains. Near the source and upper reaches of the Euphrates, these mountains diverge into two separate chains: the Pontic range extending along the southern shore of the Black Sea and the Taurus Mountains projecting along the northern shore of the Mediterranean. Between these ranges lies the central "plateau"—a somewhat misleading term since this zone is full of high-lying plains, river basins, and mountainous massifs of varied origin and nature, including volcanic peaks that rise as high as 13,000 feet. Steep slopes abound; but in comparison with the rugged, craggy relief to the north, south, and east, the plateau is more undulating, and movement and communication are relatively easy. West of the central plateau, the peninsula terminates in another series of mountain ridges that descend toward the Aegean Sea.

The river systems of Anatolia played a minor role in the life of the region's people in antiquity. Though the Euphrates and the Tigris both originate in Anatolia's eastern mountains, neither had much impact on Anatolia itself. The Halys, meanwhile, for most of its 600-mile length, flows too far below the level of the plateau to be suitable for irrigation. In its middle sector, the region of the great loop of the Halys through the central plateau, it is difficult even to ford the river. Cultivation is impossible except for narrow strips of land along the valley floor. The final, northern sector of the river, where it breaks through the Pontic range and descends to the Black Sea from the plateau, both effectively impedes communication and inhibits agriculture.

Anatolia's international role in antiquity was primarily dependent on its abundant metal and obsidian deposits. Probably the Near East's main source of obsidian (a hard volcanic rock used to make tools, weapons, and the like), Anatolia also supplied copper, silver, lead, and timber to its southern and eastern neighbors.

The major seventh millennium B.C. site of Çatal Hüyük, in the Konya plain of south-central Anatolia, is one of the most important early village sites in ancient western Asia. Although its economy was based chiefly on agriculture, trade in obsidian from nearby sources was surely another important component. Çatal Hüyük is perhaps best known for its intricate architecture (139 mudbrick and wood structures have been excavated) and unique wall paintings. The paintings were often multicolored and occasionally were combined with molded relief decoration. Some of the painted designs are so similar to traditional Turkish flat-woven rugs (*kilims*) that the excavator believed this craft had already developed 8,000 years ago. More than any other site in Anatolia, Çatal Hüyük has revealed to the archaeologist's spade and trowel the cultural sophistication and complexity of early sedentary village life.

Difficulties in communication and expansion presented by the Halys River precluded the political unification of the Anatolian plateau until the second millennium B.C. The unifiers, known as the Hittites, were probably not dependent on irrigation, since rainfall on the plateau was usually adequate for agriculture. The Hittites and other Anatolian peoples therefore developed societies different from those of the **hydraulic civilizations** in southern Mesopotamia and Egypt that were based on irrigation.

URBANIZATION: THE EMERGENCE OF CITY LIFE

The emergence of cities and states in the Near East involved interaction among people rather than the interaction between people and their environment that had characterized the de-

(© James Mellaart)

Shrine VI.A.50 at the Neolithic site of Çatal Hüyük, Turkey, with wall paintings of kilim-*like designs and a figure believed to be a goddess, and with molded reliefs of bucrania.*

velopment of agriculture. Many factors converged to bring about the development of the first cities in the Near East, notably those of Mesopotamia. Most early cities evolved from farming villages. Improvements in agricultural practice, especially irrigation, produced a stable food base that allowed increases in population and in the density of settlement. Irrigated agriculture necessarily promoted differences in land productivity, since the land closest to the rivers was the most fertile and was assured of an adequate water supply. This situation led to variations in wealth among farmers and gradually to the emergence of distinct social classes. At the same time, the complex system of canals, ditches, dikes, and other contrivances essential to irrigation demanded cooperation among diverse labor forces and social groups. Scarcity of pastureland, which made the cultivation and storage of fodder vital to the well-being of domesticated animals, called for the management of herds. Access-to-water rights, storage and re-distribution of food surpluses, and the need to import basic raw materials also helped to create a growing need for concerted decision making, regulation, and control.

At the same time, food surpluses made it possible for some individuals to give up farming to become craftsmen, laborers, merchants, and administrators. Gradually a central economic authority—either temple administrators or a propertied elite class—began to fulfill the need for centralized control. It is impossible to sort all the factors into a linear, cause-and-effect relationship. Sedentary agriculture, irrigation, food surpluses, the need for imported raw materials, social organization and co-operation—all worked together in a complex system that produced dynamic economic and social results.

Urban Culture in Mesopotamia

A city is an area permanently inhabited by people whose numbers are significantly larger and whose relationships are more complex than those of a family, tribe, or clan. But what do we mean when we talk about prehistoric cities and about urbanization in ancient times? The essential characteristics of the first cities were a series of new economic institutions: social classes, hierarchical administrative systems, and a highly centralized economy.

The first innovation identifiable in the Mesopotamian archaeological record is the construction of temples. Although the earliest identifiable temple (at Eridu in the South of the country) has been dated to about 5000 B.C., these structures assume more monumental proportions toward the end of the fourth millennium B.C. New attitudes and new modes of social interaction appear to have crystallized around these massive undertakings; at the same time, they united people in new social groupings. The authority represented by these temple structures probably assumed much of the responsibility for organizing and directing urban society.

Written records that would allow detailed discussion of the role of these temples within early urban society do not exist. Nevertheless, the temples obviously represent a physical manifestation of religious beliefs and ideological precepts. Third millennium B.C. textual references suggest that these early temples housed the priests, the human representatives of the gods, in their roles as lords of the temple estates and directors of the daily economic activities of the urban centers. Without written evidence, however, it is impossible to know precisely what these temples represented for the people who built them or why they were built. From archaeological evidence that reveals the careful planning, construction, and elaboration of the earliest cities' monumental buildings, it is clear that craft specialization and eventually full-blown ceramic and textile industries began to mature during the fourth millennium B.C.

Trade and commerce came under the control of either the temples or a few families whose wealth and power were based on control of the most fertile tracts of land. These religious and landed elites constituted the upper strata of society. By controlling the production of crafts or the distribution of imported goods and agricultural products, these central authorities within the cities would have accumulated greater wealth, which may in turn have instigated social conflict or warfare.

Resolution of conflict surely required the creation of civic institutions (judicial, military, managerial), which probably further entrenched the position of the central economic authority. This authority increasingly controlled the productive resources of society and, in so doing, further sharpened social divisions.

Thus the earliest cities were products of many interacting forces, all of which operated in such a way that the area surrounding a city became increasingly dependent on the city's numerous services, while the city relied on the agricultural surplus of its hinterland. Certain villages tended to attract adjacent developing settlements; eventually the main settlement and its satellites formed a single urban cluster.

The late fourth millennium B.C. site of Uruk (Erech in the Bible, Warka today), on the banks of the Euphrates in southernmost Mesopotamia, may be taken as a typical early urban center. The city may have covered as much as 30 acres, and its population may have numbered as many as 10,000 souls. Although there must have been large areas with domestic architecture and craftsmen's quarters, the two sectors most thoroughly excavated are both presumed to have been religious precincts. The structures were very elaborate, with colonnaded halls, mosaic courts, and finely niched walls, the whole built on a raised platform with combinations of ramps and steps for access. Constructed of complex mudbrick-work or of limestone blocks brought at least 40 miles from the Arabian plateau, these monumental buildings stand as eloquent testimony to the powerful impact that the divine—or their human caretakers—made upon the urban inhabitants of late prehistoric Mesopotamia.

Much of Mesopotamia's socioeconomic and political development occurred in response to what has been called "the deficient environment." Mesopotamia relied heavily on external trade. Almost all basic raw materials, including wood, metal, and stone, had to be imported—especially to southern Mesopotamia, where the rich alluvial soil was the most vital resource. This lack of essential raw materials fostered and encouraged trade and, eventually, territorial expansion. And the exchange of goods, local and imported, along with the redistribution of agricultural produce further promoted the process of urbanization. Such utilitarian materials as timber, flint, limestone, and perhaps bitumen began to be imported in quantity, while more precious goods like metal and stone trickled in from distant sources. In exchange, the inhabitants of Mesopotamia may have traded manufactured goods like textiles and leathers, as well as foodstuffs.

Three distinct cultural periods characterized the fifth and fourth millennia B.C.: the Ubaid (about 5000–3600 B.C.), the Uruk (about 3600–3300 B.C.), and the Protoliterate, consisting of the Late Uruk and Jemdet Nasr phases (about 3300–2900 B.C.). During the Ubaid period, modest farming villages began to grow into large population centers, and the temple or temple complex originated. Monumental architectural structures, such as the temples uncovered at Warka, characterized the Uruk period. By the Protoliterate (Early Literate) period, the temple clearly played the central social, economic, and political role in early Mesopotamian cities.

Irrigation was instrumental in the growth of village size and population during the Ubaid period. At the site of Eridu, in extreme southern Mesopotamia, the sequence of temples first built in the Ubaid period and rebuilt over the next 2,000 years represents the earliest evidence of organized religious activity in southern Mesopotamia. These early temples at Eridu were small in comparison with the much larger structures of the Uruk period, just as the size of the site at Eridu in the Ubaid period was only about 4 acres in comparison with the 30-acre extent of Uruk in the later period. Apparently the status and power of the temple grew together with the size of the buildings and the extent of the settlement itself.

If the temple at Eridu attests to the existence of a religious hierarchy in Mesopotamia by the Ubaid period, the monumental religious architecture of the Uruk period suggests a powerful elite commanding an organized, skilled, resourceful labor force. Meanwhile the temple itself had evolved into an elaborate architectural complex. The White Temple unearthed at Uruk is a prime example, and Uruk remained a pinnacle of Mesopotamian achievement throughout the Uruk and succeeding Protoliterate periods. The three-part plan of the White Temple—with its long central room bordered on either side with rows of smaller rooms and with its architecture sporting buttresses and niches—was very similar in size, general plan, and individual features to the later Sumerian temples of the historical period (see page 48).

Lacking comprehensive written records, and as a result of limited archaeological excavation in Ubaid- and Uruk-period levels at Mesopotamian sites, we can only make inferences about social organization and social classes. Given the size and elaboration of the temple complexes by the Uruk period, the administrators or personnel of the temple must have had access to wealth quite disproportionate to that of the other members of society. High-status goods—finely worked objects of gold and silver, or beads and pendants of imported semiprecious stones such as carnelian, turquoise, and **lapis lazuli**—were found in the greatest concentrations within the temples. Their occurrence elsewhere, however, suggests that wealth was not confined to members of the temple institution. It is not even possible to speculate on the makeup of the labor force that constructed the temples, on the role of slaves or priests (if such there were), or on the nature of the families or individuals who built, maintained, and presumably served or worshiped at these temples.

(From H. and R. Leacroft, *The Buildings of Ancient Mesopotamia*, Leicester, 1974)

"Cut open" reconstruction of the White Temple at Uruk (Warka) in southern Mesopotamia. Uruk period, late fourth millennium B.C.

By the end of the fourth millennium B.C. (the Protoliterate period), population centers that can be called urban by virtue of both size and function existed not just in southern Mesopotamia but also at Tell Brak and perhaps Nineveh in the north and at Habuba Kabira in Syria. By this time, the temple had become the center of what may have been a redistributive economy—one in which goods were collected and redistributed by a centralized authority. The temple hierarchy presumably controlled such matters as land ownership, employment of workers and craft specialists, and management of long-distance trade. The temple authority wielded a strong influence on technological developments (e.g., introduction of the plow, invention of the wheel) and exercised clear political dominance over the city and its hinterland.

Each city and its surrounding area functioned as an irrigated island separated from other such islands by open stretches of desert and swamp. The irrigated islands, many of which eventually evolved into full-fledged city-states (see Chapter III), developed strong separatist tendencies that were to be a recurring theme in the political history of the country; the nonarable regions ultimately came to be a source of strategic dispute. This pattern, imposed by the geography of southern Mesopotamia, always hindered attempts to unify the country. The deep-rooted particularism of the fully developed Mesopotamian city-states may plausibly be traced to this economic and political dependence between a town and its encircling territory.

The Ubaid and Uruk cultures may have spread along the burgeoning trading network. In any case, pottery and architecture characteristic of the Uruk period spread throughout the Mesopotamian plain and beyond. Contact with areas beyond Mesopotamia increased during the Protoliterate era. The site of Habuba Kabira, on the Euphrates in northern Syria, shows so many similarities with southern Mesopotamia that it must have been a trading outpost. By the beginning of the historical period, an extensive trade network connected Mesopotamia with other parts of ancient western Asia. Rivers—especially the less turbulent Euphrates—and their tributaries served as trade and transportation routes, and boats were the chief means of transport. Besides carrying imported commodities, the rivers provided for the movement of people, redistribution of goods and supplies, and transport of military contingents.

The achievements of the Ubaid, Uruk, and Protoliterate periods were considerable. Agriculture, nourished by irrigation, became the primary method of subsistence. Sometime during the fourth millennium B.C., farming was simplified by the introduction of the plow. The first use of wheel-made pottery in the Uruk period indicates that the wheel had been invented by the fourth millennium B.C.

Before the end of the Protoliterate period, orchards began to be cultivated; dates proliferated in southernmost Mesopotamia; figs in the northern, upland areas, and olives in the eastern Mediterranean and the Levant. Sheep and goats had been the most useful animals in the early, upland villages, but settlement in the hot and dry Mesopotamian plain made cattle much more important. Sheep raising continued, however, because of the wool, which together with flax served the needs of the urban textile makers. The overall efficiency of farming and the resultant food surpluses were essential for the administrators, craftsmen, laborers, and merchants of a complex society.

Craft specialization and industries (ceramic, metallurgical, textile) began to mature during the fourth millennium B.C. Direct evidence for this exists in the careful planning, construction, and elaboration of the monumental buildings of the earliest cities. **Cylinder seals**, which in historic times indicated personal ownership, also became common during the Protoliterate era. These cylindrical stone seals, one or two inches in height, were engraved with images (and later with brief inscriptions) that were reproduced when the cylinder was rolled over a wet clay surface.

The Protoliterate period is so named because of the first appearance of **pictographic writing** on clay tablets, the single-most momentous invention of Mesopotamian civilization. The earliest writing dates from about 3100 B.C., during the Late Uruk phase. Because it was purely schematic and at least partially pictographic (see page 55), the language of the earliest tablets remains unidentified. By the succeeding Jemdet Nasr phase, however, enough **phonetic elements** were employed in the tablets to certify what scholars had expected: the language was Sumerian (see the next section, Prehistory and the Sumerians). Writing proved to be the most effective way of collecting and disseminating information in a complex society. By making it possible to keep records and to speed up communication, writing facilitated the further development and and centralization of the cities.

All these innovations—writing, craft specialization, the wheel, the plow, and monumental architecture—stand out in the archaeological record of the earliest cities. Yet the most significant developments were in the area of socioeconomic organization. Social classes appeared, administrative systems were arranged hierarchically, and the economy (managed by the powerful temple-institution) became highly centralized. Ultimately these developments would affect all of Western civilization. During the first millennium B.C., the political and commercial em-

(Giraudon/Art Resource, NY)

Cylinder seal of the Protoliterate period, with seal impression.

pires of the Near East came into direct contact with the Greeks and Romans. These sophisticated urban cultures were clearly influenced by Near Eastern systems of agriculture, technology, art and architecture, writing, and even administration.

Prehistory and the Sumerians

Cuneiform tablets written in the Sumerian language demonstrate the decisive influence of the Sumerians on Mesopotamian law, religion, literature, art, architecture, and science after 3000 B.C. Although the preeminence of the Sumerians in southern Mesopotamia lasted at least from 3000 to 2350 B.C., their origin and first appearance in the region have long remained a mystery and thus sparked scholarly debate.

Who were the Sumerians? Where did they come from, and when did they arrive in Mesopotamia? Did they initiate the developments of the Ubaid and Uruk periods, or did they simply elaborate on foundations built by earlier inhabitants?

Since Sumerian beginnings necessarily predate written records, questions about those beginnings cannot be answered solely by considering written records from the historical period. The mute evidence of prehistoric archaeology must be carefully evaluated in conjunction with later historical documents.

Archaeological data strongly point to continuity in population, in architectural traditions, and in pottery styles within southern Mesopotamia from the fifth through the third millennium B.C. The sequence of temples built at Eridu beginning in the fifth millennium B.C.—the Ubaid period—contained all the basic features of later third millennium B.C. Sumerian temples: three-part plan, construction on a raised platform, the use of regular buttressing and niches. In fact, some scholars associate fishbones found in the early shrines at Eridu with worship of the Sumerian deity Enki. Symbolized by fresh water, Enki was the city-god of Eridu in historical times. The White Temple of mid-fourth millennium B.C. Uruk was closely comparable to later Sumerian temples in its monumental size, three-part layout, and design; it was clearly the prototype, if not the direct antecedent, of the Sumerian structures.

The prehistoric civilization of Mesopotamia had reached a high level of achievement by the Protoliterate period at the end of the fourth millennium B.C. Moreover, the rapid succession of interrelated material accomplishments (e.g., invention of the wheel and first use of wheel-made pottery; introduction of the plow and the increasing sophistication in irrigation techniques, both of which made agricultural surpluses for urban dwellers possible) and the continuity in ceramic and architectural tradition both suggest that a single culture was responsible for this achievement. Since no written evidence exists to reveal the language spoken in southern Mesopotamia between 5000 and 3000 B.C., attempts to identify the ethnolinguistic composition of this culture must remain speculative. Yet we know that during the Protoliterate period (about 3100 B.C.), when textual evidence intelligible to us first becomes available, the main ethnolinguistic group in southern Mesopotamia was Sumerian.

These converging streams of archaeological and written evidence make it reasonable to suggest that the Sumerians had been in Mesopotamia since the beginning of the Ubaid period, about 5000 B.C. But because it is impossible to demonstrate that the Ubaid and Uruk temple builders spoke Sumerian, the case must be argued differently.

During the period from 5000 to 3000 B.C., a single culture developed in southern Mesopotamia. Cultural developments similar to those of the Ubaid period occurred somewhat contemporaneously in neighboring southwestern Iran (Khuzistan) and along the Gulf coast of Saudi Arabia, but there is no indication that they preceded the events in southern Mesopotamia. Although the ethnic identity of this Mesopotamian population remains unknown, sufficient reason exists to associate the Sumerians with southern Mesopotamia, and there is no longer any evidence to derive them from elsewhere.

Finally, the fact that the earliest tablets *intelligible* to us were written in the Sumerian language helps to resolve the problem of Sumerian origins. The population of the southern alluvium must always have been mixed. Yet archaeological evidence—the continuities in material culture—and linguistic evidence—the fact that the Sumerian language was used in the Protoliterate tablets—both allow us to argue that the Sumerians must have been present in southern Mesopotamia since about 5000 B.C.

The Levant and Egypt in Late Prehistory

The Levant did not participate in the evolutionary developments in agriculture that eventually fostered the urban transformation in Mesopotamia. Until the late fourth millennium B.C., the economy and social organization of Levantine settlements remained at the level of the agricultural village.

The urban center at Habuba Kabira near the great bend of the Euphrates River in northern Syria owes its importance to a pivotal location on trade routes that ran in all directions. Nonetheless, the impetus for such a major urban center seems to have stemmed from trade associated with Mesopotamian (Sumerian) civilization, not from commercial expansion within Syria itself. There are as yet no other contemporary sites in Syria that reveal such strides toward urbanization.

The absence of irrigation in the Levant meant that people were less strictly bound to the riverbanks. The topographical variety of the region—coastal plains, mountain ranges, intermontane valleys, steppe, and desert—led to the formation of small territorial units rather than politically unified states. Topography also delimited the routes that could be used for migration and commerce. Gradually, however, the Levant came to serve as the crossroads for Near Eastern and eastern Mediterranean trade.

North-south traffic moved freely, but the few east-west passages—Damascus, Qatna, Hamath, Ebla (and earlier, Habuba Kabira), and Alalakh—became vital commercial lifelines. The Levantine coast, with its many harbors, boasted some of the best-known ports of trade in antiquity: Ugarit, Byblos, Tyre, Sidon, and Akko.

Commercially Syria-Palestine was a bridge between Egypt, Anatolia, and Mesopotamia. Politically and militarily the entire area often served as a battleground where the more powerful states of ancient western Asia struggled for supremacy. Yet this region's greatest impact on history was to be its religious and cultural legacies, notably Hebrew monotheism and the Phoenician alphabet. Empires rise and fall, but beliefs and ideas defy the passage of time.

An agricultural way of life had become as firmly entrenched in Egypt as in Mesopotamia by the Gerzean or Late Naqada period (about 3600–3000 B.C.). When we consider the phenomenon of urbanization in Egypt, we fall into a dilemma. With few exceptions (Tell el-Amarna, Abydos, Tell ed-Daba), the ancient towns of Egypt remain largely unexcavated and unstudied. While archaeological investigations in Mesopotamia, Anatolia, and the Levant concentrated on town sites, archaeologists working in Egypt have usually chosen temple sites and cemeteries to excavate and study. Scholarly debate further clouds the issue. According to **philologists** who specialize in the study of ancient Egyptian writing and language, early Egyptian civilization lacked towns: the Egyptian language made no distinction between towns and other types of settlements. Archaeologists, on the other hand, have uncovered towns as well as secure evidence of urban life in ancient Egypt: archaeology works with its own designations and allows comparisons with other urban cultures as well as among ancient Egyptian settlements themselves.

Casting aside what is essentially a matter of semantics, complicated by a dearth of archaeological exploration in town sites, it is clear that the ancient Egyptians lived in towns, some of which were almost certainly urban centers. In theory, we may suggest that the stimulus for urbanization in late prehistoric Egypt arose, as it did in Mesopotamia, from the juxtaposition of several factors: agricultural surpluses derived from the fertile alluvial soil of the Nile; the availability of precious goods and desirable raw materials (copper, gold, ivory, ebony) in the immediate area; the stimulus to increase food surpluses by intentional ("artificial") irrigation (see pages 39 and 42). As in Mesopotamia, all these factors required divisions of labor, concentrations of population, supervision, and centralized organization—prerequisites for an urban center with a hierarchical social structure.

Some of these developments may even have been the direct result of Mesopotamian influence. During the late prehistoric period, Egypt appears to have assimilated some foreign influence that may have stimulated its own rise to civilization. These intrusive cultural elements, most obvious in the Naqada region of Upper Egypt, have a distinctively Mesopotamian flavor. Any contact between Mesopotamia and Egypt would probably have occurred along one of the wadis that provided access to the Red Sea.

Besides various architectural and artistic elements, such as cylinder seals, Egypt's most significant borrowing from Mesopotamia—if such it was—would indisputably have been the *concept* of writing. Mesopotamia's primacy in writing is not disputed, and its gradual evolution has been traced (see pages 53–59). In Egypt, by contrast, writing appeared rather abruptly and, from the start, employed elements characteristic of an advanced stage of writing. The two writing systems are so dissimilar that if borrowing from Mesopotamia did occur, it was limited to the idea that a standardized picture can convey a specific word and that words difficult to depict can be expressed phonetically by the rebus principle (see page 58).

Technical, artistic, and cultural borrowings from Mesopotamia may have exercised formative influence during Egypt's transition to the historical epoch. Yet foreign stimulus was at most a catalyst: Egypt promptly and radically transformed these and other innovations into forms distinctively Egyptian. Little trace remained of the presumed Mesopotamian prototypes.

Gerzean cultural remains of the late fourth millennium B.C. are found in both Upper and Lower Egypt. Hunting of wild animals declined, and farming became the basic economic activity of Gerzean society. People lived in small, rectangular huts fitted with a wood-framed doorway in one side. Metallurgy was introduced, and craftsmen began to fashion and cast ribbed daggers, flat axes, and knives. The richness of some Gerzean tombs and the exotic imports (copper, lead, silver, gold, lapis lazuli) suggest that society was becoming stratified. Not only do the imports imply that some people in Gerzean society were wealthier than others, they also indicate increasing Egyptian participation in the major trading networks of the Near East in the late fourth millennium B.C. Although there is no indication of the large monumental structures or the temple complexes that characterized late prehistoric Mesopotamia, a successful agricultural economy in Egypt had probably produced a wealthy elite— landed, religious, or both.

Later written documents imply that political institutions began to develop in Egypt during late Gerzean times. Although this may be a backward projection of later events, it can be assumed that the Gerzean period was a time of regional rivalry. At the dawn of the historic period, before Egypt was unified under a single ruler, there were several centers of power. Favored by a strong agricultural economy and the possibility of trade, these centers developed into political and economic constellations that, if not urban, offered all the key conditions for urbanization.

For unknown reasons, a long period of hostility prevailed between the towns of Upper and Lower Egypt. As a result of this prolonged conflict, the power of military leaders evidently increased and became permanent. Herein lay the conditions that were later to lead to the unification of Egypt and the rise of the pharaonic state. Urban developments were nipped in the bud as a centralized government came to monopolize trade. The former towns were stripped of their political and economic strength as power was concentrated in a single monarch and in his royal residence. The surge toward urbanization in Egypt, theoretically very similar to that in Mesopotamia, appears to have been rapid and intense. The independent centers of the Gerzean period passed through a rapid, competitive phase of economic and technological (irrigation) development and effectively adopted a national, state system.

FROM PEBBLE TO WEDGE: THE EVOLUTION OF WRITING

Writing was held in the highest regard in the ancient world. Its origin and invention were associated with gods or heroes. Egyptians credited Thoth, the god of wisdom, science, and medicine, with the creation of writing. In Babylonia, Nabu, divine scribe and patron deity of scribes, revealed the secrets of writing to humans. For the Sumerians, the role of Nabu was filled by Nisaba, the wife of Enlil, the god of the earth's atmosphere. Later, Jewish tradition regarded Moses as the inventor of letters. The Greeks, Chinese, and Hindus also believed in the divine origin of script. Through writing, the rich technological, religious, literary, and political lore of antiquity has survived into modern times. Writing, in sum, gives permanence to human knowledge.

There are three main types of writing. In pictographic/logographic writing, such as **hieroglyphic** systems, a given picture or sign stands for a particular word or idea. In syllabic systems, such as cuneiform, words and ideas are spelled out phonetically, syllable by syllable. (Note that hieroglyphic writing is not entirely pictographic, nor is cuneiform wholly syllabic.) Finally, in alphabetic writing, each sign represents a particular sound.

People have lived without writing throughout most of human history. Yet images, symbols, and other devices were used to transmit thought long before the advent of writing. During the Upper Palaeolithic era (Old Stone Age), about 30,000 to 12,000 years ago, incised bones may have been used to keep track of lunar time. If so, these bone artifacts represent the earliest known system of counting, or "reckoning." Whether these records were intended for use by people other than their makers is uncertain. In any case, most such developments ended with the decline of Paleolithic cultures by the end of the last ice age, about 10,000 B.C.

Throughout the Near East, from Iran to Khartoum in the Sudan, small clay or, less often, stone tokens of varying shapes have surfaced in archaeological excavations. Dating from as early as the eighth millennium B.C., these objects were originally thought to be gaming pieces or marbles, as if the ancient world sat constantly at play. Purposely fire hardened, their function must have necessitated some permanence. These diminutive (.08–.8 inch, or 3 millimeter to 2 centimeter) spheres, rods, discs, cones, and tetrahedrons may represent counters in an archaic recording system. If so, they are closely linked to the origins of writing.

The use of pebbles, sticks, bones, and other natural materials for purposes of computation characterizes many cultures, ancient and modern. The human mind's need to visualize mathematical calculations is well served by such devices; the abacus is perhaps the best-known example. Each of the clay tokens of the ancient Near East is thought to have stood for a different item or commodity.

Although this still-evolving theory of the origin of writing is not fully accepted by all scholars, its comprehensiveness strongly suggests that we are on the right track. It is believed that the geometric forms of many tokens were symbolic in nature and unrelated to the shapes of the items they represented. Some tokens represented a unit of a particular good (for example, a measure of grain) while others represented commodities (see Chart 2–1). Tokens would have been used for taking inventory or keeping records of transactions, for bartering, and conceivably for tabulating animals in a flock or the fruits of the harvest. The token system remained markedly stable from the eighth to the fourth millennium B.C. The abundance of tokens in archaeological levels dating from about 3500 B.C. attests to their popularity and widespread adoption. It has been deduced that this system transcended language barriers; that is, its meaning was readily perceived by those who came into contact with it.

The next stage in the evolution of writing, it is argued, occurred shortly after 3500 B.C., during the Uruk period. The ear-

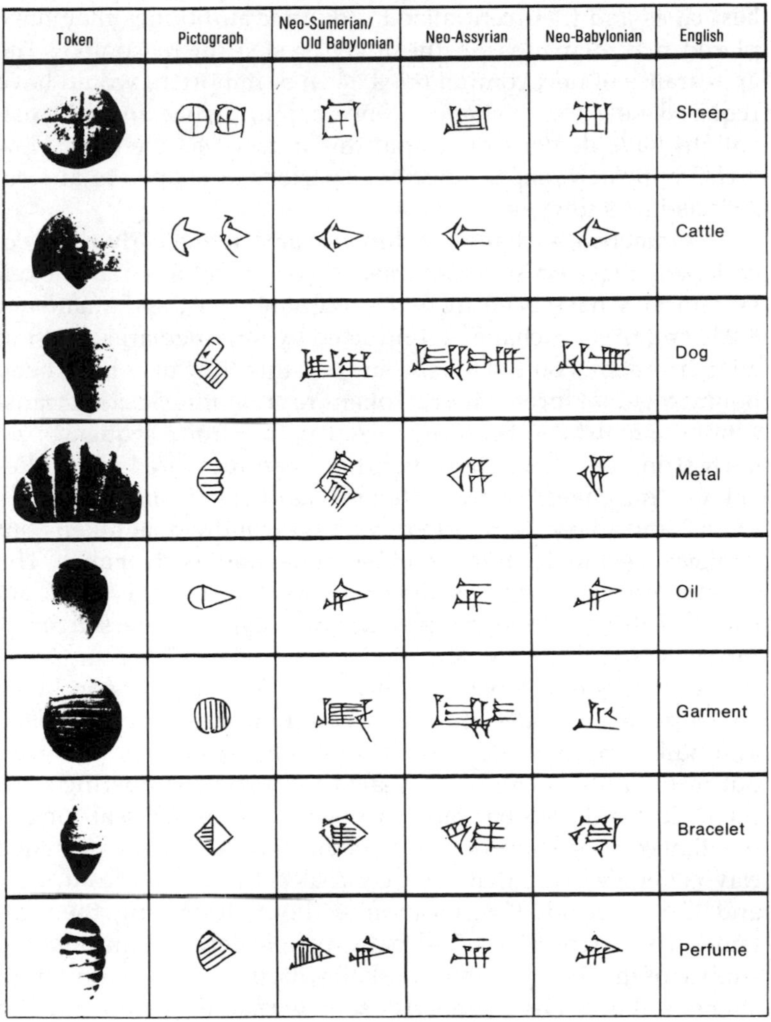

Token	Pictograph	Neo-Sumerian/ Old Babylonian	Neo-Assyrian	Neo-Babylonian	English
					Sheep
					Cattle
					Dog
					Metal
					Oil
					Garment
					Bracelet
					Perfume

Courtesy of *Archaeology Magazine*, Archaeological Institute of America

Chart 2–1 Evolution from Token to Cuneiform Writing

liest cities and their centralized economic authorities may have placed new demands on the token system of reckoning. The appearance of new commodities, local or imported, would have required new token shapes. Once again, archaeological excavations have demonstrated that this in fact was the case. New forms appeared, expanding the repertory of shapes to at least 250 distinct subtypes.

Commercial exchange within and among the early cities occasionally required intermediaries. Two innovations in the token system may have been made to accommodate the demands of trade and other exchanges conducted by intermediaries. First of all, perforations on the tokens suggest that they may have been bound together for transport. Tokens representing specific transactions might have been organized in a definite sequence; no such string of tokens, however, has been recovered intact. Resultant "messages," such as "ten loaves of bread, sixty measures of oil," and so on, were no longer merely individual tokens but connected symbols understood by sender and receiver alike. The creator or seller of the product presumably sent this "official" count of the goods to the prospective buyer via messenger or intermediary.

A parallel development—the use of a small, spherical clay envelope called a *bulla*—further secured the exchange of tokens. The bulla, approximately the size of a baseball, was hollowed out to hold tokens and was sealed to prevent tampering with them. It could also be impressed with a cylinder seal for authentication or to show ownership. The drawback of these opaque clay envelopes was that they concealed the tokens from view and thus precluded verification without destroying the container. To overcome this drawback, people began to impress the surface of the fresh, pliable clay ball with the number and rough shape of the tokens within. These new markings were applied on top of the seal, either by using the tokens themselves or by means of a stick or thumbprint.

These marks are the crucial link between the three-dimensional token system and a two-dimensional writing system. Anyone familiar with the tokens could now "read" the clay balls. Once these impressed bullae began to be used, it would soon have become apparent that tokens were superfluous: the requisite information could now be provided in full on the outside of the bulla. At this stage, the bullae are fully representative of the dynamism of writing as a symbolic linkage of symbols.

The earliest tablets, which also functioned as economic records, resembled the bullae in size, shape, and even convexity. In place of geometric tokens enclosed in a clay ball, the tablets used written characters inscribed on a clay ball. The signs on the earliest impressed tablets, although very similar in form to the spheres, rods, and cones on the clay balls, were so imprecise that they were first supplemented and then rapidly supplanted by incised signs. The use of a stylus to incise the signs allowed a better approximation of the geometric shapes and peculiar markings of the tokens.

According to the token theory, therefore, the signs used on the earliest tablets were not actual pictographs. That is, they portrayed not specific objects but symbolic tokens. From the outset, then, writing employed a system of symbols whose meanings were widely understood regardless of language. In time, these signs became simplified, and small drawings of the tokens were incised on the tablets with a pointed stylus. Newer vocabulary words came to be depicted by true pictographs in the likeness of the objects represented. The adaptation of a special stylus, usually made from reeds, ultimately gave the Sumerian script its standardized cuneiform (wedge-shaped) character.

This theory argues that, earlier assumptions to the contrary, writing was a step in the evolution of an ingenious computing system. A marginal invention—the use of bullae—transformed an accounting method into writing, one of the dynamics of civilization. The tokens may well have functioned as a common language of accounting for a number of prehistoric and early historic cultures of ancient western Asia. While the token system eventually reverted to its original computational function, the cuneiform system of writing it spawned continued in use for almost 3,000 years until Aramaic, an alphabetic writing system, replaced it. Sumerian, the earliest known language represented in cuneiform, uses a logographic system wherein each sign or sign group corresponds to a single word. Initially the system included over 2,000 signs. By the end of the Early Dynastic period (see Chapter III), about 2350 B.C., however, this number had been reduced to about 600.

Another important development in early Mesopotamian writing was the *rebus principle*, whereby a word or idea is represented by depicting objects whose names suggest the word or idea they represent. Consider, for example, the English word *treaty*. Difficult to render in a picture or pictograph, its rebus representation might be a *tree* plus a *tea*cup or a *tea* bag. The rebus principle simplified writing, reduced ambiguity, and immeasurably increased the range of expressible ideas. The ultimate consequence of rebus writing was phonetization: representation of the sounds that express an idea, rather than depiction of the idea itself. Only after the phonemic system had progressed to the point that signs were more syllabic than logographic could writing be used to express the full range of sounds and ideas encountered in spoken language. This too had been accomplished by the end of the Early Dynastic period.

The earliest tablets were purely economic documents, but cuneiform writing was eventually used to express political, juridical, literary, philosophical/religious, and scientific ideas. Treaties, letters, contracts, accounts, court decisions, and law codices written in cuneiform survive. Most cuneiform archives, however, contain a large percentage of economic, bureaucratic, and commercial documents.

The mixed syllabic-logographic cuneiform system was eventually used for many languages: Sumerian, Akkadian, Eblaite, Hurrian, Hittite, Elamite, and Urartian. Writing greatly facilitated communication and interaction between people in different areas. The discovery of identical or nearly identical lists at widely separated sites, such as Ebla in northern Syria and Tell Abu Salabikh in southern Mesopotamia, attests to efforts to standardize the writing system and to facilitate interregional communication.

Most important, writing fostered the swift exchange of information in a society that was rapidly becoming bureaucratic, where economic transactions had become too complicated to rely on human memory. The development of the computer is a comparable surge forward in our own times. The growth, centralization, and maintenance of Mesopotamian cities depended on the rapid transmission of information by writing.

NOTE

1. Translation by J. A. Wilson, in *Ancient Near Eastern Texts Relating to the Old Testament*, 3d ed., ed. J. B. Pritchard (Princeton, N.J.:Princeton University Press, 1969), p. 372.

SUPPLEMENTARY READINGS

Adams, R. M. 1981. *Heartland of Cities: Surveys of Ancient Settlement and Land Use on the Central Floodplain of the Euphrates*. Chicago: University of Chicago Press.

Braidwood, R. J. 1974. *Prehistoric Men*. 8th ed. Glenview, Ill.: Scott, Foresman.

Butzer, K. W. 1976. *Early Hydraulic Civilization in Egypt*. Chicago: University of Chicago Press.

Cauvin, J., and P. Sanlaville, eds. 1981. *Préhistoire du Levant. Chronologie & Organisation de l'Espace depuis les Origines jusqu'au VI Millénaire*. Colloque Internationaux du Centre National de la Recherche Scientifique 598. Paris: Centre National de la Recherche Scientifique.

Childe, V. Gordon. 1954. *New Light on the Most Ancient East*. London: Routledge & Kegan Paul.

Edwards, I. E. S.; C. J. Gadd; and N. G. L. Hammond, eds. 1970. Prolegomena and Prehistory. *The Cambridge Ancient History*, vol. 1, part 1, 3d ed. Cambridge: Cambridge University Press.

Flannery, K. V. 1973. "The origins of agriculture." *Annual Review of Anthropology* 2, pp. 271–310.

Hoffman, M. A. 1979. *Egypt before the Pharaohs: The Prehistoric Foundations of Egyptian Civilization*. New York: Alfred A. Knopf.

Hole, F. (ed.) 1987. *The Archaeology of Western Iran: Settlement Society from Prehistory to the Islamc Conquest*. Smithsonian Series in Archaeological Inquiry 1. Smithsonian Institute: Washington, D.C.

Hole, F. 1977. *Studies in the Archaeological History of the Deh Luran Plain*. Memoirs of the Museum of Anthropology, University of Michigan, no. 9. Ann Arbor: University of Michigan.

Jones, T. B. 1969. *The Sumerian Problem*. New York: John Wiley & Sons.

Leonard, J. N., and Time-Life editors. 1973. *The First Farmers*. New York: Time-Life Books.

Mellaart, J. 1975. *The Neolithic of the Near East*. London: Thames and Hudson.

Moore, A. M. T. 1985. "The development of Neolithic societies in the Near East." In *Advances in World Archaeology*, ed. F. Wendorf and A. E. Close. Vol. 4, pp. 1–69.

Moorey, P. R. S. 1979. *The Origins of Civilization*. Oxford: Clarendon Press.

Oates, D. and J. Oates. 1976. *The Rise of Civilization*. Oxford: Elsevier-Phaidon.

Redman, C. L. 1978. *The Rise of Civilization: From Early Farmers to Urban Society in the Ancient Near East*. San Francisco: W. H. Freeman.

Reed, C. A. 1977. *Origins of Agriculture*. The Hague: Mouton Press.

Renfrew, C. 1979. *Before Civilization*. Cambridge: Cambridge University Press.

Schmandt-Besserat, D. 1986. "The Origins of Writing—An Archaeologist's Perspective." *Written Communication* 3, no. 1, pp. 31–45.

———. 1983. "Tokens and counting." *Biblical Archaeologist* 46, pp. 117–20.

———. 1980. "The Envelopes that Bear the First Writing." *Technology and Culture* 21, no. 3, pp. 357–85.

Smith, P. E. L., and T. C. Young, Jr., 1983. "The Force of Numbers: Population Pressure in the Central Western Zagros 12,000–4500 B.C." In *The Hilly Flanks and Beyond*, ed. T. C. Young, Jr., P. E. L. Smith, and P. Mortensen. Studies in Ancient Oriental Civilization, volume 36, pp 141–161. Chicago: Oriental Institute.

Smith, P. E. L., and T. C. Young, Jr. 1972. "The Evolution of Early Agriculture and Culture in Greater Mesopotamia: A Trial Model." In *Population Growth: Anthropological Implications*, ed. B. J. Spooner, Cambridge, Mass.: MIT Press, pp. 1–59.

Trigger, B. G. 1983. "The Rise of Egyptian Civilization." In *Ancient Egypt: A Social History*. B. G. Trigger, B. J. Kemp, D. O'Conner, and A. B. Lloyd, pp. 1–70. Cambridge: Cambridge University Press.

World Archaeology. 1986. Vol. 17, no.3, contains several articles on early writing systems in Egypt, Mesopotamia, Anatolia, Iran, and the Aegean.

III

THE THIRD
MILLENNIUM B.C.:
DIVERSITY OF
DOMINION

By the end of the fourth millennium B.C, the prehistoric societies of Mesopotamia and Egypt had taken a momentous step: the adoption of writing, chiefly to keep records for their burgeoning economies. Syria did not lag far behind; about 2500–2400 B.C., scribes at Ebla in northern Syria had begun using the cuneiform script of Mesopotamia to keep track of their far-flung economic affairs. With the advent of writing, the prehistoric period drew to a close in ancient western Asia.

In addition to writing, another very important change characterized the transition to the historic eras in ancient western Asia: the development and increasingly widespread use of copper and bronze tools, weapons, assorted implements, even jewelery. Archaeologists traditionally have divided the entire span of tool-using, human activity worldwide into Stone, Bronze, and Iron ages; such a concept may be found already in 2,000-year-old classical (Greek and Roman) and ancient Chinese literature.

The prehistoric past has been divided (and further subdivided, although that need not concern us here) into the Paleolithic and Neolithic periods (see page 15). By the beginning of the third millennium B.C., bronze became increasingly common, although it never totally replaced the use of copper or stone tools and implements. Because bronze became the metal most widely used during the third and second millennia B.C., that 2,000-year era is commonly known as the Bronze Age. By the first millennium B.C. (for reasons that will be discussed in Chapter V), iron had replaced bronze or copper in this role. Archaeologists therefore typically refer to that era as the Iron Age. Following this classification procedure through to its logical conclusion, the early modern era (seventeenth–nineteenth centuries A.D.) might be called the age of steel, and our own era ought to be designated the plastic age.

Because copper had been in frequent use throughout the fourth millennium B.C., that period is often referred to as the **Chalcolithic** (Copper-Stone) Age; alternatively it is known as the Final Neolithic. During the third millennium (3000–2000 B.C.), the development of a many-faceted metallurgical technology ushered in what has come to be known as the Early Bronze Age. In sites from Greece to the Iranian plateau, archaeologists have uncovered objects made of gold, silver, electrum (a natural alloy of gold and silver), and lead.

The greatest technological advance in the third millennium B.C., however, was the use of tin (most commonly), arsenic, or antimony—ideally in proportions from about 1:7 to 1:10—as an alloy with copper to produce objects of **bronze**. As often happened, developments in Egypt took a slightly different course: to the virtual exclusion of tin, elaborate use was made of arsenic as an alloy. The addition of small amounts of tin (or slightly less of arsenic) made the resultant bronze alloys easier to cast as well as harder and more durable. Yet the final product was virtually as malleable as one made purely of copper.

The extraordinary innovations in metallurgical technology were part and parcel of a wide range of cultural (especially writing), economic (especially the growth of long-distance trade), and sociopolitical developments that characterize the third millennium B.C. Urban life necessitated changes in social organization: loyalties were redirected from kin to kings. It is quite likely that more efficient bronze tools and weapons expedited the construction of massive public buildings within the cities and concomitantly necessitated the erection of fortifications that surrounded and protected the cities. Economic growth, supported by extensive long-distance trading, in turn provided the wherewithal for professional craftsmen and an increasingly wide range of other specialists devoted to the maintenance and management of the urban (and later, state) bureaucracies. Arguably the most significant component of this new urban organization and outlook was the adoption of writing and its proliferation and development by a scribal elite.

Culturally the advent of writing prompted remarkable, sociocultural innovation in third millennium B.C. Mesopotamia, Syria, and Egypt. In Mesopotamia, cuneiform writing became an art in itself; in Egypt, hieroglyphics. Mesopotamian scribes early assumed unique importance by teaching and developing skills in cuneiform writing, the most important medium in ancient western Asia for the maintenance of culture and the transmission and preservation of legal, literary, and religious information.

Innovations in art and architecture were widespread. The Egyptians constructed their most magnificent monuments—including the pyramids—in stone, whereas the Mesopotamians made extensive use of mudbrick, a material highly susceptible to time and the elements. Consequently Egyptian architectural remains today seem much more impressive than the crumpled heaps of debris that represent the once-splendid **ziqqurats** (temple towers) and palaces of Mesopotamia.

In what we might call the spiritual realm, a very pessimistic worldview permeated Mesopotamian religious attitudes. This stands in sharp contrast to the confident, harmonious outlook of ancient Egyptian religion. Differing impressions of the divine-human relationship (master-servant in Mesopotamia and shepherd-ward in Egypt) underlay many sociocultural differences in these centers of the ancient Near Eastern world. Such attitudes probably also influenced political leanings toward centralization (Egypt) and decentralization (Mesopotamia).

Politically the third millennium B.C. was a period of trial and error in the ancient Near East. New configurations emerged and collapsed in an ongoing struggle to establish and maintain he-

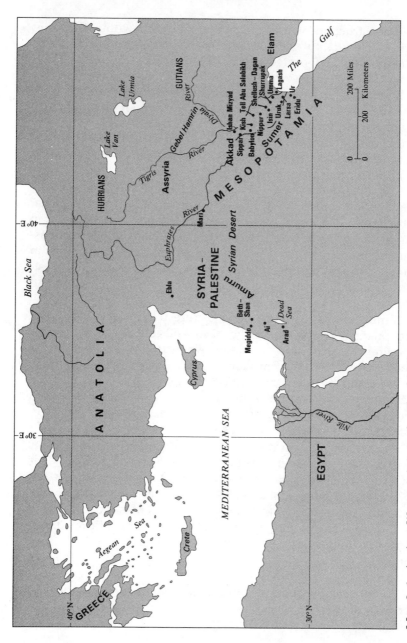

Map 3–1 Ancient Western Asia in the Third Millennium B.C.: Sites and Geographic Features

(Marburg/Art Resource, NY)
The pyramid of Sneferu, first pharaoh of the Fourth Dynasty, represents an early stage in pyramid construction.

gemony. During this formative period, each region evolved distinct institutions in response to its own needs and circumstances. The Mesopotamian city-states remained intensely individualistic, even during attempts at centralized rule. In Syria, the goal of the ruling elite seems to have been to gain some sort of economic dominance over a wide-ranging commercial network. In Palestine, the great, walled urban centers may well signify more localized political and economic aims. Meanwhile, Egypt, with its divinized ruler, consistently adhered to the ideal of political unity, even when centralized control faltered toward the end of the third millennium B.C.

MESOPOTAMIA: CITY– STATE, NATION–STATE, EMPIRE

The course of Mesopotamian history cannot be understood solely in **unilinear** terms. The recurrent trend toward *local* rule was repeatedly punctuated by political systems that tended toward more complex organization and more extensive dominion. Local rule is best exemplified by Mesopotamia's most characteristic and resilient political institution: the city-state. Political control by individual city-states typified the Sumerian dynasties of the early third millennium B.C.

With the advent of the Akkadian and Ur III ruling dynasties in the latter half of the third millennium B.C., the characteristic Mesopotamian political structure had shifted from localized city-state rule to territorial or federalized nation-state rule. The operative goal became territorial expansion. The alternation between local, city-state rule (decentralization) and monarchic, nation-state rule (centralization), which would be repeated throughout the course of ancient Near Eastern history, had thus already begun to characterize the Mesopotamian political landscape by the mid-third millennium B.C. Both centralized rule and local rule had merits; in fact, they seem to have been almost interchangeable options. The long- term pattern of localized city-states could be transposed readily with that of centralized nation-states. The individual urban centers of third millennium B.C. Mesopotamia thrived as irrigated islands amid a sea of desert or steppe. The political and environmental reality made both systems—centralized and decentralized—viable (see pages 45 and 68).

In later periods, the trend toward centralization and territorial expansion would lead to a concentration of widespread political and economic power within a single ruling city-state. During the second millennium B.C., Babylonians, Assyrians, and Kassites subjected increasingly extensive areas to direct rule. This intensification of organizational complexity reached its peak under the Assyrians and Persians during the first millennium B.C. At that time, local rule by city-states and more extensive rule by nation-states gave way to the third basic political structure of Mesopotamian tradition, the highly centralized, direct rule by empire.

The Early Dynastic Period (2900–2350 B.C.)

Mesopotamian history is divided into periods characterized by significant changes in society, economy, politics, and culture. Throughout Mesopotamia, the early third millennium B.C. witnessed the rise of the first recorded dynasties—ruling families in various cities that passed political power from one generation to the next. In consequence, the time span from about 2900 to 2350 B.C. has come to be known as the Early Dynastic period.

The chronology of this period is based on archaeological data, and only rarely can it be correlated with known political events. Thus, even after the advent of writing, archaeological evidence initially remains central to historical interpretation. However sketchily the archaeological and textual sources portray Early Dynastic Mesopotamian culture, far more is known politically about this period than about any prehistoric era.

The main written sources for the Early Dynastic period are numerous cuneiform tablets from the cities of Ur, Lagash, Kish, and Shurrupak; an important collection of literary tablets from Tell Abu Salabikh; and detailed royal inscriptions from Lagash. Some later tales, notably the epic of Gilgamesh, hark back to Early Dynastic times. The Sumerian King List, composed early in the second millennium B.C., provides the names of kings and ruling dynasties and the temporal extent of their dominion in Mesopotamia. Yet this scheme represents only the barest outline of the political history of Sumer and Akkad from prehistoric times. As it approaches the period of its compilation, the king list becomes increasingly plausible. Although valuable to historians, it is misleading in that it treats overlapping and contemporaneous city-state dynasties as successive. Even for the enthusiastic would-be chroniclers of the Sumerian King List, the remote past was difficult to portray with any sense of accuracy.

The Sumerian city-state

The urbanization process that had begun in the fourth millennium B.C. culminated during the Early Dynastic period in the rise of what became a deeply ingrained Mesopotamian institution: the city-state. (On the origins of the city-state, see Chapter II, pages 38–47.) Early Dynastic Sumer was a loose-knit collection of territorially small city-states whose associations with one another ranged from vassalage to equality, but never unity. For one thing, central and southern Mesopotamia lacked a natural focal point. Even Nippur, the religious (and approximate geographical) center of the land, wielded no political power (see pages 69–70).

Each city-state consisted of an urban center and the dependent communities surrounding it. Sumerian cities grew in size during this era, and their number increased to at least twelve. Some rural settlements were abandoned as their former inhabitants swelled the urban population; others continued to supply the cities with much-needed agricultural products in return for military protection, traded and manufactured goods, and all the other services provided by the city. This symbiotic relationship between each city and its hinterland was both symptom and cause of Mesopotamia's perennial political division. The political configuration is paralleled by the environmental setting: in effect, each city-state was an independent, irrigated "island" isolated from other irrigated islands by the arid steppe or plain. Despite their lack of natural defenses and perhaps partially because of their close proximity to one another, Mesopotamian city-states always remained intensely independent.

At a very early stage, this independence became a deep-rooted cultural norm, reinforced by the belief that each Sumerian city-state was the personal, inviolable estate of a particular god: the moon-god Nanna at Ur, the sky-god An at Uruk, the sun-god Utu at Sippar, and Larsa, the earth-god Enki at Eridu. Inanna, the goddess who represented the human passions of love and war, had temples and shrines in several cities. The undisputed supreme divinity was Enlil, god of the air, the national divinity whose principal shrine was in Nippur. In a land of jealously independent city-states, Enlil's position seems almost paradoxical. But Enlil reigned supreme in divine—not human—society, and Nippur's religious status served to minimize conflict between it and other, competing Sumerian city-states (see pages 69–70).

Regarded as patron deities of their city-states, the gods were also believed to guard their holdings jealously and to punish their human servants severely if some other city-god usurped their claim. This attachment to local gods worked against full acceptance of centralized rule; such a central authority would always be widely regarded as foreign. Particularism—the tendency for each city-state to function independently and to resist centralized control—was thus a strong cultural value supported by religious belief; it proved to be an enduring current in Mesopotamian political history.

This tendency toward decentralization was partly counteracted by the rivers and large canals that linked Sumerian cities. Interregional trading systems must have provided needed raw materials for the manufacturing and crafts industries of individual cities. Standardized measurement and numerical systems and the basic similarity of school tablets for would-be scribes attest to intercity cooperation. The very spread of Sumerian culture from the Zagros Mountains in the east to the upper Euphrates in the west also implies some degree of economic and cultural interdependence. Yet waterways and other potential avenues of unification that served primarily as commercial thoroughfares in times of peace may also have served as routes of attack in times of war.

Temple and palace: The Sumerian economy and Sumerian society

The temple was the central institution of the Early Dynastic urban economy, and temple and city were thoroughly interdependent. Since supreme authority derived from the gods, all temple officials were divine servants. No distinction was made between sacred, secular, and economic duties. The temple accommodated the entire divine entourage, an elite that included religious priests as well as the secular ruler. The architectural grandeur of the temples testifies to the economic power of this religious elite.

Nippur, centrally located between northern and southern cities, was the country's religious nucleus, the Vatican City of ancient Sumer. As such, it enjoyed extraordinary status. Nippur almost never became embroiled in the chronic intercity strife of ancient Sumer. Enlil, as lord of the state and patron deity of Nippur, received votive gifts from booty taken in successful military campaigns. Various Early Dynastic rulers constructed monuments in this religious center. As "Trader of the Wide World," Enlil—and consequently his temple—enjoyed a prominent position in commercial exchanges with foreign countries. Nippur's resulting prosperity is apparent in its thousands of clay tablets, mostly economic in nature.

The temple elite of each city-state owned a sizable proportion of that city's land. Priests, scribes, stewards, and other officials administered the temple's holdings and directed commercial and industrial projects. Temple dependents cultivated the temple's lands, and agricultural surpluses filled its granaries. The temple's primary economic role was to redistribute the surpluses of its own agricultural and industrial workers and craftsmen. In the course of so doing, however, the temple increasingly promoted trade, warfare, and technological and craft specialization, all of which contributed in turn to expansion and urban growth. Wide-ranging foreign contacts promoted prosperity and technological advance. Over time, the temple became one element among many in an increasingly intricate and secular social structure.

The rise of secular political power.   Gradually the temple's grip on the Sumerian economy loosened. The earliest known secular palaces, as monumental in scale as the temples, arose at Kish and Eridu in southern Mesopotamia and at Mari in the mid-Euphrates region. Cuneiform records of the Early Dynastic period are virtually silent about the origins of this secular power base. Some scholars, relying on later epic literature such as the tale of Gilgamesh, hypothesize a process of political development from a "democratic" assembly to a monarchy. Though plausible, this sequence of events cannot be verified in contemporary Early Dynastic written documents.

Warfare likely was instrumental in the rise of secular power and the accompanying institution of kingship. One tempting explanation for the origin of Mesopotamian kingship is that as society became more complex and military threats more frequent, capable war leaders retained their power in peacetime. In Sumerian, such a leader was called LUGAL, meaning "big man." As the LUGAL became dominant in the Sumerian city-state, the scope of his judicial and ritual functions grew accordingly, and royal authority eventually became hereditary. As the secular ruler, the LUGAL also performed such sacral duties as building and reconstructing temples and maintaining irrigation canals on temple lands. Yet even as the palace encroached on the temple's wealth and influence, the city-god and his residence remained the foremost expression of the city's identity. The grandeur of the temple fluctuated along with the city's fortunes, and rebuilding the temple was always a prime preoccupation of Mesopotamian rulers.

The titles *EN* and *ENSI* also designated leaders of city-states. Although at one time the *EN* exercised both sacral and secular powers, particularly in Uruk, his political role declined early, and *EN* came to designate the highest priest. The position of *ENSI*, meanwhile, was almost exclusively secular, although he was thought to be appointed by the gods. A number of Early Dynastic rulers at Lagash and Umma were called *ENSI*, but the title was used in later periods not only for independent rulers but also for governors of city-states.

To modern scholars, these terms present formidable problems of definition and interpretation. In different cities and different eras, the same title designated different functions. Generally speaking, though, *LUGAL* and *ENSI* were predominantly secular positions, while *EN* was primarily a religious position with important practical and, consequently, political ramifications. From the viewpoint of the Sumerians, however, all power—whether we deem it religious or secular—derived from their gods.

The interplay between this new, divinely ordained kingship and the well-established and well-endowed temple priesthood deeply affected the class structure of Early Dynastic Sumer. Documents from a temple at Lagash, dated about 2500 B.C., indicate that most land unclaimed by temple or palace was owned by the nobility—the ruler and his family, administrators, and priests. Free citizens who owned land did so as members of a family or clan, not as individuals; such land could be transferred or sold only by designated family members. Because the price of land in Early Dynastic Sumer was extremely low, holdings were rarely sold except in times of adversity.

Agricultural lands were gradually redistributed among the royal, priestly, or noble classes. Many commoners or free citizens were reduced to the status of dependents, or "clients," of the palace, temple, or noble estate. Although some dependents of the temple or palace received gifts of land for services rendered, others existed on rations of cereal, oil, dairy products, fish, and clothing doled out by their new masters. Slavery did not play a central economic role, because the duties of most slaves (refugees of war or famine) were largely domestic, not agricultural or industrial. Nonetheless, the client system increased social and economic distinctions, and some citizens were enslaved because they were unable to repay loans made by members of the elite classes. The debtor's animals, movable goods, or even small plots of land were liable to seizure.

The class structure of Early Dynastic Sumer thus mirrored the division of land into temple, palace, and community holdings. Competition for land and for clients to work the land may have aggravated social struggles among the elite classes. By the end of the Early Dynastic period, Uru-inim-gina, last member of the ruling dynasty at Lagash, had introduced legislation intended to restore the earlier balance of wealth in society by shoring up the authority of the temple—by now closely linked to secular authority—against unscrupulous officials and the nobility. Rulers, nobles, and priests, it would seem, had come into open conflict.

Uru-inim-gina and Gilgamesh: Sumerian law and literature

Uru-inim-gina (formerly read as Uru-ka-gina) sponsored the earliest known attempt at governmental and social reform. Although his motives are never made explicit, Uru-inim-gina's attempt to renew temple authority stands out as a brilliant political maneuver to shore up royal authority without seeming to do so and in a way that couldn't be criticized. His reform texts, preserved on some Early Dynastic building inscriptions, offer a candid glimpse of Early Dynastic society. Secular rulers had enhanced their own positions at the expense of the temple and had abused the privileges and powers they had usurped. Wealthy landowners unjustly appropriated commoners' land or property. Government had overstepped its bounds. Unreasonable taxes supported a bloated bureaucracy; the rich exploited the poor; social mores had become slack.

Uru-inim-gina sought to change all this. The laws he promulgated ostensibly limited royal administrative and political powers, established personal rights, and prescribed punishments. The outright and illegitimate seizure of a common citizen's property or livestock by the nobility or by wealthy landowners was forbidden. Funeral taxes and other fees were reduced and stabilized. Changes were made in family law—the marriage of a woman to two men, for example, was banned—and the ruler was made the champion of widows' and orphans' rights.

The most significant feature of Uru-inim-gina's reforms was his attempt to halt further secular encroachments upon the rights and privileges of the temple and the city-god. Temple authority—by this time, an adjunct of palace authority—was reestablished over some aspects of society. The sharpest criticism and severest restrictions seem directed at well-to-do landowners, the chief threat to the palace regime. These reforms benefited the socially weak and economically inferior classes while reinforcing central authority. Thus Uru-inim-gina's legal reforms earned popular support for their sponsor and simultaneously thwarted the political aspirations of ambitious groups and individuals. By reaffirming temple authority, Uru-inim-gina was in effect stabilizing his own position. By championing the rights of common citizens against petty officials and noble landholders, Uru-inim-gina solidified the royal power base.

If the reforms were ever enacted, however, they had no immediate effect. Immediately following Uru-inim-gina's reign, Lagash and the rest of Sumer fell under non-Sumerian rule, and new mores and mandates came into play. Yet the reform measures of Uru-inim-gina foreshadowed a long series of later cuneiform law codes, Sumerian and Babylonian, that aimed at redressing social and economic injustices. Maintaining personal rights and relieving governmental abuse seem to be logical corollaries of the Sumerian penchant for localized rather than centralized rule.

In the historical figure Uru-inim-gina, we encounter the Sumerian king as lawgiver; the Gilgamesh epic celebrates the Sumerian king as tragic hero. Familiar to modern readers as the masterpiece of Mesopotamian literature, the epic recounts the pursuit of fame and immortality by the semilegendary king of Uruk. Based on at least five earlier Sumerian legends, the epic was amalgamated into a unified whole early in the second millennium B.C.

The story recounts the adventures of Gilgamesh and his exuberant adversary-turned-comrade, Enkidu. The gods had created Enkidu—a wild, untamed creature—in the hope that he might challenge the arrogant and ruthless Gilgamesh and thus temper his excesses. After an initial confrontation, Gilgamesh and Enkidu become fast friends. On an expedition to the west, they confront an evil monster, Humbaba, in the Cedar Forest. Enkidu slays Humbaba and, in retribution, the gods take Enkidu's life.

Enkidu's death so haunts Gilgamesh that he undertakes to seek everlasting life. This is the turning point in the epic: Gilgamesh the mighty hero is transformed into Gilgamesh the broken mortal. The pursuit of immortality—guiding theme of the epic—leads Gilgamesh into further adventures. The most famous is an encounter with Utnapishtim, an ancient hero who had survived a catastrophic flood. His tale, recounted in the epic, bears so many resemblances to the Biblical story of the Flood that Utnapishtim is often called the Babylonian Noah. Gilgamesh, following Utnapishtim's advice, finds a plant capable of rendering him immortal, only to have it filched by a snake while he sleeps, exhausted from his quest. On this vexing note, the epic of Gilgamesh ends.

Judging from the myriad ancient copies of the tale and its translation into such languages as Hurrian and Hittite, the poem was already renowned in antiquity. The epic clearly fascinated the Sumerians and perhaps served as a means for them to understand and describe their remote past. On one level, the initial conflict between Gilgamesh and Enkidu may reflect the theme of a secular ruler with religious power and ritual responsibilities (the "priest-king") defending his position against any adversary. On another, the taming of Enkidu by Gilgamesh and their ensuing friendship may be a literary allusion to the advantages of civilized society as perceived by the Sumerians. The flood tale within the epic represents the very real, natural threat posed by the springtime floods of Mesopotamia's rivers, especially the Tigris. Thus magical, martial, and natural elements are woven into the theme of an individual's search for immortality. Viewed strictly from a literary viewpoint, we may speculate whether the epic was regarded as a commentary on human estrangement from the divine that accompanied the rise of secular power in the Early Dynastic period.

Does the tale of Gilgamesh shed any light on the existence of a historical Gilgamesh? The epic credits Gilgamesh with erecting a massive defensive wall around Uruk; archaeological excavations have uncovered the remains of a wall about 5.6 miles (9 kilometers) long enclosing an area of about 1,000 acres (400 hectares). The Gilgamesh tradition demonstrates remarkable familiarity with the Early Dynastic period (for example, in the tale of Gilgamesh and Agga; see below); the epic obviously contains kernels of historical truth. Gilgamesh should probably be regarded as an historical figure, and his era, Early Dynastic II (about 2700–2600 B.C.), as the earliest phase of Mesopotamian history.

Despite the Sumerian emphasis on temple and palace institutions, individualism also exercised some influence within Early Dynastic society. A certain tension is apparent: individualism in legal, political, and cultural matters is counterbalanced by collectivism in the economy. Sumerian law, politics, and culture are fused together by the common themes of particularistic city-state rule and individual citizen's rights. Gilgamesh's private search for fame and immortality extends this theme to Sumerian literature.

The Sumerian economy, however, provides a counterpoint. The communal system of temple, palace, or noble estates was a closed system that downplayed individual initiative. Elites not only dominated trade, politics, and technology, they also laid claim to most arable land within the city-state. In the end, however, corruption within the secular branches of the elite led to Uru-inim-gina's attempt to restore the mandate to individual citizens. On quite another level, the Sumerian respect for the individual took its most dramatic expression in the supreme political and institutional power that came to be vested in one man, the Sumerian king, as the representative of the city-god.

The entrenchment of urban particularism: Sumerian political history

Warfare between Sumerian cities appears to have been chronic. Early Dynastic inscriptions are replete with references to battles between city-states, and the massive walls that Sumerian cities erected at this time imply a strong secular authority primed for military action. The epic of Gilgamesh and Agga, written much later but preserving traditions from the Early Dynastic era, describes one such war between Uruk and Kish. Although this specific conflict cannot be considered historical, inasmuch as no contemporary evidence exists to confirm it, at least it portrays accurately the conditions of Early Dynastic warfare.

(En)Mebaragesi, whom the Sumerian King List names as Agga's father, is mentioned in two contemporary inscriptions ascribed to the Early Dynastic period on archaeological grounds. These inscriptions single out (En)Mebaragesi as the earliest authenticated figure in Mesopotamian history. (Only documentation that can be dated to the period in question qualifies as primary historical evidence.) The inscriptional documentation for (En)Mebaragesi makes it likely that Gilgamesh and Agga were also historical kings, whatever subsequent literary embellishments may have been embroidered around them.

(En)Mebaragesi's city Kish, in the northern reaches of Sumer, was clearly a very important center. Rulers of his era, and later from cities over all of Sumer, adopted the illustrious title "King of Kish" to signify overlordship of the land. At Ur, the excavation of the famed royal graves has revealed the extraordinary splendor and wealth of that southern port city in the final phase of the Early Dynastic era. Gold, silver, lapis lazuli, and carnelian turned up alongside metal vessels and implements, delicately inlaid furniture, and musical instruments. These graves attest to a high degree of artistic accomplishment and offer indisputable evidence of social and economic stratification. The royal burials at Ur also confirm the decisive shift in the locus of power from temple to palace.

Only at Lagash, though, do the preserved documents provide a detailed political history. Eannatum (about 2450–2425 B.C.), the most prominent ruler of Lagash in the final Early Dynastic (III) period, defeated his city's unremitting rival, the neighboring district of Umma, and commemorated his victory on the surviving "Stela of the Vultures." Eannatum typified early Mesopotamian rulers in his dual preoccupation with war and water rights, as well as in his energetic construction of canals and waterworks. Although Uruk and other regions remained independent, Eannatum's subsequent victories over other Sumerian city-states—and over Mari in the northwest, Elam in the east, and distant states to the north—distinguished him as the first known Sumerian ruler to achieve any sort of political dominance over Mesopotamia.

The Akkadian Era (2350–2170 B.C.): Sedentism, Seminomadism, and Semites

Discussion thus far has concentrated on the internal development of the Sumerian state and the sedentary lifestyle of the Sumerians. Other groups of people, however, resided in or migrated through Mesopotamia and frequently interacted with the Sumerians. Throughout the course of ancient western Asiatic history, none of these groups was more significant, more pervasive than the **seminomadic** Semites. The dynamic interplay between these roving pastoralists and the sedentary farmers of the land is, in fact, another recurrent theme in Near Eastern history and one that both characterizes and complicates our understanding of Mesopotamian social systems.

Since the ongoing habitat of the seminomadic peoples of ancient western Asia was the steppe zone that rimmed the Fertile Crescent and since most of these seminomadic groups spoke Semitic languages, it is usually assumed that all Semitic-speaking people originally were nomads. Although this is true to a certain extent, it cannot be proven that the Akkadians in Mesopotamia or, for example, the Eblaites in Syria (see pages 130–32) were ever nomadic. Although much ado has been made over major ethnic invasions of seminomadic, Semitic-speaking peoples into Mesopotamia throughout the historical era, such theories are fatally simplistic and fail to consider the long-term ebb and flow,

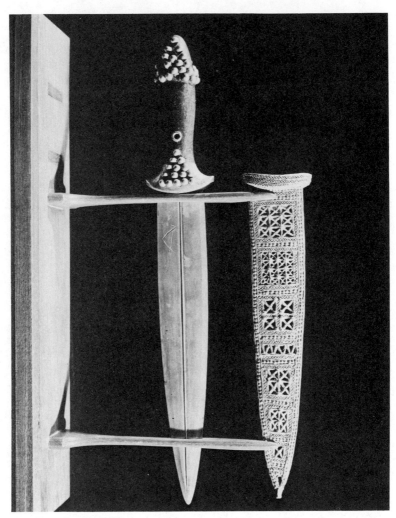

From the Royal Cemetery at Ur: solid gold dagger with lapus lazuli handle and golden "wickerwork" sheath.

(Giraudon/Art Resource, NY)

From the Royal Cemetery at Ur: lyre (restored) with golden bull's head.

(Maurice Chuzeville/Courtesy of Pierre Amiet)

Stela of the Vultures, commemorating the defeat of Umma by Eannatum of Lagash (Early Dynastic III period)

the give-and-take that characterizes relations between sedentary and seminomadic peoples.

Sedentism and seminomadism. Seminomadic, or pastoral, peoples are consistently underrepresented in both archaeological and written records. The complex interaction between sedentary and pastoral populations was basic to the urban-centered Mesopotamian social system, but urban scribes seldom took notice of environmental, social, and political pressures at work on seminomadic people.

The availability of water constrained early seminomads in the Near East; only the foolhardy moved farther than one day's travel from a reliable water hole. The traditional theory that would derive all nomadic people from the heart of the Syrian or Arabian deserts—where virtually no water exists—confuses nomadic and seminomadic traditions and ignores long-term historical and cultural patterns. Only when the camel came into general use for transportation in the desert, during the latter half of the second millennium B.C., could nomads be found roaming this harsh and barren wasteland.

Within the steppe zone of the Syrian and Arabian deserts, however, seminomads grazed their herds on seasonal vegetation. Their flocks regularly followed the retreating and advancing vegetation from steppe or plain in winter and spring to mountain pasture in summer and back again. Often these seasonal migrations encroached on the settled population of the Mesopotamian alluvium. Such other pressures as overpopulation, drought, famine, and the expulsion of weaker by stronger tribes also impelled seminomadic encroachments, as did intermarriage and service as mercenaries in the armies of settled states.

Mutual need also played a significant role in encounters between seminomads and agriculturalists. Seminomadic tribes often bartered their animal products for crops, metal utensils, or weapons. Settled farmers and townspeople in turn often wished to have their herds driven and fed alongside those of the pastoralists. While mutual need prompted such contacts, mutual hostility typically characterized them. The resulting conflict is well documented in the written records of the ancient Near East.

Interaction between seminomadic and settled people, however complicated and antagonistic it may have been, facilitated assimilation and sedentarization of seminomadic tribes. Yet seminomads who adopted the settled way of life almost always did so under economic or political compulsion. The desire for land or wealth probably did not enter in. Land meant hard work, and seminomadic pastoralists were more accustomed to herding animals. Also, raiding and looting settlements has been an economic mainstay of nomads and seminomads through the ages. Only when the steppe proved inadequate to their basic needs did seminomadic tribes begin to settle.

Though the concept of invading nomadic hordes may appeal to modern romantic notions and spur the literary imaginations of novelists and filmmakers alike, cultural processes and historical change are rarely explained so neatly and efficiently. Nonetheless, the documentary record of the Near East gives evidence of periodic large-scale ethnic movements: the Amorite about 2200–2000 B.C.; the Aramaean about 1200–1000 B.C.; and the Arab beginning about 800 B.C. Although these movements ultimately led to political dominance by seminomads and their descendants, such dominance came at the expense of semi-nomadic cultural tradition. The adage "Culture conquers more surely than the sword" is apt: the seminomads wielded the sword, but the settled inhabitants of the plain possessed the superior culture.

Mesopotamian civilization as a whole generated a much stronger influence than could any of its component parts. Once the seminomads had settled and gained political and economic dominance, the process began all over again. Stragglers from the most recent incursion or forerunners of the next seemed always to be present, conducting raids or intermixing with the settled population. But even if the culture of the settled population remained preeminent, the resulting shift in population engendered demographic, socioeconomic, and ultimately polit-ical change.

Semites and Akkadians.   By 2350 B.C., Semitic-speaking people who lived in the more northerly reaches of the land united north-ern Mesopotamia with Sumer in the south. At least in principle, Semitic rule extended from the **Gulf** to the Mediterranean Sea. These Semites, known to us as Akkadians, altered forever the course of Mesopotamian history. Because their capital city was called Agade (or Akkad), the country came to be called Akkad and the Semitic ruling dynasty and their people Akkadians.

Who were the Semites? Where did they originate? What is meant by "Semitic-speaking" peoples? Semite and Semitic-speaking are terms traceable to the biblical passage Genesis 10:21–31, where Shem (i.e., the Semite), son of Noah, is identified as the father of Ashur (Assyrians), Aram (Aramaeans), and Eber (Hebrews). The Assyrian, Aramaic, and Hebrew languages share many points in common and are usually described—along with Arabic, Ethiopic, Akkadian, and others—as being members of the Semitic language "family." Some of these languages are still spoken (live); others are not (dead).

Similarly our own English language has affinities with several other live and dead languages: French, German, Italian, Latin, Greek—even with Hittite, which was first used in Anatolia shortly after 2000 B.C. (see pages 143–45). All these belong to the Indo-European language family, whose speakers almost certainly originated in the plains of central Asia and spread slowly toward Europe and the Near East throughout the course of the fourth and third millennia B.C. Like Indo-European, Semite and Semitic-speaking are convenient and acceptable *linguistic* or *cultural* terms but have no validity in biological parlance. In other words, there are Semitic-speaking and Indo-European–speaking peoples, but there is no such thing as a Semitic or Indo-European *race*.

Since most ancient Semitic-speaking peoples lived and thrived predominantly within the great arc of the Fertile Crescent (see pages 17–22), this area is often regarded as their homeland. But without written records, it is impossible to know how early in prehistory the Semites inhabited that region. By about 2900 B.C., people with Semitic names had settled in considerable numbers in cities such as Kish on the northern fringes of Sumer. Throughout Early Dynastic times, these people lived in close cultural and often political dependence on Sumer. Gradually this Semitic-speaking group, known as the Akkadians, adopted the urban attitudes and habits of the Sumerians, and some rose to positions of political power, finally even to kingship.

The Akkadian nation-state

After the fashion of many Sumerian kings, the rulers of the Akkadian dynasty commemorated their exploits in dedicatory inscriptions at the temple of Enlil at Nippur. The originals have never been found, but a devoted scribe meticulously copied them; the surviving tablets are our main source for the history of the Akkadian era. These dedicatory inscriptions are supplemented by literary texts (e.g., "The Curse of Agade") and by later written documents including the Sumerian King List. Much later epic tales of Sargon and his grandson Naramsin—the best-known rulers of the Akkadian period—mix fact with fiction and complicate the historian's task of selecting and utilizing appropriate materials. The sparse archaeological evidence for this period has also left a decisive gap in our knowledge; even the capital city of the Akkadians has yet to be positively identified.

The last rulers of the Sumerian Early Dynastic period had attempted to unify all of Sumer under their rule. This inclination toward centralization was institutionalized by the Akkadian kings. The Akkadians replaced the Sumerian system of local autonomy with an extended nation-state whose administrative center was the king and his court at Agade. Dominance by the temple or city-state gave way to national monarchy. The task of controlling a more extensive area required innovation, and the Akkadians' administrative achievements were considerable. The Akkadian king did not exercise direct political control of annexed territory; he was represented instead by an Akkadian troop garrison. This garrison also ensured the uninterrupted shipment of tribute in the form of local raw materials.

The transition from Sumerian to Akkadian rule also prompted ideological changes. Different traditions governed the two peoples: the Akkadians recognized royal and private ownership of land, while the Sumerians had a long tradition of temple and communal ownership. Ethnic antagonism, however, was deliberately minimized. The ethnic composition, administration, and governing institutions of conquered lands were left intact. The Akkadians participated in Sumerian religious observances and adopted the Sumerian cuneiform script to write their own Semitic language, which became the dominant spoken tongue. Though Akkadians and Sumerians were two different peoples who spoke different languages, they were not two different cultures. The prevailing civilization was neither Sumerian nor Akkadian: it was, first and foremost, Mesopotamian.

The rise of Akkad

According to later legend, a high-ranking Semitic official in Kish overthrew his former master in a palace revolt about 2350 B.C. and became the first Akkadian king. To exculpate himself for usurping power and to legitimize his kingship, he adopted the throne name Sargon (in Akkadian, *Sharrum-kēn*), which means "the king is legitimate."

Sargon waged a series of thirty-four battles against Sumer, united at the time under Lugalzagesi, and ultimately succeeded in incorporating the Sumerian city-states into his Akkadian national state. He then undertook victorious military campaigns against Ebla and Mari in the west and northwest, Shubartu in the north, and Elam in the east.

But maintaining control of Sumer proved difficult for Sargon and his successors. Sargon's own fifty-six-year reign ended ignominiously with uprisings throughout the land. Although he claimed to have crushed the rebels, his sons Rimush and Manishtushu both faced similar revolts upon ascending the throne, and palace revolutions terminated both their reigns. Naramsin, however, continued the aggrandizement of the state that his grandfather Sargon had begun. Though his reign too was blighted by rebellion, the Akkadian state probably reached its greatest magnitude under Naramsin (about 2250–2220 B.C.).

The palace: The Akkadian economy and the quest for raw materials

However decisive the military victories of the Akkadian kings, the real foundation of the Akkadian nation-state was economic. The king and his court, not the temple, served as the nerve center of economic activity. Economic and social innovations had their basis in the structure of the Akkadian state and were perpetuated by the king in his role as chief entrepreneur of the state.

The kings of such a vast state had to have considerable wealth at their disposal; the court at the capital city Agade had formidable expenses. Like their Sumerian predecessors, the Akkadian kings took full financial responsibility for building and maintenance projects, the movement and redistribution of agricultural products and other provisions, and the purchase of necessities as well as luxury items.

The organization of the newly expanded state required new personnel to maintain contact between the king and all the territories and institutions dependent on him: a huge corps of royal servants and administrators had to be paid. Royal servants received not only redistributed provisions (grains, textiles) but also allotments of farmland. These farms seem to have been leased by the crown in return for a portion of their produce; thus the palace maintained its primacy in matters of wealth and land ownership.

Tribute and booty from conquered peoples contributed to the accumulation of capital, but centralized control over vital imports of raw materials was even more critical. Acquisition of raw materials, in fact, dictated Akkad's foreign policy. The aim of political control was to ensure the procurement and unimpeded delivery of basic resources to the throne in Akkad. Military expeditions were dispatched to the northwest in pursuit of Sargon's goal of reaching the Cedar Forest (the Amanus mountains) and the Silver Mountain (the Taurus Mountains), rich sources of wood, metal, and stone. Metals were sought also from Anatolia or perhaps from Iran and stone from the upland areas surrounding Mesopotamia. Dominance of overland trade was not the only priority: Sargon's inscriptions spell out the need for state management of maritime trade with the Gulf region and beyond, important sources of metal and various types of precious or building/sculpting stone.

The crown kept up its prominent role in landholdings by leasing parcels of agricultural land in return for a share of the yield. Yet private property also existed alongside the princely; legal documents attest to sales of fields, slaves, animals, and various commodities. Individual ownership of land and accumulation of wealth eventually spread and altered the social class structure of Mesopotamia. The Sumerian penchant for individualism in law, literature, and politics now extended to the economic sector. Mesopotamian society became divided hierarchically into classes based on the ownership of property and determined by economic autonomy.

Business letters, contracts, and other legal documents—all official correspondence—provide our only information on private individuals. Consequently it is difficult to elaborate further on Akkadian social structure. Generally speaking, however, Mesopotamian society maintained a strong agricultural basis throughout historical times. Cultivation was done on several levels—public, private, indentured—but exactly how much was held by each type of producer is very difficult to establish and, in any case, varied greatly in different periods, regions, and ecological settings. The trend toward individual ownership and production, however, may be traced back directly to its Akkadian origins.

Deities and dynasts: Mesopotamian religion and kingship

> In those days the dwellings of Agade were filled with gold,
> its bright- shining houses were filled with silver,
> into its granaries were brought copper, tin, slabs of
> lapis lazuli, its silos bulged (?) at the sides . . .
> its quay where the boats docked were all abustle . . .
> its walls reached skyward like a mountain . . .
> the gates—like the Tigris emptying its water into the sea,
> holy Inanna opened its gates.[1]

This vivid description of Agade, composed by a Sumerian poet early in the second millennium B.C., is one of the few pieces of textual or archaeological evidence that sheds some light on the capital city of the Akkadians. The site of Agade has still not been positively identified, and the resulting sparseness of archaeological evidence leaves a decisive gap in our knowledge. The most likely candidate, modern Ishan Mizyad, is very near Babylon, Kish, and other later capital cities of ancient Mesopotamia.

Agade was Sargon's special domain. Booty, tribute, and trade made the new capital prosperous; a multitude of officials and administrators lived and thrived there. Goods from distant sectors of ancient western Asia flowed into its storehouses, and ships from as far afield as India/Pakistan and Oman docked at its harbor.

This newly acquired wealth greatly enhanced the position of the king. "Citizens of Akkad"—members and confidants of the royal family—were placed in charge of annexed lands. Sargon appointed his daughter Enheduanna to the newly created position of high priestess of the moon-god Nanna at Ur, perhaps as a political maneuver to elicit the loyalty of the old Sumerian cities. The office of high priestess—a unifying link even in times of political division—remained a royal prerogative until shortly after 1800 B.C.

A new conception of kingship went hand in hand with the Akkadians' extraordinary enhancement of royal power and prestige. There is evidence of cultic worship of Sargon and his two sons after their deaths, and Naramsin even adopted the unprecedented titles "God of Agade" and "King of the Four Quarters of the Universe" during his own lifetime. In a culture that regarded the king as human mediator between his subjects and the divine, Naramsin's claim may seem presumptuous. Yet divinization of the ruler in this instance may in fact have been nothing more than an attempt to create another rallying point for the state's many potentially divisive elements. Naramsin's victory stela, which portrays him and his soldiers trampling their enemies, exemplifies this new concept of kingship: the king appears twice as large as his troops and wears a horned crown usually reserved for the gods. Naramsin's divinity led later Assyrian writers to portray him as a "guiding national genius" on a par with Sargon.

The principle of divine kingship was seldom followed up. Beyond these occurrences among the Akkadians, only rulers at Ur (twenty-first century B.C.) and Isin (twentieth century B.C.) claimed divine status. The intention that lay behind royal divinization is obscure; initially it may well have been adopted for political or ideological reasons. One point is clear: the divinized Mesopotamian king was completely different from his Egyptian counterpart, a god descended among men.

Within Mesopotamia, divine society was regarded as a replica of human society, with all the attendant human shortcomings or qualities. Like the Greek gods, Mesopotamian divinities were anthropomorphic (human in form), intelligent, and altruistic but subject to love, hate, jealousy, and anger. And like their human counterparts, the gods of Mesopotamia were of unequal status, each assigned to particular tasks or spheres of activity. The major gods embodied forces immanent in nature: An (Semitic, Anu) the sky-god; Enlil the air-god; Enki (Semitic, Ea) the earth-god and sweetwater-god; Nanna (Semitic, Sin) the moon-god; Utu (Semitic, Shamash) the sun-god; Inanna (Semitic, Ishtar) the goddess of love and war; Ereshkigal, the goddess of the netherworld. Astral and earthly deities were responsible for the creation and smooth operation of the uni-

Stela of Naramsin of Akkad, portraying the victorious Naramsin in divine headdress, towering over his enemies.

verse; they ruled the world through their earthly representative, the reigning king of Sumer and Akkad.

The king, in his paradivine status, served to intercede between the human and divine planes. Much of our evidence about Mesopotamian religion is based upon this regal-divine relationship, even though religious practice inevitably percolated down to the common worshipper. Mesopotamian deities remained aloof, but their care and feeding brought them into direct religious, political, and economic contact with temple and priest, palace and king, dependent and worshipper.

The key to understanding Mesopotamian religious attitudes is the relationship between the human and the divine: people had been created to serve the gods. On closer inspection, the relationship becomes more complex. Pious individuals expected to realize economic strength and spiritual security as the outcome of an intimate association with the divine. Misfortune and failure, on the other hand, implied the lack of protection from a supernatural power. The people of Mesopotamia, in other words, regarded their gods with worship and admiration but equally with submission and fear. The Mesopotamians had confidence in the divine and relied upon the supernatural much as servants rely upon their master or children upon their parents.

In order to communicate with the gods who shaped their destinies, people resorted to various techniques of **divination**— attempts to predict the future. Since the gods were believed to be the prime movers of all human and natural events, it was vital to know their intentions. Among the forecasting techniques were the interpretation of dreams, observation of a slaughtered animal's liver (**hepatoscopy**) or other exta (**extispicy**), or of smoke rising from burning incense, the shooting of arrows, and the casting of dice or lots. Eclipses or other celestial phenomena were also important but as natural rather than devised omens. Divination, of course, presumed that the gods were willing to reveal their intentions—thus the careful compliance with observing rituals and taboos and with offering prayers, sacrifices, and sustenance to the divine.

Religious ideas and attitudes practiced by the Sumerians and Akkadians in the third millennium B.C. deeply influenced the public and private life of all later Mesopotamians. People believed themselves to be constrained by divine will; obedience to that will was thus both a necessary and honorable quality. Service to the gods was essential. Interpreting this dictum quite literally, priests fed, clothed, and looked after the divine images within the temples while dutiful citizens sent food or drink offerings to the temple, observed and perhaps participated in the public rituals or great processions, offered prayers and sacrifices (especially to their personal gods), and observed countless rules and sanctions that affected their daily activities. To the individual involved, all this activity would have been regarded in social and economic terms as much as in religious terms.

The polytheistic nature of Mesopotamian religion must not be understood as some primitive form of nature worship. Its broad spiritual and intellectual dimensions contrast favorably with the narrower, one-dimensional intensity of more modern, monotheistic religions. In fact, the absence of intolerance in Mesopotamian religion and its acceptance of new or foreign deities as necessitated by political and economic events throughout three millennia of history represent a harmonious and appropriate counterpart of the shifting stresses—stability and resilience—within Mesopotamian society.

Akkad in eclipse

Naramsin's victory stela celebrates his defeat of one of the many Zagros mountain tribes. These tribes' repeated invasions of the Mesopotamian plain highlight the growing vulnerability of the Akkadian state and suggest that its decline began even while Naramsin still occupied the throne.

During the reign of Naramsin's son and successor Shar-kali-sharri, Gutian raiders from the Zagros Mountains and Amorite seminomads from the northwest steppe began to chip away at the block of the Akkadian state. At Shar-kali-sharri's death, the country plunged into three years of anarchy—a period the Sumerian King List aptly characterized by asking "Who was king?" and replying "Who was not king?" Though the events that led to anarchy are still unknown, there is no doubt that Akkad gradually disappeared from the political arena.

Akkad's Gutian successors were deeply influenced by Mesopotamian culture and traditions. They worshipped Sumerian deities and assumed Akkadian personal names. This pattern of assimilation recurred whenever seminomadic peoples or mountain tribes moved into the Mesopotamian alluvium with intent to stay. Though the extent of the Gutians' authority is uncertain, they managed to remain in the country until shortly before 2110 B.C., nearly a century after Shar-kali-sharri first confronted them.

The Akkadians were ultimately no more successful at dominating a far-flung state, or even Sumer, than their Early Dynastic predecessors had been. In their pioneering attempt to forge a unified state, the Akkadian dynasts encountered novel problems and failed to solve them. The task of ruling so extensive a state with so many particularistic components proved insuperable with the limited resources at Akkad's command.

Even so, the Akkadian experiment created the conditions for fusion of the Sumerian and Semitic peoples and left a singular Mesopotamian imprint on the resulting culture. More significant perhaps was the impetus it gave to the idea of political dominion over the entire land. The immediate beneficiaries were the Gutians and the Sumerian city-state of Lagash. The ultimate beneficiary was Ur.

The Ur III Period (2112–2004 B.C.): A Sumerian Renaissance

According to the Sumerian King List, the city-state of Ur now established dominion over Mesopotamia for the third time. Consequently the ruling kings have become known to historians as the Ur III dynasty. This dynasty brought political stability to the country while sponsoring the revival of Sumerian art, literature, and law.

Primary written sources for this period are abundant. Economic documents from administrative centers like Umma (near Lagash) and Sellush-Dagan (near Nippur) number in the tens of thousands. And in contrast to the scant archaeological evidence from the Akkadian period, the remains of the Ur III kings' extensive construction projects survive in most major Mesopotamian cities of the time.

Because Sumerian again became the official language of the land, this period is often characterized as a "Sumerian Renaissance." But by this time, the question of Sumerian versus Akkadian cultural identity had become insignificant. Sumerian nostalgia was confined to preserving traditional Sumerian literature and composing hymns glorifying the ruler in the act of addressing the gods. The "neo-Sumerian" Ur III state owed fully as much to the Sargonid dynasty as the latter had owed to the achievements of Early Dynastic Sumer.

The regal grandeur of the Sargonid state had also become integrated into the Mesopotamian worldview. Ur III kings adopted the titles of the Akkadian kings and were likewise deified. Ur-Nammu, founder of the Ur III dynasty, claimed the title "King of Sumer and Akkad," officially acknowledging for the first time the composite origins of Mesopotamia, now unified into a single state. Sumerian and Akkadian culture had truly fused into one Mesopotamian civilization.

Unification under Ur

While the Gutians maintained sporadic control over some northern cities, Lagash and Uruk regained autonomy in the south. The inscriptions of Gudea, the leading dynast of Lagash, who ruled about 2120 B.C., imply extensive political influence. Lagash's prosperity in this period is readily apparent in its architecture and fine sculpture, which show Akkadian influence alongside Sumerian traditions. But despite the prominence of Lagash, Ur was ultimately to lead the post-Akkadian revival of Sumerian traditions in southern Mesopotamia.

Utuhengal, a ruler of Uruk, finally expelled the Gutians from Mesopotamia around 2120 B.C. Some time thereafter, he appointed in the city of Ur a military governor named Ur-Nammu, who proceeded to displace his former benefactor, claim the title "King of Ur," and establish a dynasty that rapidly became preeminent in Mesopotamia. For a little over a century, from 2112 to 2004 B.C., Ur-Nammu and his four successors headed an absolute monarchy whose authority and influence rivaled that of their Akkadian predecessors.

Ur-Nammu's reign was chiefly devoted to the organization and administration of the new state. Nonetheless, he extended political boundaries somewhat and may well have perished in battle. Shulgi (2094–2047 B.C.) enacted further economic and administrative reforms and led a number of victorious military campaigns to the northern and eastern borders of his realm. Diplomatically, he extended control toward the southeast by marrying his daughters to local governors. Shulgi reigned over an area comparable to but much more cohesive than that of the Akkadian kings.

The Ur III state

Anxious to prevent the recurrent rebellions that had plagued their Akkadian predecessors, the Ur III rulers introduced some administrative innovations. Former city-states became administrative districts, governed by an *ENSI* dependent on the crown for his appointment and responsible to the crown for his authority. Important or troublesome districts were assigned to a military governor or military garrison commander. To prevent such governors from garnering too much power in their districts, the Ur III kings regularly rotated them to new assignments. Another strategy used to strengthen the central government at the expense of local powers was relocation. The entire poulation of one conquered city was resettled near Nippur. The most extreme instance of this policy was the resettlement of entire districts, a practice that was to become standard in the empires of the first millennium B.C.

The rulers of the Ur III dynasty were absolute monarchs of a highly organized, centrally controlled state. Military action seems to have been limited to securing the borders of the state. Though Ur-Nammu may have died in a military encounter, inscriptions dedicated to him and his successor Shulgi sound a peaceful note.

Ur-Nammu's piety led to his coronation at the ancient shrines of Nippur, an act commemorated in a royal hymn addressed to him as a god. Shulgi too was worshipped as a royal divinity at local shrines erected in his honor. Politics again mingled with culture and religion. Like Sargon and Naramsin, Shulgi was celebrated in cuneiform literature; the numerous royal hymns composed to him or in his memory reflect his patronage of Sumerian literature and culture. Shulgi also claimed to have had a scribe's education, rare among Mesopotamian kings. Even in this era of absolute monarchy, Shulgi's support and sponsorship of the arts call to mind the Sumerian quality of personal initiative.

State regulation and temple initiative: The Ur III economy

Tens of thousands of cuneiform records detail the operations of the Ur III economy. Documentation survives for literally every type of item that passed through the various government agencies, even for the individuals who conducted the transactions.

Administration of the Ur III state was a palace affair, but the temple seems to have vigorously pursued its own ends. The huge numbers of animals received and duly recorded at Sellush-Dagan (modern Drehem)—28,000 cattle and 350,000 sheep in one year alone—were redistributed to the temples of Nippur and other major cities, to the palace household, and to various royal officials in the form of salaries or gifts. State control over herds also made for a flourishing wool and leather industry. Tablets from Umma detail the daily workload of male and female laborers as well as their wages in beer, bread, oil, fish, and spices. Merchants, some of whom were private entrepreneurs unaffiliated with the palace, provided raw materials and luxuries of all sorts. Although many of these imports were paid for in agricultural products, silver had an agreed-on value and functioned virtually as cash does today.

Not surprisingly, the concentration of power in the state sector affected the class structure. Uppermost in the hierarchy stood the royal government with all its estates, factories, workshops, and trading centers near and far. The temples likewise had their own estates and factories, a concession from the state. Within both systems emerged a distinct bureaucratic class, grown wealthy on taxes from their districts or on returns from their holdings. Private merchants grew wealthy from trade—private or state directed—and represented, in effect, a middle class. The system was rooted in its working classes: impoverished citizens who became state workers; freemen who paid taxes through **corvée** or military service; small landowners and farmers; and slaves (prisoners of war, criminals, and indentured servants).

With political as well as economic power invested exclusively in royal hands, the state dominated society and severely curtailed individual enterprise.

Private land ownership had become widespread under the Sargonid dynasty. Ur III records, however, do not mention sales of agricultural land to or between private individuals. Nor do the numerous surviving Ur III court documents include decisions on land sales. Ur III records, in other words, offer no evidence of private ownership or private exchange of arable land. There are, however, numerous contracts of lease and a few records of land donations to individuals. Thus it appears that tenants on state- and temple-owned lands accounted for a significant portion of the population and that the highly centralized Ur III state rigidly controlled all agricultural properties in traditional Sumerian fashion.

Within a century after the fall of the Ur III state, private land sale documents again begin to turn up in the cities of southern Mesopotamia. Accumulated evidence thus strongly suggests a persistent cultural difference. Generally speaking, Sumerians recognized only centralized and communal ownership of arable land; private land ownership was associated more closely with Semitic rule.

The Code of Ur-Nammu: Law in Ur III times

The dearth of private documents during the Ur III period is offset by a unique public record: the law code of Ur-Nammu. Whereas the Early Dynastic texts of Uru-inim-gina represented the first known effort at legal reform, the Code of Ur-Nammu is the earliest known collection of actual laws. Preserved only in the bits and pieces of an extremely fragmentary tablet, the code consists of a brief historical prologue followed by a section on economic and social abuses. Like the reforms of Uru-inim-gina, the preamble emphasizes personal rights and correction of administrative abuses and economic inequity.

Similar in content to later codes, with its sections on bodily injury, treatment of slaves, and criminal law, the Code of Ur-Nammu represents either the beginning or an early manifestation of a long tradition of legal codification. The code's key phrase "to establish justice in the land" reappears in second millennium B.C. law codes. By that time, this phrase had come to stand for a general remission of the crippling debts that many agricultural landowners incurred due to natural disasters or high interest on loans of capital or goods from the temple or palace. Whenever a new king ascended the throne, he would "establish justice in the land"—that is, proclaim a general moratorium on debt. But such debts may not have occurred under the Ur III regime, which apparently did not tolerate private ownership of agricultural property.

Whether these royal proclamations were binding on the courts is unknown; interestingly enough, they are virtually never cited as a basis for a legal decision. Other legal procedures are well documented in local court records called *ditilla*, or "case closed," for the phrase that invariably concluded such tablets. Court cases dealt with such matters as sale, donation, and debt contracts, family law, and the rights of slaves. Evidently several judges sat on a single case and handed down a joint decision.

The fragmentary laws of Ur-Nammu manifest a concern for social and economic justice that recurs in all later collections of Mesopotamian law. Its underlying principle of monetary recompense distinguishes it from the comparatively severe *Lex talionis*—"An eye for an eye, a tooth for a tooth"—that guided the later Semitic codes of Ḥammurapi, the Assyrians, and the Hebrews.

The ziqqurat and temple precinct: Residence of the divine

In their capacity as patrons of the arts, the kings of the Ur III period were prolific and ambitious builders. Most of the large cities they controlled still contain the remains of their temples, palaces, and ziqqurats (terraced temple-towers). At Ur, the royal and religious quarter was redesigned in a manner that exudes the technical expertise and high aesthetic standards of a practiced architectural school.

A precinct wall surrounded the elaborate religious compound dedicated to the moon-god Nanna, patron deity of Ur. In accordance with the king's divine stature, the royal residence and royal tombs were situated within this compound, which also contained internal courtyards, intramural chambers, store-rooms, and the temple residence. On a raised terrace in the northwest corner of the precinct, the lofty three-staged ziqqurat of Ur towered above the surrounding plain. Ziqqurats soon became characteristic landmarks of Mesopotamian cities. The most celebrated is surely the biblical Tower of Babel, but the best-preserved example is at Ur. Its core is simple mudbrick; its excellent state of preservation results from a casing of baked bricks and from careful renovations commissioned by the Neo-Babylonian kings in the sixth century B.C.

Because virtually all Mesopotamian buildings, including temples, were constructed of mudbrick, unlimited opportunities arose for kings to repair or reconstruct temples. Such a project was an act of piety, since the temple was, after all, the earthly residence of a god. It was also a tenet of faith that the temple should always be rebuilt on the same consecrated spot. With the passing of centuries and successive reconstructions, temples and the cities surrounding them rose to ever-greater heights. The exalted status of the city-god was expressed in the increasingly elevated position of his residence within the city. It seems fitting that the magnificent architectural accomplishments of the Ur III period were sponsored by rulers who had themselves assumed the status of gods. Never again would political leaders in Mesopotamia exercise such strong influence *as* gods; later kings wielded power *through* the gods, as representatives of the divine.

The fall of Ur

Shulgi was succeeded by two of his sons, Amar-Sin (2046–2038 B.C.) and Shu-Sin (2037–2029 B.C.). Toward the end of Shu-Sin's reign, seminomadic, Semitic-speaking Amorites from the western and northwestern steppes made their first effective inroads into Mesopotamia.

Under the last of the Ur III dynasts, Ibbi-Sin (2038–2004 B.C.), the Amorite situation became critical. Major cities became isolated, and agricultural lands were abandoned. Famine followed, and eventually a spiraling inflationary cycle caused grain rices to multiply sixty times over. Ibbi-Sin finally lost even the capital

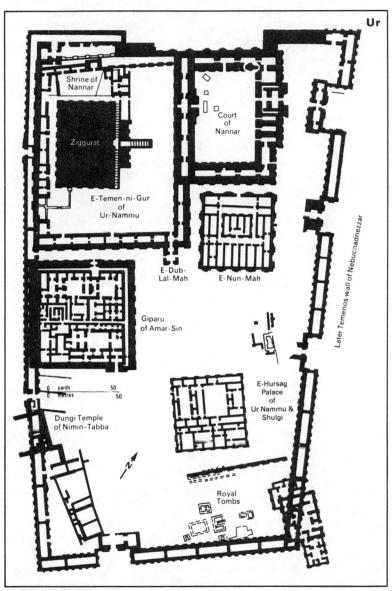

Ur

Shrine of Nannar

Court of Nannar

Ziggurat

E-Temen-ni-Gur of Ur-Nammu

E-Dub-Lal-Mah

E-Nun-Mah

Giparu of Amar-Sin

Later Temenos wall of Nebuchadnezzar

E-Hursag Palace of Ur Nammu & Shulgi

Dungi Temple of Nimin-Tabba

Royal Tombs

yards 0   50
metres 0   50

(The Robert Harding Picture Library)

Plan of the religious quarter and ziqqurat at Ur (Ur III period).

city of Ur in a devastating raid by the Elamites and some Zagros mountain tribes. The Elamites, who inhabited the southeastern stretches of the Mesopotamian plain, led Ibbi-Sin into ignominious captivity. A long Sumerian poem, "The Lamentation over the Destruction of Ur," vividly describes how low once-mighty Ur had fallen:

> Sumer is broken up by the *gishburru* weapon;
> the people groan . . .
> The destructive storm makes the land tremble and quake;
> like the flood-storm it destroys the cities . . .
> The storm ordered by Enlil in hate,
> the storm which wears away the land,
> covered Ur like a garment,
> enveloped it like linen.[2]

The Elamites had done no more than hasten the inevitable. Pressure from Amorites in the northwest and Hurrians in the north and northeast had contributed by degrees to the end of Ur's dominion. Most significant of all, however, was the resurgence of local power—the sheer unwillingness of Mesopotamian cities to tolerate centralized rule for any extended period of time.

Once again, centralized rule gave way to local. Several provincial governors seized the opportunity to dissolve their relations with Ur. Ishbi-Erra, originally a governor from the mid-Euphrates site of Mari, managed to turn the Amorite incursions to advantage. About 2017 B.C., he established a dynasty in the city of Isin, about fifteen miles south of Nippur, farther north than most of the Sumerian centers. This dynasty is considered the successor of Ur III, although its domain was much smaller.

In little more than 150 years, Mesopotamia had undergone intensive change at the political level: state rule by Akkadian kings, limited but effective domination by Gutian invaders, localized rule under autonomous Sumerian city-states, and rigidly centralized control by the Sumerian Ur III kings. The unlimited power that came to be invested in the *LUGAL* as human representative of the city-god lasted throughout three millennia of Mesopotamian political history. The concept of political dominion over all Mesopotamia had been born, nurtured, and brought to fruition.

Continuities in Mesopotamian culture .steadfastly persisted during all this political hopscotching. Although the political superstructure again shifted to the resilient rule of the city-state, Sumerian administrative and cultural practices persisted into the new era. Some facets of Sumerian law gave way to harsher, Semitic dictates, yet the concern for social and economic justice typifies Mesopotamian legal tradition in all time periods. Nonetheless, social division persisted, and secular rulers repeatedly sought equity for their subjects.

The cuneiform script continued to serve as the medium of communication, and Akkadian slowly became the language of the land. In teaching cuneiform to their students, professional **scribes** preserved and transmitted religious, legal, and literary ideas. The epic cycles of Gilgamesh and other Sumerian heroes permeate the Mesopotamian literary tradition.

Ziqqurats continued to house the city-god and soon became permanent fixtures in every Mesopotamian city. Another enduring current was the belief that each city-state was owned and protected by a patron deity. This, coupled with the concept of a master-servant relationship between the human and the divine, fostered the fierce individualism of all Mesopotamian city-states throughout the historical era. Mountain tribes and seminomadic groups, although initially hostile, soon succumbed to the overwhelming influence of these Mesopotamian city-state traditions.

The perennial economic basis of Mesopotamian society was agricultural, but this base was bolstered by related industrial pursuits such as leather, textile, and metal production. All levels of society contributed to agricultural output, but the emphasis on land ownership varied from period to period. Although an effective system of trade provided needed raw materials, foreign policy in many periods aimed only to extend direct political control over distant resources.

Mesopotamian civilization weathered the storms of political change and occasional outside intervention, internal social upheaval, and relatively severe class struggles. The tenacity of an agriculturally based urban society and the endurance of the cultural traditions that evolved and flourished in the fertile alluvial plain typify the stability and resilience of the ancient Mesopotamian world.

10/12

EGYPT: UNITY UNDER DIVINITY

For great spans of time, ancient Egyptian civilization flourished in virtual isolation from the rest of ancient western Asia. But isolation was not necessarily paralleled by unity. Egypt was divided geographically into the "Black Land" and the "Red Land," politically into Upper and Lower Egypt. During the Late Predynastic period, around 3100 B.C., political entities in Upper and Lower Egypt struggled for supremacy. According to later tradition, victory eventually fell to Upper Egypt and its leader King Menes. This legendary figure, whose name has not yet been verified on any contemporary monument, is equated by most scholars with Narmer, a southern king whose ceremonial palette portrays him conquering his northern enemies.

The Nature of Kingship and Religion

Ancient Egyptians considered the union of Upper and Lower Egypt by Menes to be the most important event in their history. How Menes achieved his conquest is unknown. Far more significant, however, is the question of how he maintained unification. What was the position of the ruler in this newly forged state? The answer, incomplete as it is, helps to illuminate the nature of Egyptian kingship and the outlook of ancient Egyptian religion.

Egyptian kingship

The kings of ancient Mesopotamia and later those of Israel ruled as mediators between the human and divine. Likewise the pharaoh, as chief priest of all Egyptian temples, served as a link between the gods and the people. Theoretically, however, the pharaoh was himself divine, and his rule was thus eternal and absolute. In Egypt, the king seems to have ruled not just *for* the gods but *as* a god.

Recent studies suggest that the ancient Egyptians, or at least those of the noble and scribal classes, could readily distinguish between the divine institution of the monarchy and the mortality of the individual pharaoh. The institution of pharaoh was divine, and whoever was pharaoh was likewise divine, a status conferred by the gods in their solicitude for that individual. Upon assuming the majestic, eternal monarchy, a pharaoh was accorded divine powers in the religious literature. Popular literature, meanwhile, portrayed the pharaoh as a mortal—eating, sleeping, aging, and dying—by no means exempt from irreverence or even disapproval.

According to this theory, the ancient Egyptians readily distinguished between the office and its occupant, between divine right and human susceptibility. In practice, whoever had the political power to seize the throne could claim divinity: over the three millennia of ancient Egyptian history, foreigners, commoners, and even a few women occupied the throne of pharaoh.

Whatever the merits of this theory, pharaoh unquestionably was the embodiment of the divinely led, unified Egyptian state. In assuming kingship, pharaoh shed his impermanent, human status and instead assumed an immutable, divine position. Such was the role that fell to Menes as unifier of Upper and Lower Egypt. Whether this dogma existed earlier or originated with Menes is unknown. In any case, divine status must have been essential to consolidate and legitimize conquest during this formative era in the development of the Egyptian state.

The new state also derived authority and stability from the concept of *ma'at*. Usually translated as truth, justice, order, or righteousness, *ma'at* is more accurately characterized as a cosmic or divine force for harmony and stability, dating back to the beginnings of time. Good rule and sound administration were forever imbued with *ma'at*. The eternal rightness of *ma'at* bespoke an ordered stability that in turn confirmed and consolidated the continuing rule of pharaoh. Suffused with the benefits of *ma'at*, the divine office of pharaoh served as a basic unifying element for the ancient Egyptian state.

Egyptian religion

The Egyptian religious system resembled the Mesopotamian in that each region, like each Mesopotamian city-state, had its own patron deity. With the emergence of strong central government, some of these local gods gained preeminence throughout Egypt.

Front view of the votive palette of King Narmer, a ruler usually equated with the legendary King Menes, unifier of Upper and Lower Egypt.

Political fortune, as well as ever-changing popularity, governed the rise and fall of individual gods. Just as Enlil of Nippur came to dominate the Sumerian pantheon, Ptah rose to state status when his city Memphis became the capital of Egypt. Later another local god, Re of Heliopolis (near Memphis), eclipsed Ptah as power waxed strong for the Heliopolitan priesthood of Re. Later still, during the Middle and New Kingdoms, Amon of Thebes in Upper Egypt rose to supremacy in tandem with the political status of Theban pharaohs.

While Mesopotamian deities were invariably anthropomorphic, Egyptian gods were often represented in the guise of animals: Horus the falcon, Nekhbet the vulture, Wedjet the cobra, Anubis the dog, Bastet the cat, Thoth the ibis, Sobek the crocodile, and so on. It would appear that animals—perhaps simply because of their nonhuman essence—possessed religious significance. Other divinities, including Ptah, Min, and Amon, were always depicted in human form; but the all-important deity Re, in his purest form, was not represented at all.

The rudimentary cosmologies of Egypt and Mesopotamia were similar inasmuch as both portrayed the gods creating order out of chaos. But the basic tenets of faith in the two countries were completely different. The Mesopotamians pessimistically viewed their universe as unpredictable, their gods as unstable, their afterlife as indistinct and undesirable. Egyptian religion, by contrast, inspired confidence in the eternal order and stability of the world, in the divinely guided rhythmic cycle of life and death, and in the belief that each individual Egyptian might share in eternal bliss.

Throughout most of ancient Egyptian history, the cults of the paramount deities tolerated the existence of other deities and thus perpetuated the size and complexity of the Egyptian pantheon. Divine functions often overlapped or interchanged as individual cults expanded or contracted, amalgamated or disintegrated. Although the major gods claimed universal powers, their cults continued to be associated with particular districts. The worship of pharaoh, on the other hand, was nationwide. By publicly worshiping local deities, pharaoh expressed his concern for local rights and interests. If pharaoh's mortality limited his stature among his immortal brethren, it was compensated

(*⁰ Andre Held, Ecublens, Switzerland)

Representation of the Egyptian god Anubis, god of embalming, who wears the double crown and holds the ankh *and scepter.*

for by his omnipotence throughout Egypt and his cosmic role as national unifier.

Religion served as a potent, unifying force in ancient Egypt, a cornerstone of Egyptian society. Unlike the master-servant relationship that characterized divine-human interaction in Mesopotamian belief, Egyptian deities are better likened to shepherds tending their human flocks. Divine forces protected the living and ensured that death would continue in the same immutable fashion. The ancient Egyptians believed that they lived in a static, unchanging universe in which life and death—all human events, in fact—were part of a continuous, rhythmic cycle. Certain patterns were expected: grain had to be sown and harvested, irrigation works maintained, pyramids and great temples constructed. Just as the sun daily rose in the east and set in the west and as the River Nile annually passed through a cycle of life (the annual flood) and death, so too all human life and death passed through predictable and regular patterns. Human life harmonized with this never-ending interchange of natural universal elements.

Inasmuch as the gods were immanent in nature, the ancient Egyptians lived within the sphere of divine activity. Yet Egyptian commoners probably had direct access to official major divinities only on a few festival days each year. For many people, religious practices involved worship of household deities such as the dwarf Bes, god of marriage and domestic happiness, or of revered ancestors, past kings, and officials. The god Osiris enjoyed a unique position. Even without an official center of worship, Osiris gained general acceptance among the lower and middle classes and exerted considerable influence on state religion, especially funerary beliefs.

Osiris, his sister-wife Isis, and Horus represented the life-death cycle: Horus as the living pharaoh or god, Osiris as his dead counterpart, Isis as lamentor and rejuvenator of the deceased pharaoh. The death and rebirth of Osiris originally represented little more than a nature myth: the receding Nile in autumn and the overflowing, life-giving Nile in spring. In time, however, certain qualities of Osiris, Isis, and Horus probably came to appeal to the ancient Egyptians; human sorrows and triumphs were seen to play a prominent part in the lives of the gods. In the end, Osiris' death and resurrection hinted at the possibility of immortality for the Egyptians themselves. The faithful follower of Osiris hoped to overcome human frailty and death just as the object of his worship had done.

As in Mesopotamia, the care and feeding of the gods required a great deal of time and attention. Although public liturgies or mortuary rites might be conducted in the forecourt of a monumental Egyptian temple, only specially designated priests could perform the cultic rites in the temple's innermost sanctum. In order to appease and insure divine presence within the temple and to maintain the temple's integrity with the rhythms of nature, the cult statue was annointed, clothed, fed, and entertained three times daily. In performing these technical duties for the cult image, the priests were simultaneously helping pharaoh to maintain the order and stability of *ma'at*, the divine force behind pharaonic rule.

Egyptian religious doctrine was rooted in the idea of a static, changeless universe. This doctrine gave form to ancient Egyptian culture and society, to literature and art, to the economy and the state. The very resilience of ancient Egyptian civilization through 3,000 years of internal change and external disruption is adequate testimony to a persistent belief in divine forces that animate and regulate the cosmos. The polytheistic beliefs of the ancient Egyptians enabled a comprehension of the otherwise inexplicable nature of the divine and prompted a pursuit of immortality that filtered down from pharaoh to every member of society. Peace and immortality came to all people as part of nature's constant rhythm.

The Early Dynasties (3100–2180 B.C.): Unification and Consolidation

With the unification of north and south about 3100 B.C., the Predynastic period of Egypt came to an end. For reasons both strategic and symbolic, a capital city was established at Memphis, just south of the apex of the Nile Delta near the junction of Upper and Lower Egypt. Thus began ancient Egypt's historical period, a long series of dynasties that was to last about 3,000 years.

Modern Egyptologists group the rulers of Egypt into thirty dynasties. In so doing, they are adopting the schema of the annalist Manetho, an Egyptian priest who wrote a history of Egypt in Greek during the third century B.C. Manetho's schema is reasonably well supported by earlier sources and serves as a basic framework for ancient Egyptian history.

The main written sources for the first six dynasties are royal annals, mainly of the Fourth–Sixth Dynasties; biographical texts beginning at the end of the Third Dynasty; the Pyramid Texts, magical spells for the well-being of the king's soul after death, dating from the Fifth and Sixth Dynasties; and the Palermo Stone, which although fragmentary offers a year-by-year record of all Egyptian kings from Menes through the Fifth Dynasty. Finally, three king lists from the Nineteenth Dynasty, at the end of the second millennium B.C., provide the names and numbers of Egypt's kings and their order of succession, albeit not with complete accuracy (in that respect, these lists are roughly analogous to the Sumerian King List).

Even after Menes had unified Egypt and established a new capital at Memphis, Egyptians continued to refer to their country as "the Two Lands," as if to stress the long-standing cultural schism between north and south. The king adopted a formalized sequence of titles celebrating his divinity, the extent of his legal and religious powers, and especially his unification of and rule over the Two Lands.

A number of innovations introduced during this period rapidly became standardized, shaping the course of ancient Egyptian life for generations. Irrigation and farming—the tending of crops and the management of livestock—formed the economic mainstay of the Egyptian state. Far and away the most influential and familiar innovation was the evolution of the pyramid as a funerary monument. During the Third and Fourth Dynasties, the resources of the country were increasingly dedicated to pyramid construction. Peasants were conscripted to labor on pyramids and temples, and on large-scale agricultural projects.

Early Dynastic Egypt appears to have been a highly organized country with an efficient administrative and accounting system. Pharaoh delegated administrative responsibilities to highborn officials, all of whom held office at the royal residence in

Memphis, where their movements could be observed and their aspirations to independent power checked. Memphis' chief deity Ptah, god of the earth and creator of the universe, provided divine justification for this new political reality. The social hierarchy, headed by the pharaoh, anticipated that of later, better-known dynasties.

Political history: Protodynastic period (First and Second Dynasties) and Old Kingdom (Third–Sixth Dynasties)

After the momentous unification of Upper and Lower Egypt by Menes (Narmer?) about 3100 B.C., little but names and titles is known about the sixteen or more subsequent pharaohs of the first two dynasties (Protodynastic period; about 3100–2700 B.C.). A few brief contemporary inscriptions testify to armed encounters with eastern desert tribes, perhaps as a result of Egyptian forays for copper and turquoise.

It is usually argued that each ruler of the first two dynasties had two separate tombs, one in the north at Saqqara near Memphis, the other in the south at Abydos, presumably to stress and reinforce the ruling dynasty's control over both Lower and Upper Egypt. Recent studies, however, strongly suggest that Abydos was the pharaohs' real burial place and that the Saqqara tombs were those of First and Second Dynasty officials. Luxury materials such as gold, silver, and lapis lazuli—the last two imported—in these and other Protodynastic tombs attest not only to a stratified society but also to an active maritime trade.

Old Kingdom.   The Third–Sixth Dynasties (about 2700–2180 B.C.) comprise the Old Kingdom proper. Tomb inscriptions highlight the importance of irrigation and farming to the economy. As the resources of the state increasingly became tied to the planning and construction of the pyramids, centralization and concentration of pharaonic power in Memphis reached its peak. The Old Kingdom, especially the Fourth Dynasty, was Egypt's most spectacular and perhaps most typical era.

With the coming of the Fifth Dynasty (about 2500 B.C.), political and religious developments irrevocably reversed the tendency toward centralization. The pharaohs of the Fifth Dynasty claimed descent from and thus promoted worship of the sun-god Re, whose principal shrine was at Heliopolis, north of Memphis. For reasons still undetermined, the absolute political power of pharaoh diminished in the face of the increasing influence of the priesthood of Re. By adopting the title "Son of Re," the pharaohs enhanced the power of the Re priesthood at the expense of the heretofore dominant Ptah, god of Memphis. This apparent effort to compound the divinity of pharaoh may instead have had the effect of diluting it.

By the beginning of the Sixth Dynasty, about 2350 B.C., the formerly appointive *nomarchs* (provincial officials) had established independent roots in decentralized power centers called **nomes**, where they had specific religious, legal, military, and adminstrative duties. No longer content to be buried in pharaoh's shadow, nomarchs built their own tombs locally, complete with inscriptions boasting of their personal triumphs and virtues. The power of the **vizier**, a sort of prime minister, and of the governor of Upper Egypt increased accordingly and unprecedentedly. Although personally ambitious, these high-ranking officials still served their masters well in military and commercial ventures.

The Pharaonic state: Ancient Egyptian economy

The Egyptian state in the Old Kingdom is often depicted symbolically as a pyramid, the capstone of which was pharaoh: military commander-in-chief, head of the administration and treasury, high priest of every temple, chief merchant and judge. Situated directly under pharaoh was the royal administration, headed by the powerful vizier. The role of the administration was, quite simply, to implement the will of pharaoh: to maintain order and collect taxes, to supervise royal estates and the storage of grain and other necessities, to levy troops, and to coordinate the myriad architectural projects of the state.

In contrast to Mesopotamia, the central institution of pharaonic civilization was not the city but the royal court, where pharaoh's officials, retainers, and craftsmen congregated. High-ranking ministers of court supervised the nomarchs, who in turn oversaw village leaders. Pharaoh owned all the land in Egypt,

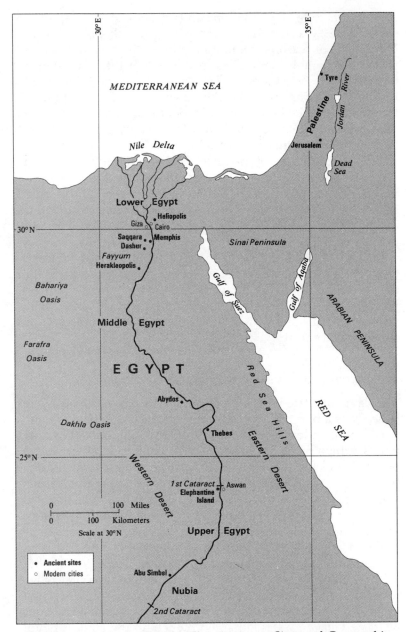

Map 3–2 Egypt in the Third Millennium B.C.: Sites and Geographic Features

and the country's economy was based on service rendered to him. In fact, the will of pharaoh largely determined the kind of work that existed. From fisherman to artisan, from farmer to scribe, most occupations served the palace or temple either directly or indirectly through a maze of officials and administrators.

To support the construction of pyramids and other state projects, as well as the ordinary functioning of the court, the economy relied heavily on taxes collected from individuals and institutions, such as temples, and on tribute from foreign conquests. Taxes were paid not in cash but in kind—that is, in animals, agricultural products, and the like—and could thus be redistributed for the direct support of royal employees (artisans, priests, officials) not engaged in food production. Use of royal land was often granted to temple priesthoods and to private individuals; such grants did not, however, confer immunity from taxes or service. Some temples were awarded large estates employing huge work forces. The economic status of the temples, unlike that of individuals, was often protected by pharaonic decree.

No evidence of private enterprise has been found, and whatever private property existed was clearly subject to the ruler's will. Localized trade was probably conducted without specific royal authorization, but large-scale movements of goods and foreign trade were carried out in the name of pharaoh. Quests for hard-to-obtain luxury goods and even for the more accessible cedars of Lebanon were undertaken by the palace. Exploitation of minerals—gold, copper, turquoise, and possibly tin—from the eastern desert and the Sinai was the prerogative of the palace, conducted by royal officials and policed by the army.

Most ancient Egyptians spent their lives cultivating the land and processing or marketing its products. During the annual inundation by the Nile, when farming became impossible, peasants were apparently conscripted to work on the construction of pyramids and other state undertakings. But unlike Mesopotamia, whose urban centers attracted many people off the land, most Egyptians maintained village-based lives, regularly punctuated by corvée labor.

The virtual lack of rainfall in Egypt forced reliance on irrigation. Basin irrigation required constant attention and supervision and made cooperation essential within each flood basin. Apparently, though, irrigation promoted unity and cooperation only on a local level. Although written evidence from the Old Kingdom makes no mention of a centralized apparatus to administer irrigation, it has long been assumed that the maintenance of the irrigation system was possible only during times of strong centralized rule. Nonetheless, it has been argued even more convincingly that flood control and irrigation were sustained locally by the population of each natural flood basin; irrigation, in other words, had no adverse affect on access to the Nile enjoyed by the next basin downstream.

In person or through his officials, pharaoh presided over economic, political, and religious spheres of activity. Whenever the breakdown of pharaonic authority threatened to erode the fiber of Egyptian civilization, the upper classes often responded by installing a pharaoh from their own, local dynasty. In such a way, the Egyptians repeatedly reinforced their ideal of maintaining a single individual at the helm of the ship of state.

Pyramids and tomb paintings: Early Egyptian culture

The pyramids of Old Kingdom Egypt are at once the most famous, monumental, and magnificent structures of the ancient world. Today they conjure up a variety of interpretations, most of which pay scant attention to this splendid architectural form in its proper context. To describe these monuments cannot do them justice. To interpret them in their sociopolitical and religious context, however, gives us a key to understanding the mentality that produced them.

The rise and decline of pharaonic power in the Old Kingdom is mirrored somewhat in the evolution of the pyramid. During the first two dynasties, a mudbrick superstructure was raised over the burial pits of royal and noble personages. This flat-topped structure, known as a *mastaba* (Arabic for bench) protected the body from exposure in sand and windstorms and ostensibly provided a secure repository for the dead person's belongings. The exterior of the mastaba was often painted and decorated with paneling, perhaps in imitation of the homes of the living.

The precursor of the Giza pyramids, and the world's earliest monumental stone structure, is the step-pyramid at Saqqara designed and built by the royal architect Imhotep for the Third Dynasty pharaoh Djoser (2663–2645 B.C). This imposing structure had its origins in a much humbler kind of burial site, the simple pit grave, which may have been used by the lower classes throughout ancient Egyptian history and prehistory. The body, arranged in a contracted position, sometimes wrapped in a reed mat and accompanied by a few possessions, was placed in a rectangular or oval pit hollowed out of the sand.

The burial place of King Djoser at Saqqara represents a major step forward in funerary architecture: construction in stone instead of mudbrick. At the same time, it testifies to pharaoh's overwhelming control of the Egyptian state. The original mastaba was topped with five more levels of decreasing size, resulting in a step-pyramid. Stone, readily available in the deserts of Upper Egypt and Nubia, increasingly became the basic building material for tombs and temples.

Even though the valley temples associated with the pyramids were used extensively for the cult of the dead king, the pyramids themselves were completely inaccessible. There is no transience here, no change. Once the pharaoh was interred, all traces of the entrance shaft were obliterated and the hermetically sealed pyramid stood—eternal, everlasting, unchanging. For a society with a religious doctrine steeped in the idea of a static universe, no monument could be more appropriate. Originally encased in smoothed limestone with virtually invisible joints, the pyramids radiate permanence and exclusion.

The earliest tomb designed as a true pyramid is the Northern Pyramid at Dahshur, thought to have been commissioned by Sneferu, first ruler of the Fourth Dynasty (see figure, page 65). The succeeding tombs of Khufu, Khafre, and Menkaure dominate the Nile landscape as their occupants in life had dominated the Nile world.

The pyramid very effectively symbolizes ancient Egyptian society and economy. In the discussion of the Egyptian economy, it was suggested that the capstone represented pharaoh, the rest of the pyramid the Egyptian state. The great pyramids at Giza, near modern Cairo, likewise reflect the extreme centralization

(© Michael Holford, Loughton, Essex)

The Step Pyramid designed and built by Imhotep for the Third Dynasty pharaoh Djoser is the world's earliest known monumental stone structure.

of the Egyptian government by the time of the Fourth Dynasty (about 2600–2500 B.C.). Permission to erect a tomb within the pyramid complex was an expression of divine favor; the tombs of princes and faithful court officials are arrayed in rows at the feet of the royal pyramids and betoken subservience to pharaoh in death as in life.

The great pyramids not only stand as the grandest expression of pharaoh's immortality and divinity, they also signify the immense power and resources of the Egyptian state. The three massive pyramids of the Fourth Dynasty represent the crowning achievement of stone construction in antiquity. The earliest and

(Courtesy of the Bettmann Archive, Inc.)

Fourth Dynasty pyramids at Giza: pyramid of Menkaure in the foreground, that of Khafre in the middle, and the Great Pyramid of Khufu in the background.

largest of these pyramids is that of the pharaoh Khufu, called Cheops by the Greeks. Khufu's pyramid, which covers about thirteen acres and contains over 2 million stone blocks weighing an average of two-and-one-half tons apiece, originally rose to a height of 481 feet. Next in size is the pyramid of Khafre (in Greek, Chephren). At the end of a long causeway from Khafre's pyramid to a valley temple near the Nile lies the Great Sphinx, an outcropping of rock carved to represent the body of a lion and the head of Khafre. The causeway and valley temple became standard features of pyramid complexes from the Fourth Dynasty on. The smallest and last of the great pyramids, that of Menkaure (Mycerinus) seems not to have been fully completed, perhaps due to Menkaure's untimely death.

Such massive construction could only be undertaken with the support of an agricultural surplus and an extensive labor pool. Farmers grew grain according to official edict and often had to remit as much as 50 percent of their harvest in kind to the state. During those periods when the Nile flood precluded planting or harvesting, Egyptian peasants were no doubt enrolled in such monumental state projects as pyramid or temple construction. Although lack of written evidence makes it difficult to decide whether labor was forced and, if so, how harshly, the

Egyptian peasant must have been indispensible to agricultural production and to the extremely complex fashioning of pharaoh's everlasting dwelling place.

Pyramids continued to be constructed intermittently throughout Egyptian history, but the achievements of the Fourth Dynasty were never surpassed. Those grandiose undertakings proved to be too great a drain on the economy. The pyramids of the Fifth Dynasty were already inferior in building quality, and today they are nothing but mounds of rubble.

As royal pyramids became smaller during the Fifth and Sixth Dynasties, artisans began to devote their efforts to private statuary and private tombs. The tomb chapels of nobles at Saqqara and other *necropoleis* (cities of the dead) near Memphis are decorated with scenes of daily life that constitute a veritable microcosm of Old Kingdom culture. This splendid mortuary art portrays people at work and at home, engaged in such pursuits as hunting, fishing, and banqueting. The tomb walls abound in scenes of agricultural life and of goldsmiths, potters, brickmakers and other craftsmen plying their trades. The ancient Egyptians believed that the depiction of foodstuffs in the tomb reliefs would provide nourishment for the deceased. In the same way, scenes of farming would have ensured a continuing supply of food. By this process of sympathetic magic, the ancient Egyptians sought to supply their eternal home with all the necessities of eternal life.

The principle whereby certain aspects of daily life were singled out for depiction on tomb walls is unknown. It has recently been suggested that the objects, plants, and animals represented categories rather than specific items. Just as Egyptian artists strove to portray universal rather than particular characteristics of plants, animals, and scenes of daily life, they aimed at generality in the representation of human figures. Occasional attempts at portraiture crop up in Old Kingdom art, but usually only the name on a statue or beside a relief drawing distinguishes an individual. With few exceptions, herdsmen, boatmen, agricultural workers, bird netters, and fishermen were portrayed as partially bald, musicians as completely bald, and herdsmen with deformed knees. Social rank was often indicated by the relative obesity of the figure. Thus Egyptian artists of the Old Kingdom tended to use physical form to represent social position.

(Giraudon/Art Resource, NY)

Tomb painting with farming scenes from the Sixth Dynasty tomb of Kagemni at Saqqara.

Egyptian mortuary art offers us a rich storehouse of ethnographic data, still inadequately understood. Funerary scenes are often portrayed on tombs, yet their emphasis is not on death but on daily life. Nevertheless, like the pyramids, mortuary art implicitly emphasizes burial and adequate provision for eternal life. As the pyramids housed the divine pharaoh for eternity,

Old Kingdom tombs ensured the nobility of everlasting sustenance.

The decline of the Old Kingdom

The most stable periods in ancient Egyptian history were those in which pharaoh dominated the government and forestalled the emergence of independent provincial power. Fourth Dynasty officials, in the course of administering the pharaoh's business, increasingly acted on their own initiative. The very forces that previously supported pharaoh's absolute, central position now began to serve as vehicles for decentralization. By the Fifth Dynasty, the increasingly elaborate state bureaucracy was functioning as a force for decentralization, and the dispersal of power to provincial administrators had begun to weaken the central government. Generally speaking, whenever royal power waxed strong, provincial posts were awarded on merit; when pharaoh's power waned, as it did at the end of the Old Kingdom, the provincial nomarchs began to claim hereditary status. As the royal pyramids diminished in size, artistic energy and local resources were poured into local tombs and monuments. The emergence of a powerful hereditary nobility is demonstrated by the tombs they constructed and elaborately decorated for themselves by the end of the Fifth Dynasty.

Economic and agricultural disaster also struck Egypt at the end of the Old Kingdom. It would probably be an overstatement to suggest that the economic history of Egypt revolved around continuous adjustment to a variable water supply. There is evidence, however, that the gradual **desiccation** of Egypt throughout the Old Kingdom was compounded during the First Intermediate Period by the Nile's repeated failure to reach adequate flood height. The resultant food shortages must have raised doubts about the powers of a ruler who, as the embodiment of the divine force within the Nile, was responsible for a successful harvest each year. The position of pharaoh may thus have become somewhat untenable and life in Egypt increasingly confused and tumultuous.

The dissolution of pharaonic rule at the end of the Sixth Dynasty was precipitated by economic and dynastic factors in addition to political ones. An already heavy-laden economy succumbed to the strain of the pharaoh's grandiose building projects. More burdensome still were the perpetual endowments designated for upkeep of royal and noble tombs. Although no obvious diminution of power accompanied the 94-year reign of the Sixth Dynasty pharaoh Pepi II, central government rapidly declined thereafter. Pepi's long rule and the simultaneous growth of provincial power are usually regarded as the major political causes of disintegration. Pepi may simply have outlived all legitimate heirs to the throne. The dynasty ended with a woman remembered as Nitocris; as at other points in Egyptian history, such lack of a male heir to the throne presaged disaster.

As the central authority of pharaoh gave way to regional power centers, the dominant and authoritarian state religion of Re lost ground. By the end of the Old Kingdom, the cult of Osiris—god of vegetation, judge of the underworld, and king of the dead—was gaining in popularity at Re's expense. Osiris' general acceptance among the lower classes prevailed even though he had no particular center of worship; Osiris could be revered in any temple. As Osiris gained general acceptance throughout Egypt, religion became more personal and less dogmatic. Even the concept of immortality became "democratized." These changes, though apparently liberating, went hand in hand with disorientation and anarchy.

The First Intermediate Period (2180–2050 B.C.): Disunity and Division

Following the lengthy reign of Pepy II, three short-lived successors presided over the rapid demise of the Sixth Dynasty and the Old Kingdom. Anarchy followed, characterized by brief reigns, palace coups, and assassinations. Manetho, with poetic hyperbole, says that in the Seventh Dynasty, "seventy kings ruled for seventy days." The Memphite pharaohs of the Seventh and Eighth Dynasties struggled to maintain control of Egypt. But the collapse of centralized rule led to petty wars between districts and to seminomadic encroachments on the Nile Delta.

An Egyptian sage, Ipu-Wer, whose "Admonitions" probably describe the topsy-turvy conditions of the First Intermediate Period, literally accused pharaoh of muddled and uninspired rule. General disorder had reversed the positions of rich and poor, dissolved law and order, encouraged violence, disrupted foreign trade, and brought agricultural production to a standstill. Egypt had become a society in ruins, where commoner could heap abuse upon king and riches-to-rags was the prevailing economic condition. Other literary works also expressed pessimism, perhaps most vividly in this meditation on suicide, in which a man addresses his soul:

> To whom can I speak today:
> Men are plundering;
> Every man seizes his fellow's (goods) . . .
> A brother . . . has become an enemy . . .
> No one thinks of yesterday,
> No one at this time acts for him who has acted.[3]

A line of rulers from Herakleopolis, a town near the Fayyum, managed to restore a modicum of security in Middle Egypt. Very little is known about these northern kings of the Ninth and Tenth Dynasties (about 2160–2040 B.C.). For slightly more than a century, they waged intermittent warfare with the vigorous ruling family from Thebes in Upper Egypt that comprised the Eleventh Dynasty (2133–1991 B.C.). As in Early Dynastic Mesopotamia, so in the First Intermediate Period more than one ruling family could prevail simultaneously. At first, the Herakleopolitan kings held sway, backed by powerful allies in Middle and Upper Egypt. By about 2085 B.C., however, Thebes under Inyotef II began to prevail. By 2023 B.C., the previously unheralded nome of Thebes had defeated Herakleopolis and laid claim to all Egypt—a claim Thebes would retain throughout most of the second millennium B.C.

The long, drawn-out sequence of internecine conflict must have gradually wearied all combatants. Scarcity and famine accompanied civil war, and cannibalism was reported in Upper Egypt. A war-weary land must have welcomed unification under Thebes. Thebes itself owed a debt to the Herakleopolitan state: their kings had restored the **Delta** nomes to Egyptian rule by pacifying Libyan and Asiatic intruders. Of the two competing powers, Thebes was weaker economically and perhaps even less advanced culturally. Yet somehow Thebes emerged triumphant and reunited the Two Lands under a single authority. As in the Predynastic era, strife between the great northern and southern confederations had ceased.

The credit for consolidating Egypt's borders and pacifying the land goes to Mentuhotpe II (about 2060–2010 B.C.). Although the regional nomarchs enjoyed more autonomy than had their counterparts during the Old Kingdom, they never disputed Mentuhotpe's hegemony over a reunited Egypt. The lengthy rule of Mentuhotpe II witnessed the resumption of state building projects, foreign trade and expeditions, and overall peace. Unrest erupted once again during the reigns of his two successors and that of the first king of the Twelfth Dynasty, Amenemhet I. But the chaos and anarchy of the First Intermediate Period had ended. Mentuhotpe may be credited with establishing Egypt's Middle Kingdom.

Cultural continuities and economic traditions revived; the rhythms of Egyptian society resumed their familiar beat. Pharaoh again began to direct all political, economic, and religious activities in the Egyptian state. Egyptian peasants returned to the cultivation of state lands or the implementation of other, state-imposed demands. Pyramids were rarely built now, but the emphasis on burial and adequate provision for eternal life continued. Belief in a peaceful, orderly, and static universe was reaffirmed, and the pursuit of immortality continued to dominate Egyptian attitudes toward the afterlife.

Certain economic and societal patterns reappear in all phases of ancient Egyptian history. The constancy of the Nile floods made secure the agricultural basis of the state and prompted seasonal planting, harvesting, and irrigation maintenance. Since pharaoh owned all land in the state and controlled trade on all but the local level, the economy literally revolved around him. The central institution of the royal court existed to serve pharaoh's will in economic, administrative, and legal matters. The divine force of *ma'at* continued to inspire peace, stability, and harmony in pharaonic rule.

Whenever the breakdown of centralized authority threatened the Egyptian state, the upper classes often sought to install a local nomarch into the position of pharaoh. The ideal of a single, powerful individual in the political spotlight was thus repeatedly reinforced even in times of decentralization. Internal disorder and political impotence in ancient Egypt seemed always to provide the seeds for the state's own rejuvenation.

This time, Egypt's reunification had been forged militarily, and the new Theban rulers had to compromise with the provincial nomarchs. Almost two centuries passed before centralized rule was firmly reestablished over all the nomes. A transformed state of Egypt emerged from this age of anarchy and strife: the foundations had been laid for a political and military machine that would gradually extend its influence into the surrounding Asiatic world.

SYRIA AND PALESTINE: TOWN AND COUNTRY

In portraying the life and times of Mesopotamians and Egyptians during the third millennium B.C., historians have invaluable written documentation in the form of cuneiform tablets and heiroglyphic inscriptions. But in evaluating the third millennium B.C. cultures of Syria and Palestine, historical interpretation has always been hindered by the lack of written records. In **Palestine**, archaeological excavations at sites such as Ai, Arad, Beth Shan, and Megiddo have revealed prosperous, walled urban centers, similar to the cities of Early Dynastic Mesopotamia. Their prosperity derived partly from trade with Egypt; but in this instance, commercial contacts and administrative need apparently never led to the adoption of writing.

Meanwhile, in northern Syria, the ubiquitous tells—many of which had revealed third millennium B.C. remains—should have suggested some sort of developed urban life. Yet the oft-presented picture of Syria at this time was one of nomadic or seminomadic tribes pursuing their annual migrations in a geopolitical landscape devoid of cities or settlements. Compared to our knowledge of the urban cultures of Mesopotamia, Egypt, and even Palestine, the history and culture of Syria in the third millennium B.C. have long remained in the dark. Recently, however, the rich and extensive finds in excavations at ancient Ebla (Tell Mardikh) by an Italian archaeological mission have begun to expose third millennium B.C. northern Syria in a clearer historical light.

The State at Ebla: Commerce and Control

The discovery of cuneiform tablets at Ebla has more than doubled the earliest known western Asiatic documentary evidence from the period between about 3200 B.C. and the advent of the Akkadian era about 2350 B.C. Previous to the findings at Ebla, the entire corpus of known cuneiform texts from this period numbered about 5,000; approximately 18,000 "tablets" have been registered at Ebla alone. Only about 2,000 of these, however, are complete. Another 6,000 are relatively large fragments, and about 10,000 are minute fragments bearing no more than one or two signs. As is true of other major cuneiform archives, most of these documents (over 80 percent at Ebla) are economic and administrative in nature. The rest are historical, legal, literary, and lexical texts and syllabaries. (The last two categories include lists of signs, bilingual vocabularies, and grammatical lists.) The finds at Ebla are so recent, since 1974, that the majority of them have yet to be published.

The archives of Ebla are believed to cover a period of about forty years. During that time, three different kings sat upon the dynastic throne at Ebla; two previous rulers are also alluded to in the documents. A very preliminary interpretation of the Ebla tablets suggests that these kings ruled the Eblaite state by sharing some of their power with the royal family, including their queens. The crown prince reportedly handled internal affairs of state; other family members helped to manage foreign matters. The elders of the city wielded considerable political influence: they administered various sectors of internal state organization and often exercised control over nearby regions directly dependent on Ebla. These high-ranking functionaries were entitled *LUGAL* "lords," two of whom were also *DI.KU₅* (in Sumerian, "judges").

Ebla's population has been estimated, on the basis of the tablets, at 260,000; if accurate, this extraordinary number must have included outlying settlements and suburbs. The tablets indicate that the entire inhabited area of the city—about 140 acres within the walls—was split into two administrative zones: the first corresponded to the acropolis (the upper, central city), the second to the lower, surrounding city. Local government matters were probably dealt with in the lower city, while state government affairs would have been directed from the acropolis. The

(© Professor Paolo Matthiae)

Western side of upper city (acropolis) at Ebla in northern Syria. The excavated squares in the background are associated with the "Royal Palace" of the third millennium B.C.

layout of the city, in other words, seems to have reflected the administrative organization of the state.

Archaeologists have tentatively identified four openings in the wall surrounding the lower city. These breaches in the wall may represent the four city gates mentioned in the texts, as well as the subdivision of the lower city into four quarters. Such close correlation of spatial organization and administrative function is unknown in Mesopotamian urban centers, where the palace or temple discharged all governmental business. This arrangement is thus far unique to Ebla.

Situated at what in later times became the crossroads of international commerce, Ebla appears to have been an important Syrian economic center of the third millennium B.C. and a precursor of the great Syrian mercantile centers of later eras. Ebla's economic boundaries were certainly far-flung, though the city did not wield political influence comparable to that of Akkad or Ur. Perhaps the strongest of Syria's city-states, Ebla reinforced its trade links through military campaigns but seems to have drawn territories into its economic sphere of influence in preference to annexing them.

Economic documents indicate that the royal flocks comprised about 80,000 sheep, 12,000 of which were slaughtered annually. And while Ebla was clearly a focal point of Syrian trade in wheat, barley, grapes, cattle, and other agricultural products, the city specialized in textile and metals. Numerous tablets from Ebla, in fact, indicate an advanced state of metallurgical technology and extensive production of a true tin-bronze (about 10 percent tin, 90 percent copper). Since the records indicate that in the course of a single year, Ebla received 1,000 pounds of silver and 10–12 pounds of gold, the city may well have controlled metal supply routes from the north.

Hundreds of place-names appear in Ebla's international trade tablets. One typical tablet records a commercial treaty between Ebrium, the fourth (or, in one radical reinterpretation, the first) ruler of Ebla's dynasty, and the ruler of an unidentified city. This tablet deals with matters typical of a commercial center—entry tax, treatment of merchants, legal problems, and the like—and with trade relations between the two cities. The treaty ends with the customary curse on the other city's ruler should he fail to abide by the treaty.

Another tablet reports Ebla's defeat of Mari, a second important Syrian center about 300 miles (480 kilometers) downstream on the Euphrates River, and reveals that a commercial colony once managed by Ebla has been liberated from Mari. Because Mari had the potential to obstruct Eblaite commerce, the dispute between Ebla and Mari may have involved not just intra-Syrian trade but all trade passing through Syria. A large tribute in silver and gold was imposed on Mari, and rule was turned over to the victorious Eblaite general. Perhaps more than any other evidence yet published, this tablet underlines how important it was for Ebla to maintain its integral commercial orbit. When that economic balance was eventually upset by the military and commercial expansion of the Akkadian kings, Ebla—if not all of Syria's urban centers—suffered serious decline.

Ebla's political history can be reconstructed only in the barest outline. Exactly when and how long its foremost dynasty ruled is still open to debate. The style of cuneiform writing suggests the period 2600/2500–2350 B.C., prior to Sargon's rule in Mesopotamia; yet stylistic comparisons of ceramics, sculpture, and minor arts argue for the era of the Akkadian kings, 2350–2200 B.C. Not least important for dating this era at Ebla was the discovery of a **cartouche** of the Old Kingdom pharaoh Pepy I (Egypt's Dynasty VI). Found on an alabaster lid in the "palace" at Ebla, this object may be dated to about 2350 B.C. and thus gives support to the lower dating. The eventual destruction of Ebla may have been wrought by Sargon's grandson Naramsin of Akkad, as he claimed in his own inscriptions.

Even though debate lingers over which Akkadian king destroyed Ebla, the economic motives for the attack are patently clear. The timber and metal deposits of northern Syria and southern Turkey would have provided sufficient incentive, as would Ebla's wealth and markets. Ebla survived this catastrophe without undergoing any significant change in its material culture. The old "royal palace," which housed all the cuneiform tablets, was leveled; a temple was later constructed on its foundation. The lack of written evidence for the postdestruction period makes it more difficult to evaluate Ebla's economic status; its mention in documents from the Mesopotamian center of Ur might even indicate that during the twenty-first century B.C., Ebla had become economically dependent on the Ur III state.

Religion and Literature: Early Syrian Culture

The Ebla tablets have provided an unexpected glimpse of religious practices in Syria in the third millennium B.C. Given the mention of a wide variety of deities, domestic and foreign, Ebla's cults seem quite tolerant. It has been suggested that two groups of deities may be identified in the Ebla tablets: an offical and a popular pantheon. The popular cult included such west Semitic deities as Ba'al, Damu, Lim, Malik, and Rasap; the official cult was comprised of the Semitic deities Adad and Shamash and the non-Semitic gods Kura and Idakul, heretofore virtually unknown in the texts of ancient western Asia. Dagan, originally a weather god associated with fertility, also appears frequently in the Ebla tablets and thereby upholds his Old Testament reputation as an important Semitic deity.

Semitic divinities familiar from other sources appear at Ebla: Rasap (Rashap) the god of pestilence and war, Sipish (Shamash/Shapash) the sun-god, Ashtar (Ishtar), Adad the weather-god, Kasalu (in Ugaritic, *ksr*), and Kamish (in Moabite, Kemosh). Tablets describe bread offerings, libations, and animal sacrifices in temples sacred to Dagan, Ashtar, Kamish, and Rasap. Such Sumerian gods as Enlil, Enki, Inanna, and Utu appear alongside the Hurrian deities Adamma and Ashtabi, for whom two months of the Eblaite year were named. One of the long Eblaite vocabularies lists correspondences between Sumerian gods and their Syrian counterparts (Nergal = Rasap, Utu = Sipish, Inanna = Ashtar, and so on). Two tablets record that members of the royal family made animal offerings to different gods within the same month. Texts of myths, hymns to deities, incantations, and proverbs have been found at Ebla, but too little has yet been published for more definitive interpretation.

Ebla's archives also attest to a flourishing scribal and literary tradition. Scribes at Ebla had imported cuneiform writing from Sumer and used it to write texts in both Sumerian and Eblaite, the local Semitic language. Foreign scribes from Mari and Emar and a mathematics scholar from Kish traveled to Ebla to avail themselves of the city's rich scholarly resources. On the tablets from the scribal school, the unsteady marks of pupils are visible next to the masterly strokes of their teachers.

The cuneiform textbooks found at Ebla number in the hundreds. The lists of Sumerian words spelled out syllable by syllable are of incalculable value in helping modern scholars determine how Sumerian was pronounced. There are also cuneiform sign lists arranged by similarity of appearance and of sound: words beginning with *nì*, followed by those beginning with *ka*, and so on—in principle equivalent to our own alphabetic order. Still other encyclopedic lists catalog goods, objects, professions, and flora and fauna. Since very similar lists have been found at Early Dynastic sites in Mesopotamia, it is difficult to determine which influence was dominant: the Mesopotamian or Eblaite tradition. It seems, however, that some of the lists are unique to Ebla.

Perhaps the most valuable of all the school-type texts are three bilingual word lists in Sumerian and Eblaite. The Sumerian words are arranged **acrophonically** and accompanied by their

Eblaite equivalents, making these the earliest known dictionaries. Unilingual lists of words and grammatical texts in Eblaite represent a priceless key to understanding this heretofore unknown and unexpected language.

The finds at Ebla have provided new clues for the understanding of Syrian history and culture during the third millennium B.C. Having borrowed the cuneiform script of Sumer, scribes at Ebla put it to work, organizing and administering politics, education, and trade at this important commercial center. The state expended much effort on maintaining its influential role in Syrian trade; only a concerted push by the expansionistic Akkadian state brought Ebla to its knees.

While it is clear that Mesopotamia significantly influenced Eblaite culture, many artistic, commercial, and literary aspects of that culture were indigenous to Syria. The spatial organization of the city closely corresponded to its administrative functions, an urban concept unique to Ebla. Even though the few religious and literary texts thus far published seem to follow closely their Mesopotamian counterparts, Syrian religion and literature still cannot be evaluated in any detail. Some of the Ebla tablets were written in the local Semitic language (Eblaite) but the majority were written in Sumerian. These tablets have already enabled Sumerologists to read and better understand third millennium B.C. Sumerian texts; they are certain to provide further insight into linguistic, religious, and socioeconomic phenomena of the second and first millennia B.C. Most important, the image of third millennium B.C. Syria rendered by the Ebla discoveries suggests that it would be inaccurate to think in terms of a dominant Mesopotamian culture that set the pace for all of ancient western Asia in the third millennium B.C. This period was a time of balance, tension, and contrast between the high cultures of Mesopotamia in the east and Syria in the west.

The Amorites in Syria: Urbanism in Decline

About 2000 B.C., Ebla was destroyed a second time. This time the material culture of the rebuilt city underwent a transformation. Although some of this change may be attributable to Ebla's involvement in a new system of interregional trade, the excavator of Ebla has suggested that the Amorites were to blame.

At approximately the same time, the Amorites certainly contributed to the downfall of the Ur III dynasty in Mesopotamia.

Who were the Amorites? How did they manage to effect such widespread disruption? In the discussion of seminomads and sedentism (see pages 80–82), it was suggested that seminomadic society in the ancient Near East took two distinct forms. Alongside the complex interaction between settled and tribal society, tribal society itself might be partly pastoral and partly dependent on agriculture. This configuration was apparent during the Ur III period, when Semitic-speaking Amorite intruders encountered other Semitic-speaking people, farmers and laborers who had settled in Mesopotamia.

Like the Eblaites and Akkadians, the Amorites spoke a Semitic language, but it differed dialectically from both of the others. Another distinction is their indisputable seminomadic background. The Sumerian term *MARTU* (in Akkadian, *Amurru*) referred both to an ethnic group settled in Mesopotamia and to a geographical direction, west, suggesting that the Amorites had entered Mesopotamia from that area.

Amorites had first come into conflict with the settled populations of Sumer and Akkad during the reign of Shar-kali-sharri in the Akkadian era. What began then as a trickle of migrants engulfed the land during the reigns of Shu-Sin and Ibbi-Sin in the latter Ur III period (see pages 98–100). Large-scale movements of this kind were far more disruptive than occasional raids or gradual assimilation.

Texts from Mari dated to the late nineteenth and early eighteenth centuries B.C. permit a more detailed look at Amorite tribes, albeit from a slightly later period of time. Although they ordinarily confined their movements to the steppe zone on the periphery of cultivated land, the Amorites occasionally mingled with settled peoples to barter for foodstuffs, utensils, and weapons.

They also had some experience with agriculture, sometimes stopping long enough to sow or reap a harvest, sometimes leaving part of the group behind to tend crops. A persistent aim of these Amorite tribes seems to have been the appropriation of arable lands, better provided with water and pasture than the steppe zone. Meanwhile they worked in settled areas as mercenaries, administrators, and even farmers. The palace at Mari attempted to enlist some tribes for military service and corvée work and even tried to tax them. The Mari texts thus portray two Amorite ways of life: as seminomad and shepherd where environmental conditions allowed, as peasant and citizen elsewhere.

No similar evidence sheds light on the social milieu and the course of events in Syria at the end of the third millennim B.C. Documentation from Ebla ends about 2200 B.C., almost 200 years before its final destruction. Archaeological evidence from Ebla and other Syrian sites suggests that a reversion from urbanism to village life followed these latter destructions, but it is too scarce and circumstantial to draw any further conclusions. The Amorite inroads into Mesopotamia that led to the fall of Ur about the same time do not necessarily prove simultaneous movement toward Syria. In any case, Amorites were already subsisting in Syria, partly as seminomads and partly as city dwellers. Whoever destroyed Ebla and brought about the decline of Near Eastern urban civilization must have encountered them.

By the end of the nineteenth century B.C., when the archaeological evidence from Syria again becomes clear and written data are once more available, the Amorites dominated not only the city-states of Syria and northwestern Mesopotamia but those of the Mesopotamian alluvium as well. The complex interaction between sedentary and seminomadic groups, a basic component of the urban-centered social system in the ancient Near East, is well illustrated by the Amorite episode. Although the Amorites achieved political dominance over a broad area, it is obvious that their passage from seminomadic pasture to palatial throne was long, indirect, and fraught with cultural crises.

NOTES

1. Translation by S. N. Kramer, in *Ancient Near Eastern Texts Relating to the Old Testament*, 3d ed., ed. J. B. Pritchard (Princeton, N.J.: Princeton University Press, 1969), pp. 647–48. Author's note: I have changed Kramer's reading of "lead" in line 3 to "tin."
2. Ibid., p. 459.
3. Translation by J. A. Wilson, in *Ancient Near Eastern Texts Relating to the Old Testament*, 3d ed., ed. J. B. Pritchard (Princeton, N.J.: Princeton University Press, 1969), pp. 405–7.

SUPPLEMENTARY READINGS

Adams, R. M. 1984. "Mesopotamian Social Evolution: Old Outlooks, New Goals." In *On the Evolution of Complex Societies: Essays in Honor of Harry Hiojer 1982*, ed. T. K. Earle. Other Realities 6, pp. 79–129. Malibu, Calif.: Undena.

Adams, R. M. 1978. "Strategies of Maximization, Stability, and Resilence in Mesopotamian Society, Settlement, and Agriculture." *Proceedings of the Amercian Philosophical Society* 122, no.5, pp. 329–35.

Baines, J., and J. Malek. 1980. *Atlas of Ancient Egypt*. Oxford: Phaidon Press.

Bottero, J.; E. Cassin; and J. Vercoutter. 1967. *The Near East: The Early Civilizations*. New York: Dell.

Cooper, J. S. 1983. *Reconstructing History from Ancient Inscriptions: The Lagash-Umma Border Conflict. Sources from the Ancient Near East* 2, no.1. Malibu, Calif.: Undena.

————. 1973. "Sumerian and Akkadian in Sumer and Akkad." *Orientalia* 42, pp. 239–46.

Diakanoff, I. M. 1974. "Structure of Society and State in Early Dynastic Sumer." *Materials from the Ancient Near East* 1, no. 3, pp. 1–16. Malibu, Calif.: Undena.

Edwards, I. E. S. 1986. *The Pyramids of Egypt*. Rev. ed. Harmondsworth, U.K.: Penguin Books.

Edwards, I. E. S.; C. J. Gadd; and N. G. L. Hammond, eds. 1971. The Early History of the Middle East. *The Cambridge Ancient History*, vol. 1, part 2, 3d rev. ed. Cambridge: Cambridge University Press.

Falkenstein, A. 1974. "The Sumerian temple city." (Translation and introduction by Maria de Jong Ellis). *Materials from the Ancient Near East* 1, no.1, pp. 1–21. Malibu, Calif.: Undena.

Foster, B. R. 1981. "A New Look at the Sumerian Temple State." *Journal of the Economic and Social History of the Orient* 24, pp. 225–41.

Frankfort, H. 1948. *Kingship and the Gods*. Chicago: University of Chicago Press.

Frankfort, H. and H.; J. A. Wilson, and T. Jacobsen. 1949. *Before Philosophy*. Harmondsworth, U.K.: Penguin Books.

Gardiner, A. 1961. *Egypt of the Pharaohs*. Oxford: Oxford University Press.

Gelb, I. J. 1979. "Household and Family in Early Mesopotamia." In *State and Temple Economy in the Ancient Near East* I, ed. E. Lipinski, pp. 1–97. Leuven, Belgium: Departement Orientalistiek.

Hallo, W. W. 1971. "Gutium." *Reallexicon der Assyriologie* 3, pp. 708–20.

Jacobsen, T. 1957. "Early Political Development in Mesopotamia." *Zeitschrift für Assyriologie* 52, pp. 91–140.

Kemp, B. J. 1984. "In the Shadow of Texts: Archaeology in Egypt." *Archaeological Review from Cambridge* 3, pp. 19–28.

————. 1983. "Old Kingdom, Middle Kingdom, and Second Intermediate Period, c. 2686–1552 B.C." In *Ancient Egypt: A Social History,* B. G. Trigger, B. J. Kemp, D. O'Conner, and A. B. Lloyd, pp. 71–182. Cambridge: Cambridge University Press.

Lipinski, E., ed. 1979. *State and Temple Economy in the Ancient Near East,* vols. I, II. Orientalia Lovaniensia Analecta 5, 6. Leuven, Belgium: Departement Orientalistiek.

Matthiae, P. 1981. *Ebla: An Empire Rediscovered.* Garden City, N.Y.: Doubleday Publishing.

Oppenheim, A. L. (Rev. ed. completed by E. Reiner.) 1977. *Ancient Mesopotamia.* Chicago: University of Chicago Press.

Perrot, J. 1979. *Syria-Palestine* I: *From the Origins to the Bronze Age.* Archaeologia Mundi Series. Basel, Switzerland: Nagel.

Pettinato, G. 1981. *The Archives of Ebla.* Garden City, N.Y.: Doubleday Publishing.

Postgate, N. 1977. *Making of the Past. The First Empires.* Oxford: Elsevier-Phaidon. Vol. 4.

Trigger, B. G.; B. J. Kemp; D. O'Conner; and A. B. Lloyd. 1983. *Ancient Egypt: A Social History.* Cambridge: Cambridge University Press.

Weeks, K. 1979. *Egyptology and the Social Sciences.* Cairo: American University in Cairo Press.

Weiss, H., Ed. 1985. *Ebla to Damascus: Art and Archaeology of Ancient Syria.* Washington, D.C.: Smithsonian Institution.

————. 1986. *The Origins of Cities in Dry- Farming Syria and Mesopotamia in the Third Millennium* B.C. Winona Lake, Ind.: American Schools of Oriental Research/Eisenbrauns.

IV

THE SECOND MILLENNIUM B.C.: THE ERA OF INTERNATIONALISM

Intensifying commercial, political, and social contacts among the various states of ancient western Asia and Egypt characterize the second millennium B.C. (2000–1000 B.C.). Although no dramatic innovations in metallurgical technology are evident, material and cultural change overall (especially in Syria-Palestine) has prompted archaeologists to call the period of about 2000–1600 B.C. the Middle Bronze Age and that of about 1600–1100 B.C. the Late Bronze Age.

Earlier sources of copper and tin (Oman, Anatolia, Afghanistan) were supplemented and occasionally replaced by newly exploited sources (Cyprus, perhaps parts of Europe or the western Mediterranean). The trade in metals became a vital component of an ever-expanding area economy. Disruptions in that trade played a significant role in the cultural collapse and the demise of internationalism at the end of the Late Bronze Age, between about 1200 and 1100 B.C.

Mesopotamia's political systems and commercial networks grew increasingly complex during the second millennium B.C. Although city-state particularism still prevailed, the eighteenth century B.C. also saw the rise of two larger political entities: Assyria under Shamshi-Adad and Babylonia under Hammurapi. The Assyrian polity appears more cohesive, but both states relied on precarious alliances and coalitions to support their expansionistic aims, and both collapsed soon after the deaths of their founders. Decentralization again prevailed for about two centuries, until Kassite newcomers succeeded in dominating the region. The Kassites unified Babylonia around 1460 B.C. and ruled thereafter for over 250 years.

By about 1500 B.C., political and economic initiative had shifted decisively westward. The cities of Syria-Palestine—coastal ports and inland emporia astride major trade routes—came to occupy pivotal positions in a complex regional economy linking the Levant to Egypt, Mesopotamia, Anatolia, Cyprus, and the Aegean. The economies of these cities centered on the production of raw materials and of commodities, varying from **copper ingots** to ivory-inlaid furniture to purple-dyed garments, and on the transportation and exchange of these and other goods to neighboring states. The powerful inland territorial states, such as those of the Hittites and Kassites, depended on these Levantine cities for goods and services otherwise unobtainable without massive military expansion or economic reorganization.

Eventually Egypt, a self-regulating territorial state with a highly centralized economy, came to rely on the Levantine cities as mediators with its trading partners in Babylonia and northern Syria. This arrangement drew Egypt into the elaborate international network of alliances and commercial relations that ensured access to markets and freedom of trade. Political dominion was elusive and often contested; Egypt and Hittite Anatolia were the chief adversaries whenever the balance of power was upset.

BABYLONIA AND ASSYRIA: NEW NATION–STATES

Properly speaking, *Mesopotamia* refers not only to the culture of the area between the Tigris and Euphrates but also to the geographic region itself. During the second millennium B.C., Mesopotamia was divided into two geopolitical areas of great historical importance: Babylonia and Assyria. Because the city of Babylon did not become a significant political force until this time, the term *Babylonia* has not been used previously as a geographic designation. From here on, however, the northern sector of the land—up to the Zagros foothills—will be called Assyria; the southern part—to the Gulf—Babylonia. The two parts are divided by the Gebel Hamrin (Red Mountain), a low-lying mountain ridge that extends southeastward from Ashur to the Diyala River basin.

Historical sources multiply in the second millennium B.C. Thousands of cuneiform tablets from this era have been unearthed in Babylonia, northern Syria, and Anatolia. King lists from Isin, Larsa, Ashur, and Babylon and lists of date formulas (whereon each year of a king's reign was given a name) reveal synchronisms and serve as a useful chronological framework. International treaties, letters, accounts, contracts, and legal documents from Babylon and Ashur in Mesopotamia, Mari and Alalakh in Syria, and Kanesh and Hattusha in Anatolia illuminate the centuries 1900–1600 B.C. like few others in ancient Near Eastern history. For the period of Kassite rule in Babylonia (about 1600–1200 B.C.), source materials are far scarcer: only about 900 tablets from the Kassite era have been published, although thousands more are known to exist in museum collections.

By forming widespread, if insecure, political coalitions, Shamshi-Adad of Assyria and Hammurapi of Babylonia forged two extensive and partly contemporaneous territorial (or national) states. As in the bygone eras of the Akkadian and Ur III dynasties, the goals were to acquire territory and to secure the constant flow of vital raw materials into the bountiful but resource-barren alluvial plain. The reemergence of forcefully unified nation-states in both Assyria and Babylonia at this time must be attributed chiefly to the great military and administrative capabilities as well as the personal charismas of Shamshi-Adad and Hammurapi.

The establishment of nation-states dislodged external trade, warfare, and diplomacy from the control of local city-states or communities. Increasing political centralization forced the smaller, localized city-states into an increasing reliance on the central Assyrian or Babylonian governments for the procurement and allocation of basic resources, the formation of a standing army, and the implementation of the legal system. Only those people who spoke for or represented the nation-state were in constant contact with foreign leaders or groups who controlled access to needed resources or determined the sociopolitical, economic, and military stance of their own polities. Local city-states competing for critical basic or luxury imports were thus inevitably drawn into the sociopolitical web woven by state leaders.

Although both Shamshi-Adad and Hammurapi failed to establish enduring national states, henceforth political power and cultural traditon in ancient Mesopotamia centered on these two polities. Even the Kassites, who built their own fortress-city nearby, maintained Babylon as their political, commercial, and religious center.

The Early Old Babylonian Period (2000–1800 B.C.): Competition and Flux

The dynasty Ishbi-Erra established at Isin (see page 100) perpetuated the political and cultural patterns of the Ur III era. He took over intact the administrative and communications system and adhered closely to the military policy of the Ur III kings. Toward the end of the twentieth century B.C., however, Isin lost control of the southern cities. Larsa seized the old capital city of Ur and thereby invalidated Isin's claim to be the sole successor of the Ur III state. A series of competing Amorite-dominated city-states vied for preeminence in Babylonia, and the history of the Sumerians drew rapidly to a close.

Around 1900 B.C., a new age emerged in Babylonia. The Amorites consolidated power in new centers such as Larsa, Eshnunna, and Babylon and ignored formerly prestigious Sumerian cities like Kish, Ur, and Uruk. Sumerian ceased to be spoken, and the prevailing Semitic speech no longer vocalized the Old Akkadian dialect but rather the Old Babylonian. Old Babylonian was not a new language but rather a later form of Akkadian; it is designated as Old to distinguish it from later dialects, and as Babylonian to differentiate it from Akkadian.

Although Larsa's predominance grew steadily, a fluctuating power struggle continued between that city and Isin. Control of Nippur was the basis for overlordship, and neither city managed to gain the upper hand permanently. Competing local dynasties

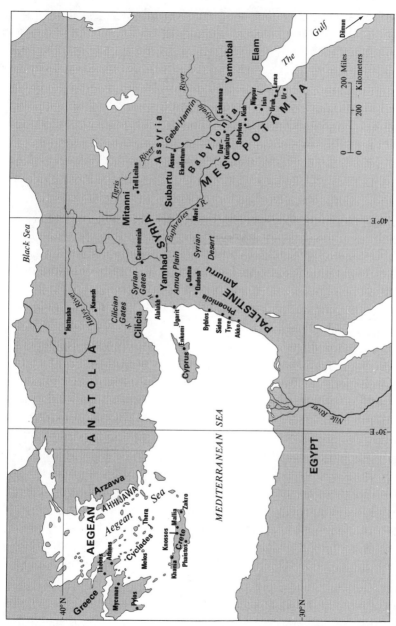

Map 4–1 Ancient Western Asia, the Aegean, and Anatolia in the Second Millennium B.C.: Sites and Geographic Features

from Uruk, Eshnunna, and Babylon shared the political spotlight with Ashur in Assyria and Mari in the northwest. No single dynasty prevailed. As in Early Dynastic Sumer, smaller states continually raided their neighbors' territory. Grander schemes had to await the formation of city-state coalitions.

Amorite assimilation in the east

During the Ur III period, some Semitic-speaking Amorite immigrants had assimilated into Mesopotamian society, intermarrying, adopting the local dialect, and forsaking tribal customs. Yet the older, settled elements among the population had continued to regard them with suspicion and contempt. By about 1900 B.C., settled Amorites finally attained prominent positions in Babylonia, even including kingship over independent states. This process was, however, very gradual and probably resulted more from individual initiative than from tribal or military pressure.

The process of assimilation cannot be reconstructed step by step with any certainty. Whenever an Amorite tribe entered an economic or military relationship with a sedentary leader, its ruler, called *abum* (father), shouldered a double responsibility: to the king for his tribe's loyalty and to his tribe for their proper treatment and due compensation. Some tribes may have passed through an intermediate stage of dependence on their settled neighbors. Eventually, however, the tribe and its leader acquired familiarity with settled ways and urban culture.

An instructive example is Kudur-Mabuk, an Amorite tribal leader who steered his son Warad-Sin to the throne of Larsa in 1834 B.C. One of Kudur-Mabuk's titles, Sheikh of Yamutbal, suggests that his tribe had spent time in Yamutbal, an area east of the Tigris. His name, which is Elamite, implies that he had once been in the service of the Elamites—a distinct, non-Semitic-speaking ethnic group (sometimes friend, sometimes foe) that occupied the southeastern stretches of the alluvial plain. Thus introduced to urban culture, Kudur-Mabuk gave his sons Akkadian names and his daughter a Sumerian name. He also consecrated his daughter as priestess of the moon-god Nanna at Ur—the office established by Sargon of Akkad as a symbolic link between Sumer and Akkad. Although a descendant and chieftain of seminomads, Kudur-Mabuk clearly had learned how to maneuver the paths to power in urban society.

The process of assimilation was finally completed when the Amorites adopted the sedentary culture, including the cuneiform script. By degrees, Amorites thus mastered many Babylonian city-states. But mastery came—as always in this complex process of settling down—at the expense of their own cultural traditions.

The Old Assyrian Period: Assyria and Anatolia

Like the Amorites, who had assumed power in Babylonia, the Assyrians also spoke a Semitic language. According to the Assyrian king list, compiled during the first millennium B.C., Assyria's earliest rulers were seventeen kings "living in tents," presumably a reference to their seminomadic roots. Next came ten kings called "ancestors," followed by the Puzur-Assur dynasty. Early in the twentieth century B.C., the Assyrian king Puzur-Assur established Assyria's independence from the Sumerian rule of the Ur III dynasty. Gradually thereafter, the city-state of Ashur became a major entrepôt for the metals trade between northern Mesopotamia and Anatolia.

By the end of the twentieth century B.C., Ashur had established a stable trading relationship with the Anatolian city of Kanesh. Anatolia was, by this time, the ancient Near East's primary source of such raw materials as copper, silver, and wood. Textiles and tin were dispatched from Assyria to Anatolia, where they were traded for Anatolian precious metals, especially silver, used in turn to finance further exports.

Old Assyrian civilization thus had two distinct components: the independent city-state of Ashur on the upper Tigris and a group of trading colonies and satellite stations in Anatolia and northern Syria, operated by Assyrians. Much of what is known of Ashur in the Old Assyrian period is based on finds from the excavations at the primary trading colony Kanesh (modern Kültepe) in central Anatolia, where more than 13,000 cuneiform tablets have been unearthed. The 3,000 tablets thus far published constitute our best primary source for this era, highlighting developments back in Ashur and spotlighting the mercantile ventures of the colony.

The Kārum Kanesh: Entrepreneurs and Interregional Commerce

Excavation of the *kārum* (merchant community) at Kanesh has revealed four distinct archaeological levels, the two earliest of which produced no written evidence. Level 2, dating from about 1920–1840 B.C. and thus approximately contemporaneous with the Puzur-Assur dynasty, acccounts for most of the texts. The next level, IB, which corresponds to a much shorter period partly overlapping the reign of Shamshi-Adad (see pages 145–46), also produced documentary evidence.

Because this written evidence has survived the ravages of time, the political and commercial activities of the Kanesh colony are fairly well known, but relatively little is learned of Ashur itself. Kingship and temple were closely allied; a city assembly worked with the king, and together the two constituted the highest legal authority in Assyrian society. Political authority in the colonies derived from the king and city assembly in Ashur and was supervised by special envoys. Diplomatic relations between the *kārum* and the host city were handled by envoys from Ashur in collaboration with colony officials. The Assyrians who resided in Anatolia did not enjoy preferred political status; they paid taxes to the native rulers, who had a vested interest in the trade.

Anatolia in the early second millennium B.C. was divided into provincial city-states, each under the control of a prince; Kanesh was one of the most influential. The merchant colony at Kanesh was the commercial hub of at least nine other colonies and ten or more subsidiary stations in northern Syria and central and eastern Anatolia. Like Kanesh, each colony and station was attached to an existing Anatolian city.

Individual agents of family companies and private institutions in Ashur conducted the venture trade in which all these outposts were engaged. When tin and textile imports reached Kanesh, most were taken on credit by retail traders who traveled widely in Anatolia. The return shipments of silver had an established value vis-à-vis tin and textiles and functioned much the same as money does today.

The Kanesh archives offer an unexpectedly detailed view of an ancient market economy; they present a mass of information on limited aspects of a very complex commercial transaction. The archives' detailed evidence on such matters as transportation, turnover, prices and profits, accounting methods, and systems of clearing and credit is of incalculable value for the history of commerce. Nonetheless, the wider economic and institutional context within which these colonies briefly flourished can still only be glimpsed.

The entrepreneurial basis of the Assyrian market trade contrasts somewhat with the situation in Babylonia, where crown bureaucrats increasingly kept a watchful eye on individual merchants. The use of silver as a medium of exchange in the Assyrian system suggests a similar practice in Babylonia. The textiles Assyria traded probably originated in Babylonia and the tin perhaps in western Afghanistan (or in southern Anatolia's Taurus Mountains?); the complexity and scope of this trade typify the internationalism of the Near East during much of the second millennium B.C.

Disruption of Old Assyrian trade: Advent of the Hittites in Anatolia?

Archaeological excavations have revealed evidence of a complete rupture in Old Assyrian trade patterns between Kanesh and Ashur in the latter half of the ninteenth century B.C. The cuneiform tablets from Kanesh contain a few Hittite personal names and loan-words, the earliest written evidence of Indo-European–speaking peoples in Anatolia. Although scholars still dispute the origin of the Hittites and the date of their arrival on the Anatolian plateau, struggles between Hittites and the native (Hattic) rulers of Kanesh may have suspended temporarily the economic activities of the Assyrian colonies.

As the Old Assyrian tablets demonstrate, Kanesh was one of Anatolia's most powerful city-states; the earliest Hittite texts give the same impression. In addition, these very early Hittite documents mention two princes, Pitkhana and Anitta, lords of the still unidentified city-state of Kussara, who "conquered" Kanesh and made it their capital. There is good reason to believe that close ethnic affinities existed between Kussara and Kanesh. Based on the evidence of names, the population of Kanesh seems to have been predominantly Indo-European. Later Hittite documents trace the lineage of early Hittite rulers back to Kussara, but no mention is made of Pitkhana or Anitta. It therefore remains uncertain whether these two rulers were Hittites or native Anatolians. Similarly it cannot be proven that their conquest of Kanesh disrupted Old Assyrian trade, but a dagger found in the main citadel at Kanesh and inscribed with Anitta's name is suggestive.

Anitta's use of horse-drawn chariots and chariot warriors—once in an attempt to obliterate the Anatolian city-state of Hattusha—virtually revolutionized Near Eastern military tactics; his expansionist ambitions eventually brought much of Anatolia under his control. The horse—originally from the steppes of central Asia—was probably introduced into the Near East by the Indo-European–speaking Hittites or one of the other "mountain peoples," Hurrians or Kassites. (The Hurrians spoke a language unrelated to any other known language, living or dead. The Kassite language is so sparsely attested that it cannot be associated with any known language.) The advent of the horse gave armies greater scope and range and consequently broadened the ambitions of more-powerful states; it brought previously isolated areas, such as Babylonia and Anatolia, into increasing contact with one another. The horse, in other words, significantly contributed to the increasing international contacts among Near Eastern cultures of the second millennium B.C.

Meanwhile, at Kanesh, trade relations with Assyria were briefly reestablished early in the eighteenth century B.C. But the exchange was less intense; the Kanesh archives no longer refer to a caravan trade of tin and textiles. The actors of trade had also changed: Hattic natives were increasingly involved in struggles with the Hittites for supremacy in Anatolia. The Assyrians, now under the Amorite ruler Shamshi-Adad, contested both Babylonians and Zagros mountain tribes for mastery over interregional trade. Within Anatolia itself, the economic and po-

litical power center shifted—some time between 1850 and 1750
B.C.—from Kanesh to Hattusha, soon to become the fabulous
capital city of the Hittites in Anatolia (see page 192).

The Old Babylonian Era (1800–1600 B.C.)

Assyria under Shamshi-Adad

The penultimate ruler of the Puzur-Assur dynasty sent an Amorite named Shamshi-Adad into Babylonia with an army, perhaps
to retaliate for Babylonian interference in Assyrian commercial
affairs. On his return, Shamshi-Adad took up residence in the
city of Ekallatum, not far south of Ashur on the opposite bank
of the Tigris. After three years there, he marched on Ashur and
usurped the throne from the last member of the Puzur-Assur
dynasty. Over the next thirty-two years (1814/13–1781 B.C.),
Shamshi-Adad established a powerful Assyrian political and
commercial state. From his newly built capital city Shubat-Enlil
(the site of Tell Leilan in northeast Syria), Shamshi-Adad rapidly
gathered under his wing the entire **Jezirah** area as far as the
Euphrates bend.

In contrast to the competing independent Amorite-ruled city
states of the nineteenth century B.C., the state that Shamshi-
Adad founded in Assyria and northwest Mesopotamia signaled
a brief trend toward a new political configuration: the nation-
state. Shamshi-Adad's polity thrived, not only on commerce but
also on the produce of the fertile Assyrian plain and the villages
of the Euphrates and its tributaries. Cuneiform records from the
important Old Babylonian city-state of Mari on the middle Euphrates—where Shamshi-Adad established one of his sons as
king—characterize the Assyrian monarch as a vigilant administrator in tight control of his domain. Yet his state was not
peaceful. Its unwieldy size made it vulnerable to attack, and the
various independent states to the west and south—Yamḫad,
Eshnunna, Larsa, and Babylon—were too powerful to fend off
simultaneously. Seminomadic peoples also posed problems, both
as caravan raiders and as unruly mercenaries.

Shamshi-Adad's death splintered the unity of the northwest.
His son Ishme-Dagan maintained rule in Assyria but lost the

remainder of the upper Euphrates region, probably to Zimri-Lim of Mari or his supporters. Thus Shamshi-Adad's brief attempt at unification did not outlive him, and decentralization predominated once again.

Mari and Alalakh: Emporia of the West.   Upper Mesopotamia and Syria were split into numerous small kingdoms during the first two centuries of the second millennium B.C. The **Jezirah** (see page 23), which cuts across the entire area, functioned as a corridor for commercial, migratory, and military movements. In extending his nation-state west to the Euphrates, Shamshi-Adad's most important prize was the seizure of Mari, always a mainstay of international trade. Farther west, beyond the Euphrates and thus beyond Shamshi-Adad's dominion, lay another important Old Babylonian city-state, Alalakh. Well known from archaeological excavations that uncovered their extensive cuneiform records, both states offer a glimpse of sedentary Amorite culture in the west and of international cultural connections between the regions of western Asia and the eastern Mediterranean.

Mari is located on the middle Euphrates just within the eastern border of Syria; Alalakh lies on the northernmost stretch of the Orontes River, twenty miles from the Mediterranean in western Syria. Although Alalakh was located on a fertile plain, its wealth, like that of Mari, was based not on agriculture but on trade; Alalakh occupied a strategic position as a communications link between east and west.

Both Mari and Alalakh were distinguished by imposing palaces, undoubtedly built and maintained with the lucrative proceeds of commerce. The huge palace at Mari was a Babylonian house writ large. Chambers arranged around an open court provided air, light, and easy communication as well as security and privacy. The palace was the king's residence, the administrative center of the kingdom, the local school, a place for work and worship, a reception hall for foreign visitors and embassies, and a depot for receiving taxes, tribute, imports, and other commodities requiring storage space. The ground plan of the slightly later palace at Alalakh was quite different, although its administrative sector, palace archive, domestic quarters, and temple also sprang up around a large central court.

Both palaces were outfitted with elaborate drains to carry waste water beyond the city walls, a system similar to that of the Minoan palaces on Crete, nearly 600 miles (965 kilometers) to the west across the Mediterranean. Since certain Syrian stylistic motifs and techniques of wall painting call to mind those of Crete, some scholars have hypothesized technical and artistic exchange between the two regions. Who influenced whom is still a matter of debate. The Mari frescoes exhibit a spiralform motif common in the Aegean, but they also contain Sumerian and Akkadian elements; the wall paintings at Alalakh are too fragmentary for interpretation.

In this era of increasing internationalism, it would not be surprising to find cultural interconnections between Syria and the Aegean. Trade between Crete and Ugarit, less than forty miles south of Alalakh, is well attested by written and archaeological evidence, and Ugarit was on the main trade route to Mari.

The scope of international trade in which Mari and Alalakh were involved was astonishingly broad. Once the Ashur-Kanesh link in the tin trade was severed, Mari seems to have become the focus of a network that imported tin—perhaps from western Afghanistan—and distributed it throughout Syria, Palestine, Cyprus, and perhaps even the Aegean. The palaces at Mari and Alalakh shuttled goods and ideas across an international trade route that expanded cultural contacts to the Indus Valley (Pakistan) in the east, to Arabia in the south, and westward through portions of the Mediterranean Sea.

Babylon under Ḫammurapi

By the end of the nineteenth century B.C., three powerful Amorite states had emerged in Babylonia: Eshnunna, Larsa, and Babylon itself. The fate of smaller states in Babylonia and the northwest hinged on their shifting alliances with these three kingdoms.

Little evidence exists to document the early years of Babylon's First Dynasty, later symbolized by the aggressive but just reign of its most renowned member, Ḫammurapi. Babylon's rise to preeminence was a slow, cumulative process and owed as much to shifting political and military conditions as to its own military strength. A letter written to Zimri-Lim of Mari reveals that the kings of Babylon, Larsa, Eshnunna, and Qatna (a major power of the west, in west-central Syria near the Orontes River) each had ten to fifteen kings in alliance with them; Yamḫad (the foremost polity of the west, centered on Aleppo) had twenty. At first, the king of Babylon was one among many, forced to make alliances to effect any conquest.

During the first two decades of his forty-two-year reign (1792–1750 B.C.), Ḫammurapi fortified several cities in northern Babylonia. In 1764 B.C., Babylon defeated the coalition of Elam, Subartu (the north, including Assyria), and Eshnunna. Defeat of Larsa the following year added it to Ḫammurapi's rapidly expanding state. By 1762 B.C., he claimed to have "established the foundations of Sumer and Akkad," a phrase borrowed from Sumerian royal hymns to express the ideal of pan-Babylonian rule. With the conquest of Mari in 1759 B.C., virtually all of Mesopotamia had come under Babylonian rule. The dynasty at Babylon adhered to the standard Amorite policy of consolidating power in new Amorite centers—in this case, Babylon—at the expense of prestigious old Sumerian cities.

In extent, Ḫammurapi's state was roughly the same as that of the Ur III rulers; in duration, it was limited to his own lifetime. By the second decade of Ḫammurapi's successor, southern Babylonia had already severed its ties with Babylon. Particularism and discord again unfurled their banners.

Ḫammurapi's rigidly centralized system had prospered initially from tribute and taxes, both used to compensate state dependents and to finance extensive state irrigation and building projects. Yet these projects placed a heavy fiscal load on subject territories and created a mood of disenchantment with the state. Upon Ḫammurapi's death, distant provinces broke away immediately, and continuing loss of revenues progressively weakened the crown. Demand for increased agricultural output from Babylonian estates upset an already fragile ecological balance. In an attempt to forestall disintegration, officialdom proliferated. But the new bureaucrats tended to support local rule and responsibility, not state interference. Ḫammurapi's successors became figureheads dependent on locally controlled goods and resources. The outcome is predictable: centralized institutions collapsed, autonomous local groups reasserted control, and the city-state pattern once again prevailed.

However short lived, the nation-state of Babylonia had lasting historical significance. Babylon became the foremost metropolis of the land, the established seat of Mesopotamian kingship. Babylonia was the ultimate political achievement of the Amorites. Mid-second millennium B.C. texts still called the area "the Land of Babylon," and later Hittite documents referred to the Akkadian language as Babylonian. The association of Babylon with all of Mesopotamia long outlived Babylon's actual dominion; its mystique and grandeur still provoke all manner of reactions.

Private ownership and interests: Babylonian society and economy. The most striking structural feature of Mesopotamian society in all periods is its economic division into the haves and have-nots, into those who held land and those dependent on the landholders. Although certain aspects of Old Babylonian society still remain difficult to interpret, important private, literary, and legal documents (including the period's most important written document, Hammurapi's law code) portray a society in which individual rights again became an issue and in which political and economic dominance by Babylon became absolute.

Administrative documents from the Old Babylonian period are rare, but the many court protocols, private contracts, and private and official letters all testify to a basic change in the nature of Babylonian society. A considerable portion of the populace was now legally free, attached to neither palace nor temple. Thus the private sector of the economy—based on ownership of agricultural land and use of hired labor or slaves—flourished in Amorite-dominated Babylonia. In marked contrast to the centralized economic systems of the Ur III and Early Dynastic periods, this typically Semitic configuration most closely resembles that of the Amorites' Semitic predecessors, the Akkadians.

Private individuals, families, and partnerships seem to have conducted much of the trade during the Old Babylonian period, but crown bureaucrats may have played some role in such nongovernmental 'chains of authority.' Prosperous merchants financed private traders, and both shared the profits or losses of individual ventures. Trade by land and by water (the Gulf) brought to Babylonia foreign goods (oils, textiles, metals) and luxury items (gold, silver, semiprecious stones). By the reign of Ḥammurapi, the major merchants became loosely associated as their activities came under closer scrutiny of the central government.

Palace and temple continued to hold large plots of land worked by dependents or by other segments of the population liable for civil or military duties. The ruler was responsible for the construction and repair of city walls, temples, and irrigation projects. Although the palace had the authority to use and dispose of temple property, temples continued to pursue economic enterprises independent of the palace. The union of temple and state had almost disappeared: the temple now stood as only one among many city-state institutions. The priesthood's involvement with private interests and private rights expressed the new spirit in the land.

The Code of Ḥammurapi, discussed in more detail below, distinguishes three basic social groups: the *awīlum*, an upper class of freeman; the *wardum*, or slave; and the *mushkēnum*, whose status is still disputed by scholars. While *awīlum* simply means "man" (legally, "free man"), the intrinsic meaning of *mushkēnum* implies some sort of subordinance. Legally the *mushkēnum* was a crown dependent; socially he was inferior to the *awīlum*. These royal dependents subsisted on agricultural rations-in-kind or on the produce of nonalienable land alloted to them in exchange for royal service.

The *wardum* class had a number of components. Indebted individuals often sold themselves or their children into slavery or were seized by their creditors. Foreign captives usually became state slaves, who labored on the crown's numerous building and agricultural projects. Since landowners employed tenant farmers (often *mushkēnum*), who received a portion of the harvest in return for their labor, privately owned slaves usually worked only in domestic service. Their status thus differed considerably from that of slaves in the classical world or even in colonial America.

Although this classification of Old Babylonian society appears straighforward, accurate translation of terms like *mushkēnum*, so remote from our own experience, is difficult;

uncertainties of interpretation often abound. The social structure of ancient Babylonia must always be viewed with such qualifications in mind.

Babylonian law and literature.   *Codex Ḥammurapi.*   The Code of Ḥammurapi is the longest surviving text from the Old Babylonian period. Almost completely preserved, the code is far more significant in legal history than any of its forerunners, such as that of Ur-Nammu (see pages 96–97). Fully 282 laws, carved in 49 columns on a basalt stela, address a variety of topics in civil, criminal, and commercial law but do not categorize them (see figure on p. 152). Many of the laws treat the disposition of and responsibility for private and real property.

Like other Near Eastern codes, Ḥammurapi's does not attempt to cover all possible legal situations. Whether it represents customary law, legal innovations, amendments, or a combination of all three cannot be determined. In its epilogue, however, Ḥammurapi describes the code as "laws of Justice" intended to clarify the rights of any "oppressed man." The code was thus at least partly intended as a source of information for those seeking justice.

The Codex Ḥammurapi embodies two major departures from previous codes: the principle of talion (punishment concomitant with the offense) and the exteme harshness of its punishments, which include drowning, burning, impaling, and other mutilations:

> If a man denounced a man, and brought a charge of murder against him, but has not proved it, his denouncer shall be put to death . . . . If a man broke into a house, they shall put him to death in front of that breach . . . . If a (free) man has put out the eye of the son of a (free) man, they shall put out his eye.

Sumerian penalties for similar crimes were limited to remuneration in silver or in kind.

Future kings are instructed on the stela to pay heed to these laws, but the lack of later references to the code makes it difficult to measure its influence. Whatever its legal function, the code was valued as a literary work. If Ḥammurapi intended to preserve a record of his just and equitable reign, he could not have been more successful: numerous copies of his code were found

(° Maurice Chuzeville/Courtesy of Pierre Amiet)

Upper part of basalt stele inscribed with Hammurapi's law code. (Area with figures is 65 cm. high.)

in the library of the seventh century B.C. Assyrian king Assurbanipal, and Hammurapi's laws still serve as the standard introductory text for all students of cuneiform writing.

The opening lines of Hammurapi's law code describe how Marduk and his city, Babylon, were made supreme on earth by Anu and Enlil, the two highest deities in the land:

> When august Anu . . . and Enlil, Lord of heaven and earth, who decrees the fate of the land, decreed for Marduk, the eldest son of Ea, Enlilship (executive power) over the totality of the people, made him great among the Igigi (gods), called Babylon by its august name, [and] in the four quarters (of the universe) made it supreme . . .

According to Mesopotamian ideology, each city-state was possessed and protected by its own deity. When a city-state expanded its domain by conquest, the powers of the city-god were thought to spread simultaneously. Until the Old Babylonian period, the supreme position on earth and in the sky had belonged to Nippur's tutelary deity Enlil. Anu remained aloof, more concerned with his heavenly domain.

Even though Babylon had become the paramount power on earth by the time of Hammurapi, Marduk could be elevated to rule over Babylonia only as the appointee of the two higher-ranking divinities. Not until the end of the Old Babylonian dynasty, about 1600 B.C., did Marduk become the sovereign of his divine peers. With his ascendancy, the succession to power by deities of different cities ended: subsequently tradition made Marduk the principal god of the land.

Enūma Elish.   Marduk's supremacy in heaven, like Babylon's on earth, went unchallenged from this time forward. The great Babylonian creation epic, the *Enūma Elish*, mythically commemorated Babylon's political ascendancy. Like Marduk's elevation by Anu and Enlil in the prologue to Hammurapi's laws, the *Enūma Elish* reflects the rising authority of Babylon, nucleus of the Mesopotamian world.

The Babylonian epic tale of creation, known by its first line, *enūma elish* (when on high), may have been composed as early as the Old Babylonian period; the form in which it is preserved, however, dates from no earlier than the succeeding Kassite era. The epic describes the creation of the world as the outcome of a cosmic battle between the forces of order and chaos.

Long before anything had been created, generations of primeval deities were born to Apsu (the personification of sweet water) and Tiamat (salt water). When certain lesser deities proved noisy and troublesome, Apsu was persuaded by his vizier Mummu to slay them. When Ea the "all wise" learned of the plan, he cast magic spells paralyzing Mummu and resulting in Apsu's death. Ea then retired to his shrine, newly founded on the motionless sweet underground waters (Apsu). Ea and his wife produced a son, Marduk, who was eventually elected to battle Tiamat and her army of dragons and serpents. Marduk, however, had a price: he demanded to be proclaimed supreme deity of the land.

With the gods' approval, Marduk proceeded to battle and vanquish Tiamat, who represented the older powers of darkness and inertia. From Tiamat's corpse, Marduk triumphantly created the universe. After putting it in order and fixing the courses of the sun and stars, he created mankind to perform the toil of the gods. In return, the gods built for Marduk the city of Babylon and his magnificent temple.

Throughout the Old Babylonian era and later in Babylonian history, the priests of Babylon recited the *Enūma Elish* on the fourth day of the New Year's festival. The myth offered the Babylonians not only an explanation of the creation of the world but also a rationalization for Babylon's supremacy in that world. Perhaps the Babylonians felt, too, that the cosmic struggle between chaos and order had never ended and that the annual recital of the *Enūma Elish* would forestall further challenges to the desired order. Predictably, however, the challenges never ceased.

The Kassite Era (1500–1200 B.C.): Unification and Cultural Preservation

The Kassites, like the Hittites and Hurrians, were intrusive actors on the ancient Near Eastern stage. Their origins are still unknown. The Kassite language, as much as it can be interpreted at all, seems unrelated to any language spoken or written in ancient western Asia. And Kassite history from 1600 to 1400 B.C. is accordingly very sketchy. Kassites had first appeared in Babylonia as agricultural laborers, infiltrating steadily but peacefully. By the end of the seventeenth century B.C., 150 years after Hammurapi's death and the dissolution of his expanded state, the social position of the Kassites had risen. They had bought their way into priestly offices, and at least one Kassite had achieved sufficient social standing to entertain a foreign envoy at his house inside Babylon's city limits. Meanwhile, according to documents from the reigns of Hammurapi's immediate successors, other Kassites posed a military threat to Babylonia in the eighteenth and seventeenth centuries B.C.

A Hittite raid on Babylon in 1595 B.C. sounded the death knell of the already crippled Old Babylonian regime and helped to legitimize the Kassite occupation of the city. By 1460 B.C., the Kassites had unified the country; gradually they made Mesopotamian institutions and culture their own. For the next 250 years, Babylonia was ruled by successive Kassite monarchs and functioned as a single political entity—a unique accomplishment for any Babylonian dynasty, native or foreign.

The fourteenth century B.C. was a veritable golden age under the Kassite kings. Foreign expansion, exploration, and involvement declined dramatically, and domestic governance reached a high point. Between 1500 and 1200 B.C., political initiative had shifted decidedly to the north and west, where Hittites, Egyptians, and Assyrians competed for control of the economically vital eastern Mediterranean seaboard. Even though the Kassites remained inactive militarily, their influence extended as far south as Dilmun (modern Bahrain) in the Gulf; Kassite cylinder seals have been found far to the northwest at Thebes in Mycenaean Greece. Letters to and from the Kassite kings Kadashman-Enlil I (about 1374–1360 B.C.) and Burnaburiash II (about 1359–1333 B.C.), written in Akkadian and found at Amarna in Egypt, indicate that the Kassite and Egyptian royal families exchanged ambassadors and even intermarried. State trade consisted of such highly prized commodities as horses, chariots, and lapis lazuli from Babylonia and ivory, woods, and precious metals (especially gold) from Egypt.

Some of Egypt's wealth must have gone into the construction of a new Kassite city, Dūr-Kurigalzu (fortress of Kurigalzu), whose founder and namesake ruled early in the fourteenth century B.C. Despite both the attention lavished on this new city and its ideological importance to the Kassites, Babylon remained the focal point of commerce, politics, and religious worship. The Kassite policy of architectural preservation and reconstruction in the old power centers of Ur, Uruk, and Eridu may have helped to neutralize separatist movements in the southern city-states.

Kassite stewardship of Mesopotamian culture

Like many other peoples who came into contact with Mesopotamian culture, the Kassites thoroughly absorbed the traditions they encountered. Along with social and religious customs, they even adopted the Akkadian language. The Kassites seldom attempted to render their own tongue in cuneiform; indeed, had they not clung tenaciously to their native personal names, it would be difficult today to discern their non-Babylonian origin. Perhaps as a result of this willingness to adapt, Kassite rule was never regarded as foreign domination. It seems unlikely that the Kassites could otherwise have endured in Babylonia for over 400 years.

With evident enthusiasm and dedication, scribes of the Kassite era translated Sumerian literature into Akkadian, revised and compiled earlier texts into standard series (for example, the *Enūma Elish*), and composed scholarly **glosses** not unlike the Talmudic commentaries on Jewish scripture and law. Kassite-period scribes also began compiling divinatory (predictive) works into encyclopaedic series corresponding to the major categories of prognostication: astrology, omen literature, and **extispicy**— interpretation of the *exta* (entrails) of sacrificial animals. Divinely inspired forecasts were a crucial aspect of daily life for all Babylonians, from king to commoner.

Kassite scrupulousness in maintaining Sumerian and Akkadian traditions in literature and language may well reflect a conscious attempt by this foreign dynasty to become Babylonian in every respect. The Kassites—or the Babylonians of the Kassite era—are often inaccurately characterized as mere editors and compilers of canonical works rather than composers of new works. Whereas the Old Babylonian scribe had been a businessman or engineer as well as a man of letters, the scribe of the Kassite era was more vainglorious about his unique profession. The names of many famous scribes and scribal families have been preserved, and authorship can even be credited to some original compositions.

Kudurru *and land tenure: Kassite society and economy*

Although Kassite stewardship of prior literary and cultural conditions conveys a static impression, the Kassite era witnessed significant deviation from and alteration of earlier legal and social practices. It is uncertain whether these innovations represent Kassite tradition—and were thus foreign to Babylonia—or merely represent elaborations of Amorite customs regarding land ownership.

The hallmark of Kassite material culture is an oval or pillar-shaped monument called *kudurru* in Akkadian. These small stelae, typically about two feet high, were not boundary markers, as they are often described, but records of royal land grants. The *kudurru* itself was deposited in the temple, and the landowner retained a clay-tablet copy. The decree spelled out details of the plot of land and any accompanying remission of taxes and duties. The text of the *kudurru* also included a list of witnesses and pronounced elaborate curses on anyone who tampered with the stela or deprived the owner of his land. A typical *kudurru* was sculpted on the top or on one side with symbols of the gods. Both these symbols and the maledictions were intended to safeguard individual rights and ownership of property.

Private ownership of land was already an entrenched feature of Old Babylonian society, but Kassite legal traditions governing the transfer of land differed notably from Amorite practices. For one thing, plots of land were occasionally defined as belonging to households or to territorial districts and were regarded as tribal property. Such land was owned collectively by tribal communities and could presumably only be alienated by communal consensus.

The other innovative legal practice of the Kassite era was the official public proclamation of land sales between private persons. If no objection was raised by a third party, the trans-

Limestone kudurru *of the Kassite period, found at Susa in Elam.*

action became official and was registered in the archives. Accurate site surveys based on careful measurements also began to be included in land tenure documents. One *kudurru* records that the king himself measured a field before conferring it on the recipient. Such departures from Old Babylonian legal practices imply an accompanying growth of bureaucracy.

The end of Kassite rule

By the late thirteenth century B.C., Kassite power began to decline. Assyria to the north had established itself as a major power (known to modern scholars as the Middle Assyrian state) during the fourteenth and thirteenth centuries B.C. The Assyrian king Tukulti-Ninurta I (1244–1208 B.C.) sacked Babylon and briefly brought it under his sway. The fortunes of the two countries were to remain linked until about 1200 B.C.

The sequence of events in Babylonia after 1200 B.C. is difficult to place in meaningful order, precisely because of the lack of pertinent written evidence: documentary sources tend to dry up in times of political or military crisis. The Kassite kingdom began to disintegrate under attack by both Assyria and Elam. The Elamites even carried off two of Babylonia's most famous monuments, the stela of Naramsin and the stela bearing Hammurapi's law code (see pages 89 and 152). In 1157 B.C., approximately 300 years of Kassite rule in Babylonia came to an end. Political instability under six insignificant dynasties was to prevail in Babylonia until the rise of the Neo-Assyrian kingdom in the ninth century B.C.

EGYPT: REUNIFICATION, SUBJUGATION, AND IMPERIALISM

The glories of Egypt's Old Kingdom had vanished forever in the tempestuous decades of the First Intermediate Period (about 2180–2050 B.C.). The precarious reunification of the land by the Middle Kingdom pharaohs at first relied on support from the still vigorous and capable *nomarchs*. The powerful pharaoh Senusert III (1878–1843 B.C.) finally contained the nomarchic element and firmly reestablished centralized control over all Egypt. In the end, however, a complex array of political, dynastic, and military factors led to the disintegration of the Middle Kingdom.

By 1700 B.C., a foreign group known as the Hyksos (the full Egyptian term means literally "princes of foreign lands") had established a separate polity in the eastern Delta. Within fifty years, the Hyksos—made up mainly of West Semitic peoples— came to dominate the entire state, the first time a foreign dynasty had ever ruled over Egypt.

Hyksos rule bred and fostered a permanent change in Egyptian foreign policy. Once the warrior pharaohs of the New Kingdom (Eighteenth–Twentieth Dynasties; 1570–1150 B.C.) finally expelled the Hyksos, they embarked on an aggressive and successful imperialistic adventure. Most of Syria and Palestine fell under Egyptian control, and Egypt was thus exposed to external influences and commercial opportunities previously untried. Egypt had finally assumed a cosmopolitan role and become an active participant in the international politics of the second millennium B.C.

The Middle Kingdom (2050–1800 B.C.): Integration under the Thebans

The Middle Kingdom ushered in peace, prosperity, and even a taste of imperial expansion. Irrigation and land reclamation projects fattened the land, while administrative reforms gave rise to new wealth and a new middle class to enjoy it. Pharaoh had indeed become the "Good Shepherd" of his flock. The Middle Kingdom was also the golden age of Egyptian literature; its written language is regarded as the classical form of hieroglyphics, and its literary works became classics as well.

> The land is diminished, (but) its administrators are many;
> bare, (but) its taxes are great . . .
> I show thee the land topsy-turvy . . .
> (then) it is that a king will come,
> belonging to the south,
> Ameni, the triumphant, his name.

He is the son of a woman of the land of Nubia;
he is one born in Upper Egypt.
He will take the [White] Crown (Upper Egypt);
he will wear the Red Crown (Lower Egypt);
he will unite the Two Mighty Ones.[1]

These lines from "The Prophecy of Nefertiti" (which actually postdated the events it "foretells"), recount in verse the afflictions of the First Intermediate Period and the rise of the Middle Kingdom pharaohs—the Eleventh and Twelfth Dynasties—who reunited Egypt once again.

The founder of the Middle Kingdom, Mentuhotpe II of the Eleventh Dynasty (about 2060–2010 B.C.), restored stability in Egypt, but trouble erupted again after his death. Separatism and disorder had so dominated Egypt during the First Intermediate Period that reunification could not be instantaneous. In an effort to banish the chaos of the preceding era, the early Twelfth Dynasty pharaohs aimed their every undertaking—cultural and religious as well as political—at the restoration and strengthening of Egypt.

The efforts of Amenemhet I (1991–1962 B.C.)—"Ameni the triumphant" of the prophecy—went a long way toward restoring unity and the justice, if not the omnipotence, of pharaoh. Amenemhet's nonroyal origins (mentioned elsewhere in the prophecy) were unacceptable to many Egyptians and brought Egypt again to the brink of civil war. His eventual success must have depended in part on the support of the nomarchs, whose power and privileges he restored or maintained.

Born in Upper Egypt, Amenemhet I was a staunch devotee of a local Theban deity, Amon, whom he elevated to primary rank among the Egyptian gods. Grafted onto the sun-god Re, this minor deity became Amon-Re "king of the gods," whose role as national and (later, in the Eighteenth Dynasty) imperial divinity helped to solidify Middle Kingdom Egypt.

Amenemhet built a new administrative capital, Itj-towy, south of Memphis, an advantageous location for centralized rule over the two lands. Land reclamation projects in the Fayyum basin near Itj-towy promoted internal cohesion and prosperity and

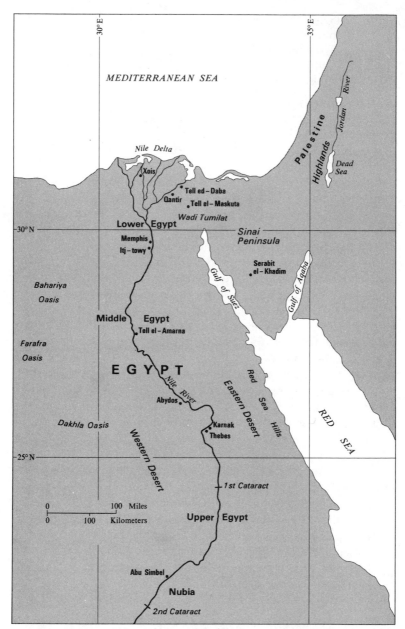

Map 4–2 Egypt in the Second Millennium B.C.: Sites and
Geographic Features

helped to balance Egypt's delicate **ecology**. Fortresses constructed in Nubia to the south and in the Wadi Tummilat in the northeastern delta served a similar purpose: the unification (and isolation) of Egypt. Even the famed Tale of Sinuhe promoted reunification, a healthy economy, and a majestic ruler (see pages 165–66).

After twenty years as pharaoh, Amenemhet made his son Senusert I coregent. This new practice became standard, providing for Amenemhet's Twelfth Dynasty successors smooth transitions of power and, because of the overlapping period of rule, long reigns. Their hold on power, however, remained precarious, dependent as it was on the support of the still-vigorous and capable nomarchs. Throughout the first 100 years of the Twelfth Dynasty (1991–1878 B.C.), the pharaohs conducted far-reaching military campaigns into Nubia for gold, other metals, and building stone. Egypt maintained good foreign relations with Syria and Palestine and traded with Anatolia and the Aegean.

Senusert III (1878–1843 B.C.), the most notable ruler of the Middle Kingdom, led further campaigns into Nubia to defend borders threatened by Sudanese tribesmen. His lasting reputation, however, is based on his sweeping administrative reforms. The nomarchs, whose power had grown excessive, were completely stripped of their ancient prerogatives; never again were their local tombs, courts, taxes, and troop-raising projects to be part of Egyptian life. Henceforth Upper, Middle, and Lower Egypt each had its own newly created department, administered from the capital under the direction of a **vizier**, whose own powers would increase inexorably with time.

How these new bureaucrats were chosen—on merit, social status, or otherwise—is unknown. But the suppression of the nobility, in conjunction with the need for personnel to run the new administrative machinery of state, gave rise to what may be called the Egyptian middle classes: officials, merchants, and artisans. Their role in the reconstituted Egyptian state may be gauged by the quantities of offerings they dedicated near the sanctuary of Osiris at Abydos and by the numerous private statuettes found throughout the land. Senusert III's administra-

tive reforms essentially replaced one troublesome force, the nomarchs, with two: the revived office of vizier and the "middle
classes."

The Hekanakht letters: Life on a Middle Kingdom farm

A series of private letters and other papers written on papyrus
and preserved in a Theban tomb render a vivid human portrait
of family life and agronomy on a small Middle Kingdom farm.
Hekanakht, a feisty, elderly landowner who lived just north of
Thebes, was called away on business, leaving his son in charge
of the farm and of the vizier Ipi's tomb, where Hekanakht was
funerary priest. To help his son manage in his absence, Hekanakht provided inventories of grain and produce for the current
year and an earlier year. During his trip, the old man wrote his
family two fussy, detailed letters specifying work to be done and
outlining the distribution of food to family members. Another
letter to a local official discussed the collection of grain by members of Hekanakht's family.

Hekanakht cautioned his son against overflooding the land
and directed him to rent some nearby land for payment in linen
cloth or emmer wheat. He complained about the stale barley he
was eating while his family enjoyed a fresh crop. Although a
cruel taskmaster toward his eldest son, Hekanakht had a soft
spot for his youngest son and for his concubine. The youngster
was to be granted his every wish, and a maidservant who had
troubled his mistress was to be sent away immediately. The first
letter ends with admonitions to report on the grain collection
and to avoid carelessness in farm matters.

This small collection of letters offers a glimpse of private
economic affairs in the Middle Kingdom. Although some of the
farm land discussed in Hekanakht's letters may have belonged
to the dead vizier, these letters nonetheless suggest that the
political decentralization of the First Intermediate Period may
have fostered a wider distribution of agricultural wealth, at least
by the Eleventh Dynasty. The democratization of central government administration under Senusert III had a similar effect
in the Twelfth Dynasty.

The Tale of Sinuhe: Classical Egyptian literature

For centuries, the richly woven tales, didactic treatises, and prophetic works of the Middle Kingdom were laboriously copied by student scribes onto papyruses, boards, and bits of pottery and thus preserved. The language used in these documents, Middle Egyptian, remained the standard written dialect of Egypt until well into New Kingdom times. In a later form used for monumental and literary purposes, it even survived until Graeco-Roman times at the end of the first millennium B.C.

Many Middle Kingdom works were based, at least loosely, on actual events and conditions. They thus contain useful historical material, although some are too stylized to be reliable sources and others—whatever their literary value—are obvious propaganda. One piece of propagandizing is the well-known Tale of Sinuhe. This clever, informative, pseudo-autobiography of an Egyptian in exile celebrates a unified Egypt, a healthy economy, and the majesty of Senusert I, Amenemhet's son.

Sinuhe, an official of the royal court, is campaigning with Senusert in Libya when word of Amenemhet I's assassination reaches their party. Senusert—without a word to the main body of the army—immediately sets out for the capital with his bodyguard, ostensibly to deal with the conspirators, although his own complicity in his father's murder is not beyond question. Sinuhe, overhearing a conversation involving the assassination and consequently fearing for his life, deserts the army on the spot and bolts to the highlands of Syria-Palestine for refuge. Sinuhe chooses his sanctuary well; it is a land of figs, grapes, olive trees, wheat, and cattle, and its Amorite ruler treats the exile like a prince:

> He set me at the head of his children.
> He married me to his eldest daughter.
> He let me choose for myself (of the choicest)
> of his country . . .
> He made me ruler of a tribe . . .
> Bread was made for me as daily fare,
> Wine as daily provision,
> Cooked meat and roast fowl . . . were laid before me.

> I spent many years, and my children grew up to be strong men.[2]

Safe from retribution, Sinuhe entertains Egyptian couriers and learns of events at home—where, despite his princely existence, he sorely longs to be. The nostalgia of all Egyptians for their homeland, the center of their universe, is a pervasive theme of the story.

Finally Sinuhe is summoned back to Egypt by Senusert, who has become secure enough on his throne to offer amnesty to a former deserter. Senusert cajoles Sinuhe with the promise of a proper Egyptian burial—as if any enticement were needed:

> Do thou return to Egypt . . .
> Thou hast begun to grow old,
> thou hast lost (thy) virginity . . .
> Recall thou the day of burial . . .
> when the evening is set aside for thee
> with ointments and wrappings
> from the hands of Tait (goddess of weavings/mummy wrappings).
> A funeral procession is made for thee
> A mummy case of gold,
> with head of lapis lazuli . . .
> Singers in front of thee,
> when the dance of *muu* is performed
> at the door of thy tomb.
> It should not be that thou shouldst die
> in a foreign country.[3]

Turning over his Asiatic holdings to his children, Sinuhe promptly returns to Egypt. Royal craftsmen construct his tomb, and he enjoys royal patronage until his death. Sinuhe's triumphant return to Egypt surely accounts for the ancient popularity of the story.

The autobiographical nature of Sinuhe's tale is remarkable, as is the historical light it sheds on the death of Amenemhet I and on the evident good relations between Egypt and Syria-Palestine. The story's propagandistic elements, however, seem most striking: Senusert I is lavishly praised throughout. Like other fictional literature of the early Middle Kingdom, the Tale of Sinuhe promoted reunification by playing on the Egyptian's nationalistic sentiments.

The decline of the Middle Kingdom

The last two rulers of the Twelfth Dynasty, Amenemhet IV and Queen Sobekneferu, probably had their hands full simply trying to maintain their predecessors' gains. As in the final years of the Old Kingdom, it was the lack of a male heir that brought Sobekneferu (1798–1786 B.C.), daughter of Amenemhet III and sister of Amenemhet IV, to the throne. And just as the reign of Nitocris had spelled disaster in the Sixth Dynasty, this abnormal situation rang down the curtain on the Middle Kingdom.

The disintegration of the well-administered, centralized Middle Kingdom at the end of the Twelfth Dynasty had multiple causes. The weakness of the dynasty's last two rulers may have aroused in local magnates latent tendencies toward autonomy. Senusert III's reorganization of Egyptian bureaucracy placed too much power in the hands of the vizier, the principal officer of the state. Meanwhile, foreign elements (mainly West Semitic) continued to be lured into the **Delta** by commercial, political, or social opportunity. Other potentially hostile factions, foreign and native, are mentioned on the Execration Texts. These were pottery bowls and rough-hewn clay figurines inscribed with curses on pharaoh's enemies and ceremonially smashed—as the cursed individuals would be, by the process of sympathetic magic. These Execration Texts contain the names of Libyans, Nubians, West Semites, and even eight Egyptians. The latter may have been members of a conspiracy hatched within the harem to place a favorite son on the throne of Egypt.

The Second Intermediate Period (1800–1570 B.C.): Foreign Domination

The Egyptian state disintegrated very gradually. While the Thirteenth Dynasty (about 1780–1630 B.C.) continued to rule from Memphis or Itj-towy, competing dynasties flourished elsewhere. The sixty pharaohs of the Thirteenth Dynasty were dominated by a strong line of viziers, who managed for about a century to run the state efficiently and to maintain some degree of Egyptian influence abroad. Another native dynasty, the Fourteenth (about 1780–1600 B.C.) apparently broke with the dominant Thebans at the end of the Twelfth Dynasty and established itself in the western Delta at Xois. Almost no evidence exists for this Xoite dynasty, and its dominion must have been strictly local.

The Hyksos in Egypt

Meanwhile, by a very complex and still poorly understood process, another group of people in the eastern Delta gradually amassed independent political power. The Egyptian term for the leaders of these people, *Heqau Khasut* "Princes of Foreign Uplands," is almost certainly the origin of the term Manetho uses for them: Hyksos. Who were these "Princes of Foreign Uplands," and what is known about their origins?

To set the scene within which events in Egypt must be viewed, it is necessary to consider briefly the archaeological record of contemporary Syria-Palestine. The urban character and massive, complex fortifications typical of many Middle Bronze Age Levantine sites reflect the resurgence of city life and culture after the sweeping collapse at the end of the Early Bronze Age, about 2000 B.C. (see pages 130–32). The imposing archaeological remains dating from about 1900–1650 B.C. represent the crystallization of Canaanite (that is, Amorite) culture. In the terminology of archaeologists working in Syria-Palestine, these are the MBIIA and MBIIB periods (MB the abbreviation for Middle Bronze).

Since a number of these fortified urban complexes had been constructed already in the MBIIA period (about 1900–1800 B.C.), Syro-Palestinian archaeologists and Egyptologists alike now question the traditional concept—inspired by documentary material from ancient Egypt itself—of Egyptian domination over Syria-Palestine during Egypt's Twelfth Dynasty (1991–1786 B.C.). A reversal of this traditional view seems to fit all the new evidence much better: parts of northeastern Egypt may well have succumbed to an increasingly sophisticated and politically powerful group of Canaanites from Palestine.

In Egypt itself, contemporary records reveal many personal names of West Semitic origin. This suggests that prior to the full consolidation of an influential Canaanite urban culture in Syria-Palestine, some "Asiatic" peoples may already have resided in Egypt. The picture is augmented by and receives some support from archaeological excavations at the site of Tell ed-Daba—almost certainly to be identified with the Hyksos center of Avaris—in the eastern Delta. There Austrian archaeologists have uncovered evidence of habitation preceding the Second Intermediate Period by a population whose material culture was virtually identical to that of the Canaanites (Amorites) in MBII Syria-Palestine.

To summarize briefly this complex scenario: Although some Syro-Palestinian people had evidently been established in the eastern Nile delta since the late Twelfth Dynasty (about 1800 B.C.), it is not clear that they were the same group that evolved into the formidable political and military force known as the Hyksos. It may be suggested that the immediate predecessors of the Hyksos Dynasty (Fifteen) in Egypt were local rulers in southern Palestine, who took advantage of the political disintegration during the Egyptian Thirteenth Dynasty to extend their influence southwest into a region with which they had long been in contact, a region in which a substantial Semitic-speaking element had long been established. The Hyksos, in other words, may be regarded as a combination of various Semitic-speaking Canaanite groups migrating directly from southern Palestine into the eastern Egyptian delta and of other Semitic elements already settled there. The latter groups may have organized a mobile force striking out against other Egyptian centers in Lower Egypt. These demographic complexities should sound a familiar note: indeed the Hyksos phenomenon must be considered as the final stage of the Amorite movements that had begun in Syria and Mesopotamia almost 300 years earlier (pages 130–32).

For the first time—and with lasting consequences—Egypt had been conquered by foreigners. Overall it appears that as centralized control in Egypt faltered, Hyksos power grew. By about 1720 B.C., the Hyksos had established a distinct political entity in the eastern Delta, effectively overcoming Thirteenth

Dynasty dominion there. By 1650 B.C., they had taken Memphis, displaced the Thirteenth Dynasty in the north, and established their own dynasty (the Fifteenth). The Hyksos reunited Lower Egypt and relegated much of Upper Egypt to vassal status. Four of the six known Hyksos rulers bore Semitic names: they are known as the "Great Hyksos" Dynasty to distinguish them from a contemporaneous "Lesser Hyksos" (sixteenth) dynasty. The Sixteenth Dynasty probably comprised vassal rulers of small city-states in northern Egypt and the Delta.

Reputedly the Hyksos introduced Egypt to the horse and war chariot, new types of daggers and swords, and the composite bow. If such warlike innovations are correctly attributed to the Hyksos, however, it may be suggested that they were adopted only toward the end of their sojourn in Egypt, when the Hyksos were increasingly threatened by a rebellious native population. Otherwise, the Hyksos respected Egyptian culture and adopted many of its features. Hyksos kings used the hieroglyphic script and worshipped Egyptian gods, especially Seth, whom they equated with the West Semitic deity Resheph. They built and repaired temples, and scribes of the Hyksos era scrupulously copied Egyptian literary and scientific works. Intellectual pursuits were encouraged, not suppressed. It appears that the majority of Egyptians accepted or at least resigned themselves to the Hyksos occupation: native Egyptians served faithfully in Hyksos administrations and intermarried with the Hyksos even at the royal level.

Expulsion of the Hyksos

Shortly after the Hyksos overthrew the Thirteenth Dynasty in the north, the Thebans had founded a new dynasty, the Seventeenth. Thus an intricate pattern prevailed in the Second Intermediate Period: Theban dynasties continued to exist, but they were challenged initially by a rival Xoite dynasty and overshadowed thereafter by Hyksos dynasties.

Unwilling vassals, the Thebans had probably retained some local power all along. Stifled between Hyksos dominating the north and Nubians (ancient residents of modern-day Sudan) controlling the south, the tributary Theban princes of the Seventeenth Dynasty became dissatisfied with divided kingship and slowly mustered their forces to expel the Hyksos. Ultimately the Theban prince Kamose drove the Hyksos ruler Apopi from middle and northern Egypt and may have taken the Hyksos capital of Avaris in the Delta. Ahmose, a younger brother of Kamose, inflicted the final blow by destroying Avaris, driving the Hyksos from Egypt, and pursuing them into southern Palestine. After at least a decade of fighting, Egypt's independence was finally secured, and Ahmose I (1570–1546 B.C.) inaugurated the New Kingdom. Paradoxically the Theban reconquest inflicted more damage on Egypt than had the entire Hyksos occupation.

Suzerainty by a western Asiatic people bred and fostered a permanent change in Egyptian foreign policy. No longer would Egypt see itself as remote from and superior to its neighbors. The warrior pharaohs of the New Kingdom embarked on an aggressive and successful imperialistic adventure that was to last more than 300 years. The Hyksos interlude may thus be seen as a stimulus to conquest of—or at least to prevent conquest by—Egypt's neighbors in ancient western Asia. Egyptian isolation became a thing of the past: Egypt quickly assumed an integral role in the commerce and cosmopolitanism that typified this era in ancient western Asia and the eastern Mediterranean.

The New Kingdom (1570–1150 B.C.): Cosmopolitanism and Imperialism

Administration and commerce

The New Kingdom took up where the Middle Kingdom left off, with the striking difference that introspection and preoccupation with internal affairs gave way to a cosmopolitan outlook. Imperial expansion, rather than mere pursuit of a favorable balance of trade, guided New Kingdom foreign policy. Military power and a professional army underpinned pharaonic rule abroad, and an expanded but carefully controlled bureaucracy mapped out administrative strategy at home.

Pharaoh continued to embody the Egyptian state in the New Kingdom. The vizier, meanwhile, remained the chief administrator. But the increasing complexity of New Kingdom bureaucracy ultimately necessitated two viziers, one each for Upper and Lower Egypt. The growth of officialdom went hand in hand with the spread of imperialism. The dual vizierate and the swollen bureaucracy prevented anyone but pharaoh from amassing much authority. Absolute power, legislative and judicial as well as executive, remained in his hands. Pharaoh made all religious, military, and political appointments. Provincial administration was in the hands of town and village mayors responsible to the viziers. Local Semitic princes were left to govern newly conquered lands in Syria and Palestine, but their sons or brothers were often brought to Egypt, educated at the royal court, and eventually sent home to serve Egypt as loyal vassals. Small Egyptian garrisons throughout the Levant discouraged insurrection and ensured the delivery of tribute.

Egyptian ships traded not only with the Syro-Palestinian port cities—Akko, Byblos, and Ugarit—but also with Cyprus and the Aegean world. Nubia and the Sudan provided Egypt with its basic raw materials and luxury goods. From Nubia came gold, semiprecious stones, and building stone. The Sudan and points south supplied African woods, ostrich plumes, animal skins, perfumes, oil, and ivory. Private commerce in the New Kingdom was limited to trading in the village marketplaces and the modest transactions of private merchants. Large-scale commerce was a function of the state or the temple, and international trade was monopolized by the state.

Since efficient administration required an educated class, the scribal profession was glorified in numerous texts, traditional and newly composed. The military and priestly classes also enjoyed the fruits of New Kingdom imperialism. Victorious soldiers were granted booty, captured slaves, and land; such land could be held as long as each new generation in the family designated one son for the military. Meanwhile the expansion of empire and, consequently, of royal donations enriched temple estates and their staffs.

The resulting tendency toward entrenched priestly, scribal, and military families could have led to a more caste-like society. But pharaoh's power to appoint and remove government officials militated against the formation of an aristocracy. The military had the distinct advantage that its officers could be granted royal appointments to civil or priestly positions. Generally speaking, officialdom was much more fluid in the New Kingdom than in earlier times. The relative social mobility of the New Kingdom allowed talented individuals of whatever origin to attain prominent positions. Women, both single and married, seem to have been legally and practically equal to men. Most people, of course, were still uneducated agricultural laborers who tilled the fields and received a share of the harvest. Though slaves were put to work for the temples and for state mining and quarrying operations, slavery was not essential to the economy. There is little evidence of power struggles between social classes. Such conflicts as there were may have been instigated by pharaoh as a means of bolstering his own supreme positon.

The Eighteenth Dynasty: Conquest and empire

The first four pharaohs of the Eighteenth Dynasty (1570–1490 B.C.) devoted their attention to Nubia and the Sudan, where they created a virtual African empire and enjoyed access to gold and other precious raw materials. Thutmose I (1528–1510 B.C.) also raided Syria, thus foreshadowing his successors' incursions into western Asia.

When Thutmose III (eventually to become Egypt's mightiest pharaoh) inherited the throne in 1490 B.C., he was only ten years old. Consequently his stepmother Queen Hatshepsut, after some years as regent, boldly assumed kingship. The contrast between the benign benefactress Hatshepsut and the warlike conqueror Thuhmose is striking. Hatshepsut concentrated on internal, domestic developments and commercial enterprises. She restored Egyptian temples that had lain abandoned or in ruins since the Second Intermediate Period, and she was responsible for numerous public works in and around Thebes. Hatshepsut's reign proved to be a noteworthy exception to the rule that female presence on the throne presaged disaster and collapse.

Among the more renowned of Hatshepsut's many peaceful undertakings was the commercial expedition she dispatched via the Red Sea to the Land of Punt. The goal of this maritime expedition was to obtain such exotic products as dogs, monkeys, incense trees, rare woods, gold, ivory, and myrrh. A pictorial and written record of this celebrated voyage decorates the walls of Hatshepsut's magnificent mortuary temple at Deir el-Bahari, opposite Thebes. Five large sailing vessels are shown bearing Egyptian products en route to Punt. The Land of Punt has been equated with the Somali coast or with coastal Arabia opposite it. More southerly lands have also been nominated, but there is at present no way to identify it positively. While this was neither the first nor the last Egyptian voyage to Punt, the prominence accorded it by Hatshepsut is in line with Egypt's pacific and tolerant foreign policy. At the same time, it exemplifies Egypt's increasing involvement in the routine cosmopolitanism and international intercourse of the second millennium B.C.

Hatshepsut's reign reflected the peaceful ideals and concerns of a state that had long regarded itself as superior and beyond challenge. The rule of Thutmose III (1490–1436 B.C.) witnessed new trends and priorities: superiority now gained expression through foreign conquest, domination, and exploitation. In his first twenty years of rule, Thutmose III waged seventeen campaigns against Syria-Palestine. His greatest victory was his first—the famed battle of Megiddo, at which Egypt defeated a coalition of Syro-Palestinian princes representing the interests of the Hurrian state of Mitanni (see pages 184–86). This conquest paved the way for an Egyptian empire in Asia.

Thutmose's aggressive imperialistic ventures brought most of Syria-Palestine under Egyptian control for the first time and simultaneously exposed Egypt to unprecedented commercial opportunities and external influence. Under Thutmose and his successors, a more world-oriented Egypt became a vigorous participant in the international politics of the second millennium B.C.

Thutmose III's successors had difficulty maintaining his empire. Thutmose IV (1413–1405 B.C.) finally established peaceful relations with the Hurrians of northern Syria and Mesopotamia by means of a diplomatic marriage—an effective instrument of statecraft employed by all the powers of ancient western Asia during the latter half of the second millennium B.C. Thutmose IV's son and successor Amenhotep III (1405–1367 B.C.) carried this practice to an extreme by marrying two Hurrian princesses of Mitanni, two Kassite princesses, and one from Anatolia.

(⁶⁾ E. Naville)

Depiction of the voyage to the land of Punt, commissioned by Queen Hatshepsut, Eighteenth Dynasty, New Kingdom.

Amenhotep III was succeeded by his son Amenhotep IV, known as Akhenaton (1367–1350 B.C.), whose worship of the sun disc Aton, among other things, marked him as Egypt's most unorthodox and controversial pharaoh.

The Amarna Revolution: Mutations in art and religion

The great national deity Amon-Re had reigned supreme in the Egyptian pantheon since the early years of the Twelfth Dynasty. Re, the sun-god par excellence, and Amon, god of the air, retained separate identities; but their merger served a very important function: Amon-Re was the supreme deity who came to represent imperial Eighteenth Dynasty Egypt in its most majestic form. During the New Kingdom, the wealth and political influence of Amon's priesthood had grown at an alarming rate; it served as a force for conservatism, maintenance of Egyptian traditions, and the expansion of the Egyptian state. When Amenhotep IV singled out the Aton—the physical solar disc—for worship and dedicated his reign to its elevation, the stage was set

Pharaoh Akhenaton and his wife Nefertiti, depicted playing with their daughters, Eighteenth Dynasty, New Kingdom.

for conflict. When the new pharaoh built a large temple to Aton near the Great Temple of Amon at Thebes, the die was cast. Amenhotep suspended worship of Amon and other gods during the new temple's construction, and gradually Amon's name was eradicated from many older monuments throughout Egypt.

In political terms, the so-called Amarna Revolution may be seen as a power struggle between the pharaoh and the priest-hood of Amon-Re—that is, between innovation in religion, mor-als, art, and literature on the one hand and aggressive maintenance of tradition on the other. The worship of Aton as a distinct deity had been initiated at least a half-century earlier: the new divinity had a temple at Thebes before the Amarna Revolution and apparently coexisted peacefully with Amon. The new, exclusive focus on Aton, however, directly threatened the vested authority of the priesthood of Amon.

The conflict was economic and political as well as religious. At stake was the traditional concept of pharaoh's independent

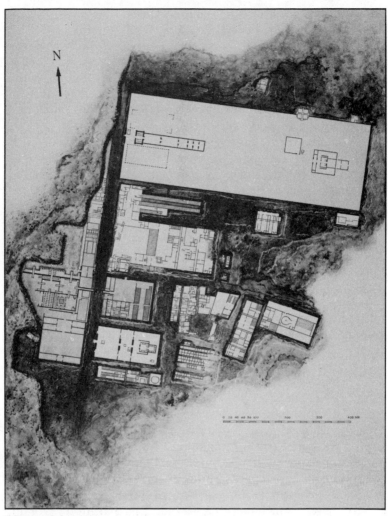

(° Equinox (Oxford) Ltd.)

Plan of palace, residence, and temple complex at Amarna. Eighteenth Dynasty, New Kingdom.

authority. The tremendous clout of Amon and his priesthood in effect challenged the power and stature of pharaoh by arguing that pharaoh was only a channel to the divine rather than himself divine.

In the new Aton temple at Karnak (Thebes) and later in tombs near the new capital city of Amarna, the radically innovative naturalistic art of the Amarna period blossomed. Murals and relief sculpture depict the royal family intimately and in ways that reveal both physical beauty and deformity. Akhenaton's peculiar physiognomy became a sort of norm on which all other portraits were modeled. The art of the Amarna period clearly represents a break with the traditional, rather stiff formalism of Egyptian art. Its novelty and grotesqueness must have repulsed more conservative tastes.

In the fifth year of his reign, Amenhotep IV changed his name to Akhenaton ("he who is serviceable to the Aton" is the most likely interpretation) and moved his capital to a virgin site in Middle Egypt, which he named Akhetaton ("place of glory of Aton," present-day Tell el-Amarna). Having abolished the traditional temples, religious rituals, and festivals, Akhenaton and his family and courtiers now worshiped the Aton in the new temple created for that purpose. The new capital, situated in a nearly uninhabited area at the desert's edge, offered unlimited space: construction could proceed without constraint. The center of the town was a huge temple complex sacred to Aton. This complex housed the royal palace and residence, temple storerooms, and an administrative center where the international cuneiform correspondence known as the Amarna Letters was uncovered in the nineteenth century A.D. (see pages 186–88).

The new religion concentrated rather exclusively on worship of the Aton. The attempt was made to suppress all memory of Amon. Shrines and temples of other gods were ignored, and texts from Amarna mentioned no gods but Aton. Even mortuary prayers were directed to Akhenaton or to Aton instead of Osiris. Yet at least some members of the royal family were named after the sun-god Re; perhaps he had been incorporated into the Aton or at least given some limited recognition.

All these factors have led to suggestions that Aton's worship was monotheistic and, furthermore, that Aton worship may have been a direct forerunner of Hebrew monotheism. In Amarna theology, however, both Akhenaton and the Aton were regarded as divine. Akhenaton and his family worshiped Aton, but that adulation remained within the palace walls: all other Egyptians were commanded to worship Akhenaton, something which served to bolster the pharaoh's own divine status. If a modern descriptive term must be attached, *monolatry*—focusing worship on one god to the exclusion of others—is more appropriate. And in comparison with Atonism, Hebrew monotheism concentrated much more on ethical concepts—right and wrong—and contained legal and ritual sanctions completely foreign to Atonism. Items and artifacts may pass easily from culture to culture, but spiritual and ethical concepts cling selectively to particular sociocultural fabrics.

The new city and the new religion proved to be an economic drain on the country. Cuneiform tablets from Akhetaton reveal Akhenaton's lack of interest or involvement in foreign affairs; the consequent loss of revenue from Egypt's Asiatic empire in Palestine and Syria must have pinched the economy. First Syria pulled out of the fold, then Palestine. But Syria was soon swallowed up by the imperialist-minded Hittites, while Palestinian city-states maintained a shaky independence. Presumably the African sector of the state also slipped from control along with access to the gold mines of Nubia and the Sudan. It is speculated that the dispossessed priesthood of Amon and the old civil bureaucracy provoked further financial and political insurrection. While upheaval during the Amarna period itself cannot be documented, civil disturbances and minor disorders were commonplace in the next quarter-century.

An eventual rift within the royal family, possibly ideological in nature, has also been hypothesized. Akhenaton's wife, Queen Nefertiti, was stripped of her throne name and exiled to a palace at the northernmost end of Amarna. Nefertiti's daughter replaced her, and her son-in-law was appointed coregent with Akhenaton. Since the son-in-law eventually returned to Thebes and reverted to worship of Amon, it could be construed that his coregency was a vehicle of compromise. If so, Nefertiti may have been the one to hold out for continuing worship of Aton (she named her new residence the House of Aton) while Akhenaton and his son-in-law favored reconciliation to the old worship of Amon.

Like Akhenaton himself, Amarna's theology and art should not be considered typically Egyptian. The Amarna Revolution represented a departure from long-standing traditions and canons of Egyptian culture and art. Although the more naturalistic aspects of Amarna's art persisted, the religious revolution proved to be an experiment, and a fleeting one. The nature of Atonism was extremely self-centered, with the royal family alone privy to render worship and loyalty to Aton. Pharaoh's entourage, like the remainder of the Egyptian state, had to devote their religious attention to Akhenaton himself. Small wonder that Akhenaton's death opened the gates to a quick and total reversion to the more traditional, less restrictive reverence of Amon.

With the full support of Akhenaton's coregent and his successor Tutankhamon, the cult of Amon was revived at Thebes shortly after Akhenaton's death. The conflict between the pharaoh and the Amon priesthood was resolved permanently. The pharaoh remained at the helm of a divine state, but he became increasingly subject to interference from priestly and bureaucratic factions. The structure of the Egyptian state changed irrevocably: the personal domination of a divine pharaoh was henceforth tempered by powerful priesthoods and official sanctions. The symbolic capstone had fallen; the pyramidal foundation had cracked.

After Akhenaton's death, the succession eventually passed to Tutankhaton (1347–1339 B.C.). This young pharaoh married one of Akhenaton's daughters and remained in residence at Amarna for two years until the traditional worship of Amon-Re was restored; he then abandoned Akhetaton and changed his name to Tutankhamon. An inscription from the fourth year of his reign certifies the restoration of the old cults and alludes to the atheism of Akhenaton's reign. "King Tut" was a minor ruler, but the wealth of his tomb—one of the few that escaped the predations of tomb robbers, ancient and modern—has made him as renowned as any ruler in the ancient Near East. It may be that his restoration of orthodoxy prompted the Amon priesthood to provide him with this lavish burial.

The Nineteenth and Twentieth Dynasties: Restoration and disruption

The Eighteenth Dynasty ended with Horemheb shortly before 1308 B.C. Horemheb, an army general, lacked an heir and consequently appointed his vizier and general, Rameses, to succeed him. Rameses I founded the Nineteenth Dynasty, whose rulers

were not Thebans but natives of the eastern Delta. Under their
sway, Egyptian foreign policy concentrated on containing Hittite
expansion in Syria. Rameses' son and coregent Seti I (1308–1291
B.C.) managed to conclude a treaty with the Hittites, but its effect
was short lived.

Rameses II (1290–1224 B.C.), son of Seti, was the last of
Egypt's great warrior-kings. During his long reign, Egypt finally
made peace with the Hittites after the hard-fought battle at Qadesh in 1285 B.C. Although conflict continued for another sixteen
years, a Hittite-Egyptian treaty—copies of which exist in both
Egyptian and Akkadian—was ratified in Rameses' twenty-first
year and reaffirmed thirteen years later by his marriage to a
Hittite princess. The resultant peace and prosperity led to a
prodigious building program: Rameses' monuments extended
from Nubia in the south to a new capital, Per-Rameses, in the
eastern Delta. Beyond Egypt proper, Sinai's turquoise and Nubia's gold continued to be exploited, but little is heard of commerce with the Mediterranean—trouble was brewing in that
quarter.

Merneptah (1224–1214 B.C.), Rameses' thirteenth son and
successor, was plagued with invasions by both the Libyans and
the Sea Peoples (see pages 212–15). Merneptah commemorated
his victory over the invaders with a poetic composition containing what may be the earliest mention of Israel. Some scholars
have accordingly assumed that it was Rameses II who enslaved
the Israelites in Egypt and that either he or Merneptah ruled at
the time of the Exodus. According to the biblical book of Exodus,
the Hebrews were forced to build the cities of Pithom and
Rameses—equated, respectively, with Per- Atum (modern Tell
el-Maskhuta) and Per-Rameses (near modern Qantir)—in the
eastern Delta, where Rameses II undertook various building
projects. An Egyptian papyrus also indicates that Ḥapiru (in
Egyptian, ⟨prw) participated in the construction of Rameses' temple. If the Ḥapiru, or any part of them, can be equated with the
Hebrews (see page 248), and if the place-name equivalents hold
up, Rameses II may well turn out to have been the unnamed
pharaoh of the Exodus and the oppressor of the Israelite people.

Upon Merneptah's death, competing factions of the royal
family traded off four brief and disturbed reigns between 1214
and 1194 B.C. Then Setnakht, a ruler of unknown origin and

brief ascendancy, established order along with a new dynasty, the Twentieth. His son Rameses III (1182–1151 B.C.) was Egypt's last notable New Kingdom pharaoh. Like Merneptah, Rameses III had to fend off invasions by Libyans and Sea Peoples. These great defensive wars may have depleted Egypt's coffers. In any case, the deteriorating economic situation in the latter half of Rameses III's reign led to worker demonstrations and the first known sit-down strike in history. Investigations into a conspiracy, evidently to assassinate Rameses, revealed that palace and harem officials, government personnel, and army officers were all involved.

Political upheaval and economic chaos may have contributed to the weakening of Egypt at home and abroad. After Rameses III's death, Egypt's Asiatic empire rapidly dissolved. Supplies of precious raw materials dried up, the land was overrun with marauding Libyans, and at least one popular uprising had to be quelled by Nubian mercenaries. The glorious days of pharaonic rule over ancient western Asia had come to a trifling and bitter end.

Throughout the New Kingdom, imperial government had increasingly extended control over all economic affairs, including foreign trade. While a professional, career-oriented army made Egypt's unprecedented geopolitical expansion possible, a cumbersome but tightly managed bureaucracy managed internal affairs. Exotic goods and essential resources—in the form of taxes, tribute, and trade—streamed into the Nile valley from Nubia, the Sudan, and points south and from Sinai, the Levant, Anatolia, and points east. Egyptian culture flourished at cosmopolitan royal courts, while Egyptian artistic canons were transformed substantially by the Amarna shake-up. Amarna religious dictates, however, disappeared as suddenly as they had arisen, and the traditional worship of Amon was successfully reinstated. Powerful priests and ambitious administrators capitalized on the Amarna episode to increase their own economic and political standing. In the end, they came to dictate pharaonic policy.

In the wake of the Sea Peoples' disruptions, centralization failed utterly, and the Egyptian state began to disintegrate. Imperial expansion in the New Kingdom had proved to be no more effective as a long-term unifying force than had the isolationism of the Middle Kingdom. By the middle of the twelfth century B.C., Egypt's world empire had collapsed.

INTERNATIONALISM IN SYRIA-PALESTINE, ANATOLIA, AND THE AEGEAN (1500–1200 B.C.)

Historical and cultural developments in Syria-Palestine between 2000 and 1500 B.C. have to be reconstructed largely with reference to archaeological data or to Babylonian and Egyptian written sources. The cuneiform texts from Mari and Alalakh illuminate events chiefly in northern Syria. During these centuries, Amorite influence and domination expanded throughout the eastern Mediterranean, even into the Egyptian delta. Although other political crosscurrents dashed any hope of overall unity, individual city-states (especially along the Levantine coast) prospered as international trading contacts blossomed.

Owing to its coastal position and its port cities, Syria-Palestine had become the commercial crossroads of the ancient Western Asia by about 1500 B.C. It was also to become a military battleground for its more powerful neighbors, a circumstance its many small city-states lacked the capacity or unity to prevent. The Levant, however, was not simply a hapless staging area: political control was constantly enriched by a lucrative international trade. The most important cultural contribution of the mid-second millennium B.C. was the creation of an alphabet—a writing system that would replace the cumbersome cuneiform and hieroglyphic systems and eventually be adopted the world over.

The fluctuating political fortunes of the various Near Eastern states during the three centuries from 1500 to 1200 B.C. can only be understood in an international context. Cuneiform letters found at Akhenaton's court in Amarna are international diplomatic documents, and similar texts spring up at sites all over ancient western Asia. For the first time and with lasting consequence, Egypt shared this international stage with other powerful states: Babylonia, Assyria, and the Hittite kingdom in Anatolia.

The Bronze Age cultures of the Aegean—Minoans from Crete and Mycenaeans from the Greek mainland—became an important part of the international scene in the eastern Mediterranean. Owing to a lack of written sources as detailed and comprehensive as those of ancient western Asia and Egypt, their exact political and economic relationship to Near Eastern states can only be established archaeologically.

At the end of the thirteenth century B.C., a bewildering sequence of population movements, invasions, and destructions upset and altered forever the essentially cooperative international relations enjoyed by major and minor political states during the second millennium B.C. Demographic, economic, climatic, and military factors in combination accounted for the subsequent disorder throughout the Mediterranean.

Syria-Palestine: Power Politics and Levantine Culture

After the fall of the Old Babylonian Dynasty under Ḫammurapi, political initiative shifted north and west. The foremost states of the era—Mitanni (Hurrians), Egypt, Hittite Anatolia, Assyria—shared imperialist ambitions as well as the military capacity to pursue conquest far beyond their own borders.

Egypt renounced its former aloofness and entered the international arena. At about the same time (sixteenth century B.C.), Hurrian newcomers moved into the Jazireh. With imperial aspirations, the Hittites expanded beyond Anatolia into northern Syria. Their consequent control of one of the most important commercial routes in the ancient world, coupled with domination over metal resources in Anatolia, put them in a very advantageous economic and political position. By 1350 B.C., the revitalized Assyrians began to extend their sway. Such developments led, in general, to frequent conflict, an elaborate system of international diplomacy, and an unstable and shifting balance of power among these four ambitious states.

The Hurrians, who probably entered upper Mesopotamia from the northeast (see page 144), moved into the political vacuum created by the decline of Assyria and Babylonia. Hurrian military power resided in the *mariannu*, a chariot-owning nobility who, like the Kassites, excelled at horsemanship and military tactics based on the horse-drawn, two-wheeled, spoked chariot. Establishing a network of small regional centers extending from Assyria in the east to Alalakh in the west, and especially in the Jazireh, the Hurrians displaced or seized the initiative from the Amorites who had preceded them. The Hurrian conquest had two distinct phases: (1) progressive domination, followed by (2) the regrouping of petty states into a Hurrian kingdom, a political

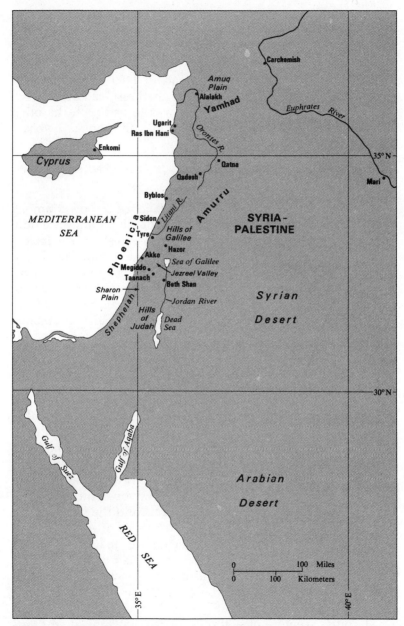

Map 4–3 Syria-Palestine in the Second Millennium B.C.: Sites and Geographic Features

grouping identified in cuneiform texts as Mitanni. The preeminence of Mitanni went uncontested until the mid-fifteenth century B.C.

Hurrian expansion southward was blocked by Egypt's thrust into Syria under Thutmose III. By about 1400 B.C., diplomatic marriages between Mitanni and Egypt had resolved the conflict, and a temporary balance of power was forged with the other competing states: Assyria, Kassite Babylonia, and Hittite Anatolia.

The Amarna Letters and the Ḥapiru: International events and provincial concerns

The complex interaction and shifting balance of power among these Late Bronze Age states and kingdoms impinged significantly on the territory in their midst: Syria-Palestine. The impact of international trade and politics on the Levantine city-states, however, was balanced and, in the end, offset by internal social change and population dynamics. And the historian gains access to these events—international and local—through one of the most significant finds of cuneiform tablets ever made: the Amarna Letters.

These Amarna tablets, discovered in 1887 at Akhenaton's capital, allow a glimpse of international diplomacy and commercial contact during the fourteenth century B.C. The approximately 380 tablets in the archive include 42 letters exchanged between pharaoh and the kings of Babylonia, Assyria, Mitanni (the Hurrians), Hittite Anatolia, Arzawa (a small state in Anatolia), and Cyprus. With few exceptions, the tablets may be dated to the reigns of pharaohs Amenhotep III and IV (Akhenaton).

Several of the Amarna documents are inventories of lavish gifts exchanged between royal courts. Envoys entrusted with delicate political and diplomatic missions and the safe conduct of great riches carried out regular exchanges of messages and gifts. The immense variety and staggering quantity of goods entrusted to these messengers, as well as the frequency of such exchanges, suggests that this was not mere royal gift-giving but the basic mechanism of trade between Egypt and its neighbors; the messengers were merchants as well as ambassadors. At the royal courts, centers of a thriving cosmopolitanism, the arts flourished while foreign princes and princesses were educated, entertained, and married off for diplomatic purposes.

Despite the strong foreign influence in Syria and Palestine at this time, the Amarna Letters and other cuneiform sources indicate that local dynasts remained the effective government of the Levant. The letters—the single most important source for interpreting internal Syro-Palestinian politics at this time—even imply that the Syrian state of Amurru successfully formed an independent political movement based on popular support.

Although Hurrians, Hittites, and Egyptians wielded some political clout, models of their social or economic structure cannot be imposed arbitrarily on the peoples of Syria-Palestine. Egyptian and Hittite overlordship had differing impact in different areas. Egyptian vassal states in the Levant had clearly defined obligations, but pharaoh had none in return. Egypt's administrative aim was clear-cut and twofold: to prevent rebellion and to extract the maximum possible tribute. Hittite treaties, by contrast, clearly defined mutual obligations between lord and vassal.

Well attested to in the Amarna archives and present seemingly everywhere in Syria and Palestine were the *Ḫapiru*, a socially restive group of people who spread throughout the Near East during the second millennium B.C. The *Ḫapiru* encompassed groups of differing ethnic composition, expatriate fugitives from various city-states and tribal communities. The fact that one could "become a *Ḫapiru*" (a phrase the Amarna Letters use frequently) implies a lack of kinship or political ties. In general, the *Ḫapiru* are best defined as a social group, not an ethnolinguistic one.

Some *Ḫapiru* served as mercenaries under successive leaders. Others formed independent communal or semitribal organizations on the borders of settled areas, often in the hill and forest country of Syria-Palestine. Subject to no state's legal authority, the *Ḫapiru* endured on the outskirts of known civilizations, where they maintained a fragile independence.

A historical relation between the social term *Ḫapiru* and the ethnic term *Hebrew* has been proposed and has found some defenders. Although the *Ḫapiru* were too broad and mixed to be considered the ancestors of Israel, it is not improbable that some Hebrews were to be found among the Ḫapiru. Both Hebrews and Ḫapiru were people without a homeland, an inferior class feared and held in contempt by the settled population.

Ugarit: International port on the eastern Mediterranean

International trade and intercultural contacts typify the archaeological and documentary record of Mediterranean ports of trade like Ugarit, Beirut, Byblos, and Tyre. These trading centers usually functioned as organs of a small, independent state. The inland powers of Mitanni, Assyria, and the Hittites depended on such ports for imports and exchange and were thus inclined to establish friendly relations and to uphold the neutrality of the harbor cities. This neutrality would have been protected by agreement with the major powers and perhaps by consensus among overseas trading powers. Occasionally, however, these ports came under the sway of hinterland states. Ugarit, for instance, was bound by treaty first to Egypt (in the early fourteenth century B.C.) and then to the Hittites. Nonetheless, history records a predominantly independent existence for Ugarit and other Levantine trading ports. Phoenician harbors such as Tyre and Sidon replaced Ugarit in this capacity during the first millennium B.C.

Ugarit (modern-day Ras Shamra on the Syrian coast) has been continuously excavated by a French archaeological team since 1929. Copious written evidence discloses that the city was already flourishing early in the second millennium B.C.; the majority of documents, however, pertain to the period 1400–1200 B.C. Most noteworthy of the chain of Levantine ports serving coastal traffic to Palestine and Egypt, Ugarit could accommodate ships of considerable size.

Situated at the intersection of land and sea routes, Ugarit was within striking distance of Cyprus and the Cilician ports of Anatolia and functioned as a link between the Aegean and the Near East. Ugarit also commanded the main overland passage north through the Amuq plain toward Aleppo and Carchemish, where the land route met the riverine Euphrates route to Assyria, Babylonia, and the east. Another road extended north and then west through the Syrian and Cilician gates to central Anatolia.

Alongside its role as middleman, Ugarit actively exported bronze weapons and vessels from its foundries, purple-dyed linen and wool, grains, olive oil, scented oil, wine, salt, cosmetics, and fine woods such as juniper and boxwood. Egyptian, Aegean, and Cypriot goods were in plentiful supply. At Ras Ibn Hani, the nearby port of Ugarit, the discovery of a unique mold for making **copper** ("oxhide") **ingots** indicates that Ugarit was closely associated with a trade in metals that touched most areas of ancient western Asia and the Mediterranean. Textual evidence indicates that Hittite and Egyptian merchants resided in Ugarit, and references to Kassite and Moabite deities suggest that Babylonians and Palestinians from Transjordan also inhabited this cosmopolitan community. The welter of scripts and languages used at Ugarit—Ugaritic, Hurrian, Akkadian, Sumerian, Hittite, Egyptian, Cypro-Minoan (the script used on Cyprus), and Hieroglyphic Luwian (an Anatolian language and script)—likewise testify to its international status.

Syro-Palestinian scripts: Origin of the alphabet

By 1400 B.C., scribes at Ugarit had invented thirty cuneiform signs to write the local Semitic language, called Ugaritic by modern scholars. The order of these signs was exactly that of the letters in the slightly later Semitic alphabet. Other early attempts at alphabetic writing undertaken within Syria-Palestine are collectively called Proto-Canaanite, and may be dated to the centuries 1500–1200 B.C. The significance of this observation is that the alphabet the world relies on today for communication first emerged in late second millennium B.C–Syria-Palestine, when numerous efforts were made to simplify the unwieldy scripts of Mesopotamia and Egypt.

The alphabet is the most recent, highly developed, convenient, easily adaptable, and universal system of writing. The Semitic alphabet was the ancestor of all subsequent alphabetic scripts, though later variations have erased any resemblances between some members of the alphabetic family: compare, for example, the Roman, Arabic, Armenian, Korean, and Indic versions. The crucial step in the creation of the alphabet was not the invention of the signs themselves but the discovery of the inner working principle: that each sound could be represented by one, and only one, sign.

Scholars still debate whether the Egyptian writing system had any influence on the West Semitic alphabet. The earliest in a series of alphabet-type inscriptions from Syria-Palestine is from Serabit el-Khadim in the Sinai, the site of Egyptian-controlled turquoise and copper mines. Dating from no later than about 1500 B.C., these few brief Proto-Sinaitic inscriptions are presumed to have been carved by Semitic workers who, having seen their Egyptian masters use writing to record language, were inspired to create their own signs. The relation of these signs to Egyptian heiroglyphs is, however, complex. If the Semites borrowed the signs or even the idea of writing from the Egyptians, they did not adhere closely to Egyptian sign forms or phonetic values. Instead they chose to give their own values to signs they had adapted or invented. And most important, they made one sign stand for one sound, thus creating an alphabet unencumbered by multiconsonantal or syllabic signs or by the nonphonetic signs (determinatives) characteristic of the cuneiform and hieroglyphic systems.

Besides the early Proto-Sinaitic and Proto-Canaanite attempts to modify extant writing systems, other, more linear second millennium B.C. scripts have turned up at Byblos (Lebanon), Tell Deir-Alla in Transjordan, and the Fayyum in Egypt. These linear systems employed about 80–100 signs, too many for an alphabet and much more reminiscent of the syllabic scripts of Crete and Cyprus. Yet this too was a step toward simplification.

Some West Semitic peoples, therefore, unbound by age-old scribal traditions, sought easier means of communicating or of establishing ownership. Early experimental scripts varied with respect to the shape of the signs and the direction of writing; no single convention had yet been adopted. But by choosing one symbol to represent each consonant, the number of signs could be reduced to thirty or less.

The resulting alphabet was the ancestor of the Phoenician alphabet, from which our own alphabet is derived through Greek and Latin. The Greeks' main contribution was to adapt and systematize vowel signs; Semitic scripts, like Egyptian phonetic

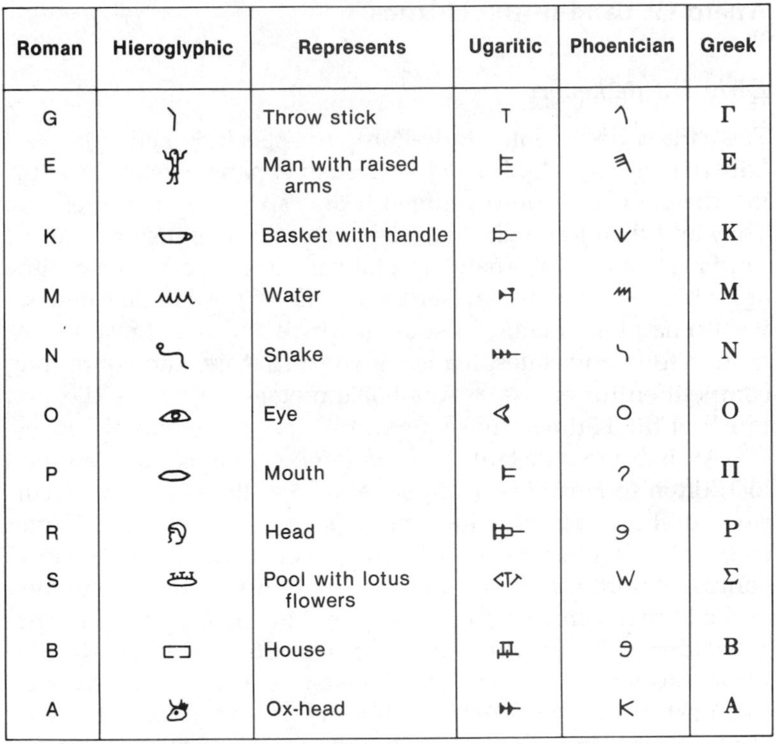

Roman	Hieroglyphic	Represents	Ugaritic	Phoenician	Greek
G	𓌙	Throw stick	𐎂	𐤂	Γ
E	𓀠	Man with raised arms	𐎅	𐤄	E
K	𓎡	Basket with handle	𐎋	𐤊	K
M	𓈖	Water	𐎎	𐤌	M
N	𓆓	Snake	𐎐	𐤍	N
O	𓁹	Eye	𐎓	𐤏	O
P	𓂋	Mouth	𐎔	𐤐	Π
R	𓁶	Head	𐎗	𐤓	P
S	𓆷	Pool with lotus flowers	𐎌	𐤔	Σ
B	𓉐	House	𐎁	𐤁	B
A	𓃾	Ox-head	𐎀	𐤀	A

Chart 4–1 Origins of the Alphabet: List of Roman, Hieroglyphic, Ugaritic, Phoenician, and Greek Sign Forms (A. Bernard Knapp)

spellings, do not express vowels in regular written characters. Scholars are still uncertain when and where the Greeks first adopted the West Semitic alphabet. At present, the proposed dates for that event range from as early as 1500/1400 B.C. to as late as 750 B.C.

While foreign armies marched the length and breadth of the Levant, striving to monopolize trade or ensure tribute, more silent cultural forces were at work. Trade patterns emerged that persisted for another thousand years. A system of writing developed that not only became universal but has endured to the present day. Armies and conquerors come and go, but cultural patterns often defy the passage of time.

Anatolia: Land of the Hittites

Early Hittite history

The earliest documented Indo-European–speaking Hittite kings—
Labarna, Ḫattusili I, Mursili I—pursued expansionistic aims during the course of the seventeenth and sixteenth centuries B.C.
They and their immediate successors took the first steps toward
unifying the central Anatolian plateau under the Hittite regime
at Ḫattusha (Hittite town) (see pages 143–45). Anatolia's mineral
wealth had long made it a strategic prize and the object of con-
tention for many states in ancient western Asia, and continuing
competition for access to Anatolia's metals must have dictated
much of the Hittites' subsequent military and economic policy.

At first, more distant lands were no sooner conquered than
lost, often to Hurrians. Ḫattusili and Mursili engaged in recurring conflicts with the Hurrians and with the powerful Syrian
state of Yamḫad, centered in Aleppo, over economic and political
control of northern Syria—the same region Ebla had dominated
in the third millennium B.C. Eventually Mursili destroyed Aleppo.
Emboldened by victory, he made a swift raid down the Euphrates as far as Babylon about 1600 B.C. He returned, however,
as quickly as he had struck, leaving the way open for the Kassite
takeover of Babylonia. Upon his victorious return to Ḫattusha,
Mursili was assassinated, initiating a series of royal murders and
bringing the fledgling Hittite state to the brink of collapse.

Telepinu, who ruled about 1500 B.C., sought to reestablish
law and order by banning the shedding of royal blood and establishing a hereditary succession to the throne. The codification
of Hittite law is also ascribed to his reign. Telepinu was forced
to secure the Hittite state by concluding a treaty with the Hurrians, who dominated his southwest border.

The Hittite New Kingdom (1400–1200 B.C.)

At the death of Telepinu around 1500 B.C., the Old Kingdom
came to an end. The Hittite state plunged into a protracted
struggle for survival. The precipitous decline of the Hittites be-

tween about 1500 and 1380 B.C. was influenced by Hurrian expansion and consolidation in the southeast and by competition from other Anatolian peoples. Conflict between Hurrians and Hittites persisted throughout this period.

Thanks to the military and organizational skill of Suppiluliuma I (about 1380–1345 B.C.), who regarded himself as both avenger and conqueror, the Hittites emerged victorious from this dismal period. Within a century, they had built the most powerful state in the Near East. Suppiluliuma took his first revenge on the Hurrians by decisively smashing the state of Mitanni. Mitanni's position of prominence was claimed by the resurgent Assyrians, who made inroads against both Kassites and Hittites. Under Assur-uballit I (1363–1328 B.C.) and his successors, Assyria emerged as a formidable military force, a role it maintained throughout the thirteenth century B.C. To counter the Assyrian threat, Suppiluliuma placed a puppet king on the Hurrian throne; thereafter Mitanni functioned as a buffer state between the Hittites and Assyria. Once Suppiluliuma had wrested eastern Anatolia from the Hurrians, its raw materials became available to the Hittite metalworking industry.

By placing his sons in control of the major Syrian states of Aleppo and Carchemish and by binding the native rulers of smaller Syrian states to the Hittites under treaty, Suppiluliuma firmly established Hittite control of the important Euphrates trade route. Soon, however, the Egyptians renewed their interest in Syria, and the two powers found themselves locked in struggle.

Suppiluliuma's son Mursili II defeated the troublesome Anatolian state of Arzawa, which bordered Hittite territory on the southwest. Arzawa had been allied with the distant power of Ahhijawa (which may well be the Hittite rendering of "Achaeans," the Greeks of western Anatolia and the Aegean). Hittite contacts with the Ahhijawa, both friendly and hostile, lasted throughout the fourteenth and thirteenth centuries B.C.

Mursili II's successor Muwatalli organized the northern boundary of the Hittite state and then turned his attention to the Egyptian threat in Syria. Hittite armies finally clashed with Egyptian troops under Rameses II at the great battle of Qadesh on the Orontes River in 1285 B.C. This encounter established, very near the site of the battle, a firm border between the two powers: Syria came under Hittite control, Palestine remained Egyptian.

While the Hittites were preoccupied in Syria, the Assyrians fought their way across the Jazireh to the very border of the Hittite state, the Euphrates River. The Hittite king Hattusili III tried to forestall the Assyrian advance by concluding mutual-defense treaties with the Kassites and with Egypt. But Hittite control faltered. The Assyrian push to the Euphrates deprived the Hittites of the copper resources of southeastern Anatolia; Tukulti-Ninurta I of Assyria (1244–1208 B.C.) then crossed the Euphrates and claimed the deportation of 28,000 Hittite subjects from their land. Their fate is unknown. Weary from its long struggle with Assyria, the Hittite empire crumbled under Suppiluliuma II, namesake of the founder.

The final blow, however, came from the opposite direction. Directly or indirectly, the movements of the Sea Peoples (see pages 212–15) and incursions by tribes from the northwest halted the economic and administrative machinery of the Hittite state. The land was pillaged, and Hattusha was burned to the ground, never to be reinhabited.

Hittite society and culture

When the Hittites first entered Anatolia, about 2000 B.C., they encountered and interacted with a firmly rooted, non-Indo-European, indigenous Bronze Age culture. Further influenced by increasing contacts with Hurrians (through whom they probably acquired knowledge of cuneiform writing) and Babylonians, Hittite culture was to some extent derivative. Hittite law, while more humane than Babylonian law, used similar phraseology. And Hittite religion and ceremony—dominated by the sun-god but including a host of other deities—show the impact of Mesopotamian belief and ritual. Yet the Hittites did not simply emulate the culture of their eastern neighbors. Once entrenched in the unique geographical and environmental surroundings of the central Anatolian plateau, Hittite culture evolved along its own distinct path.

Agriculture and metallurgy: The economic base. Life for Hittite peasants of the second millennium B.C., like that of their modern-day Turkish counterparts, revolved almost exclusively around agriculture. Many crops must have been cultivated on fertile lands just north of the capital city Ḫattusha. The gods are repeatedly asked in Hittite prayers to extend their blessings to the staple crops: grain, wine, and oil. Other Hittite texts demonstrate that fruit groves and perhaps vineyards—less certainly grain fields—were irrigated. Cattle, pigs, sheep, and goats provided protein for the diet while horses, donkeys, and dogs provided traction, transport, and control for animals. If population estimates of 30,000–40,000 for Ḫattusha are accurate, successful agricultural production would have been indispensible to the Hittite economy.

The economy also relied on the mining and production of metals. Anatolia's mountain chains are rich in copper, silver, and iron deposits; tin (stannite) deposits, vital to the copper-producing industry, have recently been identified in the Taurus Mountains. The Old Assyrian traders in Anatolia had exported copper and silver, but iron—while abundant—remained a poorly known and precious metal in the second millennium B.C. Iron objects recovered in archaeological excavations pale in number beside finds of copper or bronze. Scattered evidence attests to industrial areas associated with metalworking, but little is known of actual processes, methods of transportation, or organization of the industry. Final shaping of the metal into weapons, tools, and other products was done in the cities, not at the source.

The copious mineral deposits of Anatolia surely influenced economic policy. Although trade seems already to have been well established in the old Assyrian period, the transportation of materials always posed problems. The land was large, mountainous, and difficult of passage. Regardless of the demand from other regions of ancient western Asia and Egypt, such factors must always have limited the amount of trade and the kinds of products exchanged.

Cultural elements and political ideas, though often traced to those of surrounding peoples, took on a distinctively Hittite hue in the heartland of Anatolia. On the basis of the Hittite laws,

dated about 1500 B.C., Hittite rule seems to have been benevolent, although strict governmental guidance pervaded many aspects of Hittite society. The king ruled directly instead of through
administrators, and the success of his rule seems often to have
depended on his own personal charisma. The Hittite state, in
the person of the king, held title to all land. Military service and
tenant labor were demanded in exchange for grants of land. The
laws established prices in kind for food, clothing, industrial
products, and luxury items; they also fixed wages and fees for
services. Craftsmen and artists produced unique sculptural reliefs, depicting military or mythological scenes, and rather rigid
and ponderous temples and palaces.

Hittite literature: Hurrian sources and Greek parallels.   Many
Hittite literary texts are highly reminiscent of their Akkadian
counterparts. And like Akkadian texts, their preservation results
from the constant copying of traditional texts by scribes in training, a common practice throughout the cuneiform world.

Though clearly Akkadian in conception, literary texts
unearthed at Hattusa had an unmistakably Hittite flavor. For
example, fragments of the epic of Gilgamesh in Akkadian, Hurrian, and Hittite versions were found at Hattusha. In the Hittite
rendition, passages of special appeal to a Mesopotamian audience were shortened, while certain episodes that took place in
geographical settings more familiar to Hittites or Hurrians were
expanded. Since the epic was also found in Hurrian translation,
it may well have reached the Hittites through a Hurrian
intermediary.

Hittite omen texts, prayer and ritual texts, word lists, and
similar documents far outnumber literary texts. Myths of local
origin were closely linked to cult and ritual, a specifically Hittite
approach uncharacteristic of Akkadian myths. The basic form
of Hittite prayers may have been borrowed from Mesopotamia,
but they too were transformed into something distinctively
Hittite.

Many elements of Hurrian culture found their way into Hittite society: gods, cult festivals, art, language, probably even the
cuneiform system of writing. The foreign literary texts found at
Hattusha are predominantly Hurrian, even if some can ulti-

mately be traced back to an Akkadian source. In fact, the major Hittite epic cycle centers on the Hurrian god Kumarbi, who seizes divine kingship and unsuccessfully struggles to regain it after being replaced by Teshub, the Hurrian weather-god. Since fragments of a Hurrian version of this myth were also found at Hattusha, the Hittite account was probably based on a Hurrian original.

Even more interesting, however, are the striking parallels between the Kumarbi epic and Hesiod's *Theogony*, an important work of early Greek literature. Parallels obtain not just in outline but in specific detail. The three generations of gods in the Hittite texts—Anu (heaven), Kumarbi (father of the gods), and Teshub—correspond precisely to the Greek Ouranos, Kronos, and Zeus. Just as Kumarbi emasculates his father Anu, so Kronos mutilates his father Ouranos. In both mythologies, numerous other deities spring from this bloody act.

How could these myths have reached the Greeks? They may have been transmitted by the Hittites to Greeks in western Anatolia, where these two peoples must have met repeatedly. The most likely explanation, however, is that Hurro-Hittite traditions reached the west by way of Phoenicia. Textual evidence from Ugarit and Alalakh confirms that a sizable Hurrian contingent inhabited northern Syria in the latter half of the second millennium B.C.; Hurrian myths could have reached Phoenicia in this way. Apparently the Greeks gained more than knowledge of the alphabet from Phoenicia: the Greek epic may have acquired Hurrian motifs through Phoenician intermediacy.

Especially in its literature, the Hittites' unique cultural situation between east and west becomes apparent. Hittite culture overall may have been eclectic, but its legal, political, religious, and artistic practices reveal a distinct society of Indo-European–speaking people who made a marked impact on the Near Eastern world and expanded its horizons farther west and north than ever before.

For the better part of two centuries, the Hittites had held their own among the superpowers of ancient western Asia, controlling vital trade routes that secured and enhanced their dominion. It was sudden disaster from outside, not disintegration from within, that cut the trade routes and the economic umbilical cord of the Hittites. Their policies failed accordingly, calling an end to the Hittite interlude in ancient Near Eastern history.

Bronze Age Cultures of the Aegean: Minoans and Mycenaeans

The study of Aegean Bronze Age cultures—Minoan on Crete and Helladic (Mycenaean) in Greece—belongs more accurately to prehistory than to history. Rather than the diffusion of culture or influxes of outside populations, social and material changes within these two cultures prompted the rise of the Aegean world's Bronze Age cultures. The agricultural economies of the Bronze Age Aegean, in other words, emerged directly and naturally from their Neolithic forerunners. Stimulus from western Asia, however, especially with respect to that area's highly organized palatial systems, cannot be discounted.

Neolithic and Early Bronze Age developments

Crete became populated at least as early as the seventh millennium B.C. Neolithic settlement on the island, however, remained extremely limited until the late fourth millennium B.C., when the number and size of villages increased noticeably, perhaps as the result of new settlers from Anatolia. Yet even then, the economy of Crete's villages revolved exclusively around agriculture; there is no evidence of social stratification, craft specialization, or trading contacts.

The Neolithic farming villages of the Greek mainland appear likewise to have been characterized by little if any variation in social status. By the beginning of the Bronze Age, however, early in the third millennium B.C., innovations in transportation (the oared longship) and a shift from cereal crops to the cultivation of olives and vines seem to have radically altered social, spatial, and subsistence patterns throughout the Aegean world. Together with the advent and spread of metallurgy, grape and olive cultivation probably promoted the acquisition of wealth and the emergence of social classes. Bronzeworking techniques stimulated trade and expansion: the tin, if not the copper, needed to make bronze had to be imported. Bronze tools in turn probably

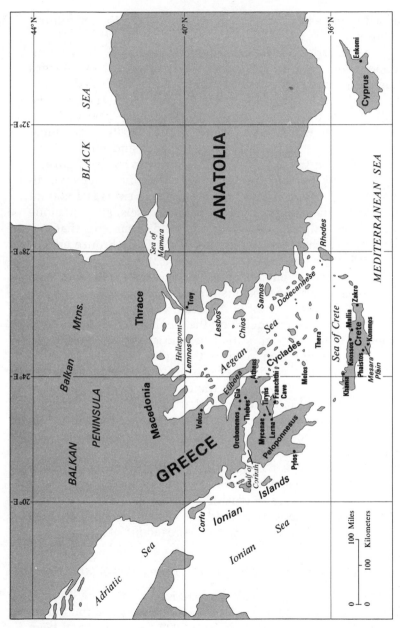

Map 4–4 The Aegean in the Second Millennium B.C.: Sites and Geographic Features

enabled farmers to increase their yields, making for agricultural surpluses.

These interlocking developments stimulated the Aegean economy, and regional diversity quickly ensued. New villages sprang up throughout Greece, Crete, and the Cyclades—the Aegean islands between Crete and the mainland. The local distinctiveness of the Early Bronze Age (about 3000–2000 B.C.) contrasts markedly with the uniformity of the Neolithic. The great House of Tiles at Lerna in Greece, the sites and tombs of the Mesara plain in Crete, and the characteristic marble figurines from the workshops of the Cyclades all testify to regional diversity. The growing sophistication of village crafts is apparent in the seals, fine painted pottery, marble vessels, efficient stone axes, bronze artifacts, and silver and gold ornaments that distinguish the archaeological remains of the Early Bronze era.

Metallurgy developed first and foremost in the Cyclades and on Crete. The achievements of early Aegean metallurgists have been linked to the rapid expansion of trade throughout the Aegean and the western coast of Anatolia. The Bronze Age metals trade may have been modeled on the Neolithic exploitation and movement of obsidian from the Cycladic island of Melos. Finds of obsidian brought from Melos to the Greek mainland (Franchthi Cave in southeastern Greece) over 11,000 years ago show that boats capable of traversing the open sea already existed in that very early period. Numerous harbors and diverse trading routes provided for easy year-round communication from coast to island and from island to island. The simple sailing craft depicted on Early Bronze Age Aegean seals were probably the vehicles of intra-Aegean contact. The resultant wide distribution of goods, techniques, and ideas promoted some degree of cultural unity in the Aegean world. Regional diversity and intercultural contact thus conditioned the development of Aegean life in the succeeding Middle Bronze Age (about 2000–1600 B.C.).

The Palatial period: Apex of Minoan civilization (2000–1400 B.C.)

The Middle Bronze Age was characterized by striking dissimilarities between Crete and Greece. Widespread destruction on the Greek mainland shortly before 2000 B.C. may have been

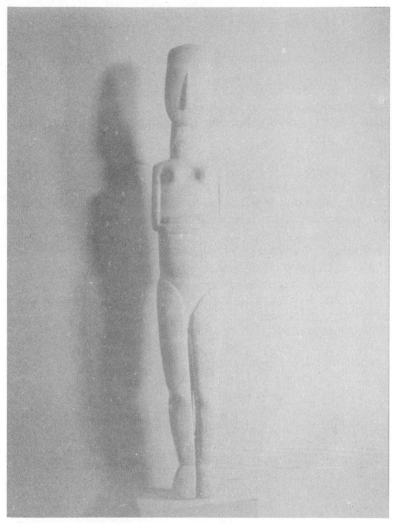

(⁰ Ekdotike Athenon S.A., Athens)

White marble Cycladic figurine from the middle phases of the Early Bronze Age (about 2600 B.C.)

caused by intruding newcomers. On Crete, meanwhile, Minoan civilization—named after the legendary ruler Minos—crystallized rapidly at the end of the third millennium B.C. The first of Crete's well-known palaces had been built by the twentieth century B.C.

Palatial society was still based on agriculture, especially on the intensive cultivation of the olive and vine. The most famous palace was at Knossos, but others arose at Phaistos and at Mallia; by 1700 B.C., another palace had been constructed at Zakro on the east coast and probably one at Khania in the west as well. These palaces were typically large structures whose sectors or rooms were grouped around a central rectangular court.

An earthquake that destroyed the original palaces about 1700 B.C. prompted lavish reconstruction and initiated the so-called Second Palace period (1700–1400 B.C.), the highpoint of Minoan civilization. Magnificent frescoes adorned the walls of the new palaces. The rich colors and gaiety of the scenes portrayed on these frescoes have usually been interpreted as indicators of a leisure class that enjoyed its games, lived peaceably on the gains of a thriving commerce, and could dispense with many of the accoutrements of warfare characteristic of other Bronze Age cultures. Delicate ceramics in floral and marine designs demonstrate a high level of craftsmanship; jewelry, gems, bronze, and ivory figurines attest to unrivaled prosperity.

Self-supporting in food and other basic raw materials (some metals may have been imported), the Minoans exported their painted pottery, food, and probably cloth. Textual evidence from Ugarit and Mari in Syria indicates that other Cretan products— oil, fermented beverages, grain, and weapons—found their way to the Levant. Intensive grape and olive cultivation, in conjunction with wide trading contacts throughout the Aegean, led to economic interdependence. A redistribution system organized and controlled by the palaces funneled luxury items, including metals, and basic goods into the economy. A rich agricultural base, combined with a wide-ranging, lucrative exchange network, carried Minoan Crete to the apex of prosperity by the end of the sixteenth century B.C.

A volcanic eruption on the Aegean island of Thera, about 68 miles (110 kilometers) north of Crete, dated now to the sev-

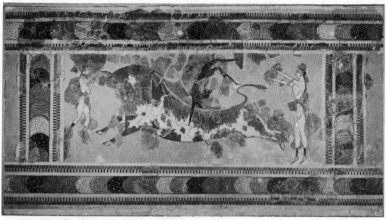

(° D. A. Harrisiadis, Athens)

Minoan bull-leaping fresco from the east wing of the palace at Knossos,
Crete. Second Palace period, about 1700–1400 B.C.

enteenth century B.C. by **radiocarbon** evidence, may have caused
some disruption to Crete and consequently to Minoan trade
networks. Shortly after 1500 B.C., numerous Minoan sites had
been destroyed or abandoned, although Knossos maintained its
status and level of development after only minor damage. Although at least 150 years separate Thera's volcanic eruption and
these destructions on Crete, Aegean historians still discuss and
debate the impact of the former upon the latter. If the scientific
basis of radiocarbon dating is accepted, it seems unlikely that
destructions on Crete dated about 1500 B.C. could have been
caused directly by a volcanic eruption that occurred on Thera
almost a century and a half earlier.

Whether these Cretan destructions were caused by human
or natural agents is not apparent from the archaeological record
alone. Yet burials of warriors, unprecedented military scenes on
frescoes at the rebuilt palace at Knossos, and ceramics reminiscent of mainland Greece suggest that Mycenaean Greek forces
may have established themselves at Crete's most powerful palatial center. And a system of writing, known as Linear B and
used to write the Greek language (see the following section),
came into use at Knossos at least by 1450 B.C.

"Marseille Ewer," one of the most famous and elegant Late Minoan IB Marine Style vases, about 1450 B.C.

By the end of the fifteenth century B.C., the palace at Knossos suffered a destruction from which it never recovered; one can only guess whether this was the work of Mycenaeans or of rebellious Minoans. Minoan culture continued to flourish at Khania in the west and at Kommos on the south coast; a few other sites experienced a modest resurgence during the fourteenth and thirteenth centuries B.C. But palatial life had vanished from Crete, and the era of Minoan predominance in the Aegean had come to an end.

Aegean writing. By the beginning of the second millennium B.C., the Minoans of Crete had developed a hieroglyphic system of writing distinct from Egyptian heiroglyphics. This script's pictorial signs were eventually simplified to linear outlines in the system known as Linear A. Inscriptions in Linear A are found on a variety of materials: stone, pottery, stucco, metal, and clay (including small clay tablets). Despite ardent efforts, the language(s) rendered by both the hieroglyphic and Linear A scripts remains unknown to this day. A number of linguists, it may be added, have argued that Semitic words occur in the Linear A texts, although this in no way proves that the underlying language of the texts is Semitic. Furthermore, since the original homeland of the people who developed Minoan palatial society is still a matter of scholarly debate, no definite suggestions can be made about the ethnolinguistic makeup of the Minoans.

By the mid-fifteenth century B.C., a subsequent script known as Linear B began to be used regularly at Knossos. Linear B was inscribed primarily on rectangular and leaf-shaped clay tablets, which were hardened and thus preserved by the fire that later destroyed Knossos.

The existing fragments of the hieroglyphic and Linear A scripts are too few to allow verifiable decipherment. Linear B, on the other hand, survives on thousands of tablets and fragments. Even before the script had been deciphered, it was obvious that these were business records or inventories. When Linear B tablets were also found on the Greek mainland at Pylos in 1939, Sir Arthur Evans (who had discovered the first Linear B tablets in his excavations at Knossos) insisted that the sophisticated Minoans had introduced literacy to the backward mainlanders. Evans' influence was such that few scholars challenged him.

Then, in 1952, Michael Ventris, a young British architect with a genius for ancient tongues, finally deciphered Linear B. What Ventris found, few had imagined: the language of the Linear B tablets was an early form of Greek. Ventris's discovery required considerable modification of Evans' theory. Eventually, however, it enabled scholars to reconstruct a more accurate scenario of indigenous developments on the Greek mainland during the second millennium B.C. (see pages 207–10). Although the Minoans had indeed introduced writing to the Aegean, Greeks and Cypriots eventually adopted the Minoan linear system and refined the script for their own purposes.

Middle and Late Helladic Greece: Rise of Mycenaean society

Mainland Greece lagged behind Crete. During the third millennium B.C., the people of the mainland had developed advanced agricultural techniques, gained some proficiency with metals, learned the potter's craft, and engaged in commercial exchange with Crete, the Cyclades, and western Anatolia. Then, shortly before 2000 B.C., disaster struck much of the mainland and swept away the old regimes. The popular hypothesis that the intruders were the first Indo-European (in this case, Greek) speakers in Greece is plausible but unverifiable: such an intrusion would conform very well chronologically with what is believed to be the advent of Indo-European–speaking peoples (Hittites) in Anatolia. What is certain is that the ensuing Middle Helladic culture represented a temporary step backward. A poorer and simpler rural economy, less impressive in its material remains, dominated mainland Greece. Recovery was slow, and the culture of Middle Helladic Greece pales beside that of Middle Minoan Crete.

Mycenaean civilization, now also termed Late Helladic, was named for Heinrich Schliemann's excavations at the magnificent southeast Peloponnesian citadel of Mycenae in the 1870s. The Late Helladic culture that evolved from these Middle Helladic roots began to flourish about 1700 B.C. By that time, Greek-speaking chieftains ruled at Mycenae. These rulers were buried in lavishly ornamented tombs, called shaft graves because each consisted of a deep rectangular shaft lined with stone and covered with wooden beams and stone slabs. The riches buried with these rulers included exquisite gold filigree work, fine ceramics with marine and floral motifs resembling those of Crete, inlaid bronze swords, and golden death masks. The material aspect of this culture has often been considered derivative of Crete. Helladic workmanship and style, however, are distinctive and characterized by military themes, an elaborate and increasingly stylized approach to the decoration of noticeably angular ceramics, and a stiffness absent from Minoan art.

While plunder might account for some of the shaft graves' wealth, it probably derived largely from Greece's extensive trading contacts: the Cyclades, Crete, Cyprus, Anatolia, Syria, and parts of southern Europe appear to have traded with Greece. A new prosperity bloomed; mainland Greece was coming into its own.

The Shaft Grave era (about 1700–1500 B.C.) was merely a prelude to the most glorious age of Helladic Greece. As Minoan Crete declined, the great fortified centers on the mainland entered a period of unprecedented power and prosperity. By the centuries 1400–1200 B.C., called Late Helladic III, palaces had arisen at Mycenae, Tiryns, Pylos, Thebes, Orchomenos, Volos, and possibly at Athens and Gla. The massive stone walls, called "Cyclopaean," that enclosed these citadels contrast markedly with unwalled Minoan palaces.

Another distinctive feature of the period is the *tholos*, or beehive tomb. Sprinkled throughout southern Greece, *tholoi* were circular, rock-lined chambers cut out of hillsides, dramatic displays of regal authority and command of labor. The majestic group of nine tholoi uncovered at Mycenae dates from the fifteenth to thirteenth centuries B.C. Unparalleled outside Greece, tholoi symbolize the peak flowering of Helladic culture.

Cretan influence may have stirred the Helladic awakening, but by 1400 B.C., influence began to flow in the opposite direction. Helladic culture pervaded virtually all of mainland Greece, and Crete and the Cyclades were also drawn into its orbit. The trading activities of the Helladic Greeks ultimately surpassed those of the Minoans in scope and volume. Late Helladic pottery has been found throughout the Mediterranean world: Sicily, Sar-

✦

(® Ekdotike Athenon S.A., Athens)
Gold funerary mask from Shaft Grave V, Grave Circle A, at Mycenae,
Greece, about 1550–1500 B.C.

dinia, Crete, the Cyclades, Rhodes, Cyprus, Anatolia, central
Europe, the Balkans, Egypt, and the Levant. In Syria, Palestine,
and Cyprus, this distinctive pottery is so plentiful that some
scholars have hypothesized Greek settlement or colonization.
Yet the absence of any other artifacts of Helladic material culture
makes Greek settlement, except perhaps by merchants, unlikely.

Trade in metals may have played a central role in Helladic
commerce. In the central and eastern Mediterranean, tin and
copper must have been in constant demand for the production
of bronze, and the Greeks seem to have developed the requisite
contacts to obtain regular supplies. Amber from the Baltic Sea

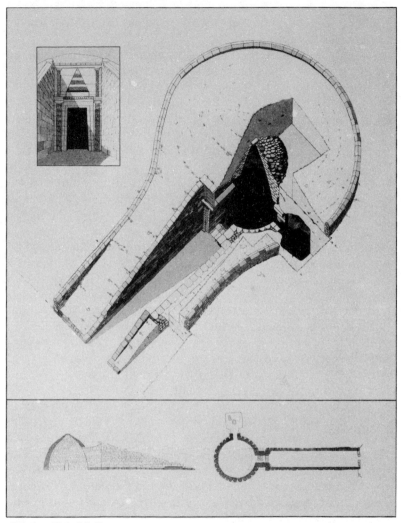

(⁶³ Equinox (Oxford) Ltd.)

Plan and section of the "Treasury of Atreus," the finest tholos *tomb excavated at Mycenae, Greece, 1400–1200* B.C.

also played a role in commerce, especially in intra-European contact and exchange. Amber was recovered in the shaft graves at Mycenae.

Regional diversity and intercultural contact characterize the elaborate commercial networks that operated in the Bronze Age Aegean and eastern Mediterranean world. The exact mechanisms of this trade (state or local domination? private control?) and the ethnic affiliation of the merchants and mariners involved (Mycenaeans? Syrians? Egyptians? Cypriots? itinerants?) are the focus of much current research. It is already clear, however, that the peoples of the Bronze Age Aegean were active and able participants in the international diplomacy and commercial exchange that characterized the eastern Mediterranean world in the latter half of the second millennium B.C.

Aegean record-keeping.   What light do the Linear B tablets shed on Minoan and Mycenaean society in the second millennium B.C.? It seems clear that writing served two main purposes in the Aegean world: to demonstrate ownership, such as on seals and pottery vessels, and to keep records. Contrary to expectations, there is no evidence that Linear B was ever employed to write literary or historical texts or even letters. Writing was confined to very few locales, and the number of people who could read and write was probably always small. Literacy, in other words, did not run deep in Aegean society.

Linear B documents consist principally of palace records: lists of commodities and goods owed to the palace or offered to the gods, all meticulously itemized, along with the names and titles of officials, administrators, clerks, and functionaries. The overall impression is one of an elaborate and carefully controlled royal bureaucracy in which all lines ran to the center. The staggering variety of skilled artisans and workers mentioned on the tablets indicates a remarkable division of labor and a high degree of specialization. There are references to woodcutters, bronze-smiths, shipbuilders, fullers, tailors, bakers, unguent-boilers, chairmakers, and even bath attendants.

Similar centralized economies based on a broad array of specialized occupations existed at the same time in western Asia, especially in other palace-oriented cultures such as those of the

Hittites and Babylonians and at Ebla, Mari, Ugarit, and Alalakh in Syria. Thus the structure of Minoan and Mycenaean society seems to have fit the context of the eastern Mediterranean world and to testify to the numerous crosscurrents that bound that world together.

Decline and fall: The post-Mycenaean aftermath

The elaborate palatial economy of Helladic Greece depended heavily on foreign commerce for luxury goods, metals, and perhaps even periodic shipments of grain and other foodstuffs. The vulnerability of this society is apparent in its overspecialized trading economy, top-heavy and highly centralized administration, overreliance on regular and efficient transport and communication (both internal and external), overpopulation, and perhaps loss of soil productivity through overexploitation. Balanced utilization of local resources might have cushioned the economy against whatever shocks—climatic change, loss of overseas contact, or other catastrophes—precipitated its decline.

In all likelihood, interlocking economic, political, and natural factors brought the thriving culture of Bronze Age Greece to an end. External problems in the eastern Mediterranean no doubt contributed to economic collapse. From the mid-thirteenth through the mid-twelfth centuries B.C., a series of destructions leveled most of the palatial centers and fortresses of mainland Greece. The burning of the palaces toppled regimes whose leaders and merchants may well have been among the Aegean corsairs and pirates so vividly described in Homer's epic poems, the *Iliad* and the *Odyssey*. These fallen princes and sailors were probably among the piratic Sea Peoples who spread out through the eastern Mediterranean.

Among the casualties was writing itself. The syllabary of the Linear B tablets survived only in a related script that continued in use on Cyprus until the late first millennium B.C. Literacy vanished from Greece for at least three centuries, to reappear in a form—the Greek alphabet—and for purposes quite different from those of Linear B. Bronze Age writing was the handmaiden of a palatial economy, the creation of a specialized class in the service of monopolistic rulers.

The fall of the palaces created so complete a break that the Bronze Age had little impact on later Greek society. Later written tradition ascribes at least partial blame for these disasters to some Greek-speaking migrants from the north: the Dorians. Most likely the Dorians descended upon an already destabilized Greece (see also the following section). A few other memories of the Bronze Age survived, most vividly in the epic traditions. Handed down orally throughout illiterate centuries, these epic traditions eventually crystallized in Homer's great poems. Bards celebrated the splendor of Mycenae and the exploits of Agamemnon (who led its army), Greece's greatest warriors Achilles and Ajax, and wily Odysseus, whose talents led Greece to its most renowned triumph, the conquest of Troy. Although the Greeks cannot be proved responsible, archaeological evidence at the site of Troy in northwestern Anatolia indicates a fiery destruction at the end of the Bronze Age.

The epic poems, largely products of the succeeding Dark Age, retain accurate images of a flourishing Bronze Age Helladic civilization. The passing of that heroic age ushered in a long, bleak era that would, nonetheless, prove decisive in the formation of the new culture of classical Greece. The element of continuity lay in the people themselves. Whatever befell the Bronze Age kingdoms, the bulk of the people—farmers and laborers—lived on.

The Sea Peoples: End of an Era

The stable and prosperous states and kingdoms of the late second millennium B.C. all collapsed, one after another, in the century between approximately 1250 and 1150 B.C.: Hittites, Egyptians, Assyrians, Kassites, the petty kingdoms of Syria-Palestine, even the citadels of Troy and Mycenaean Greece and the towns of Cyprus. Isolation and decline prevailed from the Aegean in the west to the Zagros in the east. Less severe in the Levant, the decline still resulted in struggles between Israelites, Philistines, and Aramaeans for control of the old Canaanite (Amorite) centers. In Syria-Palestine, Semitic-speaking, semi-nomadic Aramaeans set up numerous small states and subsequently expanded eastward to Babylonia, where many tribes settled in the rural stretches of the southern alluvium. Meanwhile internal dissent, possibly contributing to or in response to the overall decline, promoted the collapse of the Middle Assyrian and Kassite states.

Destructions and demographic displacements: Cause or effect?

Nobody would dispute that the archaeological and written records of Late Bronze Age Greece, Cyprus, Egypt, and the Levant depict a widespread, interlocking socioeconomic system in crisis. Disagreement among scholars persists, however, about the *cause(s)* of that crisis. Most interpretations would attribute this wide-ranging collapse to invasions or events external to the particular area in question. Although external troubles would certainly have complicated an already grave situation, it seems clear that an interplay of internal processes and external incidents must have precipitated the overall cultural and economic decline.

The events at the end of the Late Bronze Age are usually lumped together and attributed to the chaos resulting from the movements of the Sea Peoples throughout the Aegean, the Mediterranean, and the Near East. The actuality was not so simple: whatever their origin, whoever they were, the Sea Peoples were a symptom as well as a cause of widespread decline. The very term "Sea Peoples" is a misnomer, since they were not a united people and only some came by sea. But so they were called in the Egyptian records of Merneptah and Rameses III, and so they are still known today.

Two separate phenomena were intertwined in these upheavals: (1) the collapse of states and empires and (2) the movements of the Sea Peoples. While it is not clear what triggered this process, the disruption of states and the flurry of demographic movements during the twelfth century B.C. must be seen as interrelated phenomena, not as simple cause and effect. As people were displaced by disruptions, they became a source of further disruption, which displaced still more people, who added to the turmoil and helped to perpetuate the process.

The Hittite empire may have been ravaged by more northerly peoples—Kaska tribes from north-central Anatolia? migrants from the Balkan peninsula?—while Syria-Palestine was the target of

Ḫapiru as well as seminomadic Aramaeans and Israelites. Textual evidence from Hittite Anatolia, Ugarit, and Egypt suggests that famine ravaged parts of the eastern Mediterranean; perhaps climatic change played its part as well. The economic blockade that the Hittites erected against Assyria in eastern Mediterranean ports may have strained the delicate economic balance in that area.

Despite the virtual certainty of an overall collapse throughout the Aegean and eastern Mediterranean in the end, the specific features of collapse in each area were initiated by social, political, economic, or ideological factors unique to those areas. The ambiguity of the evidence, archaeological and textual, makes it difficult to distinguish between outcome and cause. Once decline in the eastern Mediterranean set in, however, it upset the economy of Mycenaean Greece, whose palace bureaucracy relied heavily on foreign commerce and trade. Many members of the Mycenaean nobility and their dependents fled eastward to Rhodes, Cyprus, Cilicia, and beyond. Greek farmers and laborers stayed behind to till the soil, as they had always done. Some Mycenaeans who ventured east may have joined with other economically depressed peoples from Anatolia, Syria, or Palestine. Had some of these dislocated peoples been former seamen, merchants, or traders in international commerce, they would readily have taken to piracy. In such a way, the motley group known as the Sea Peoples may have evolved.

Communications throughout the Aegean and eastern Mediterranean would have been seriously disrupted. On land and at sea, piracy and brigandage accelerated the breakdown of international trade. Neither was a new phenomenon. Throughout the Late Bronze Age, groups like the *Lukka* (Lycians of Anatolia?) and the *Aḫḫijawa* (Achaean Greeks?) had raided coastal cities. Other socially restive groups, such as the *Ḫapiru* and the *Garu* (mentioned in the Amarna Letters), plagued inland urban centers at the same time.

Studies of more recent eras in the Mediterranean suggest that piracy and economic health rise and wane together, not in alternation. Piracy, in other words, *depends* on flourishing commerce and shipping. The Sea Peoples' attacks on international power centers marked the end, not the beginning of an era of piracy. These marauders banded together in a desperate quest, no longer just for wealth but for sustenance. By devastating port cities up and down the eastern Mediterranean coast, they ultimately destroyed their own prey, and the disruptive process finally came to an end.

The Egyptians recorded the names of some of the raiders they defeated in the Nile delta at the gates of Egypt: *'ikws* (Achaean Greeks?), *trs* (Etruscans?), *lk* (Lycians), *srdn* (Sardinians), *skrs* (Sicilians?), *plst* (Philistines), *dkr* (Tjekker), *dyny* (Danunians), *wss* (?). Once repulsed, these groups must have scattered widely; the Philistines retreated up the coast to a land that eventually came to be known after them: Palestine. If the various invaders of Egypt are correctly identified above, the diaspora that followed their defeat touched many shores of the Mediterranean, from Sardinia and Sicily in the west to Cyprus and the Levantine coast in the east. Few of these homeless bands seem simply to have moved from their native country to a final destination. More likely they wandered for indeterminate periods of time.

What the Egyptian monuments record is the end of a chain reaction. Behind it lay a hopelessly confused series of demographic displacements and ethnic intermixings. The stable elements—farmers and minor craftsmen—remained, their horizons narrowed but their freedom regained. The age of internationalism was over. When historical sources shed light once again, in the first millennium B.C., the key to commerce was no longer international diplomacy and accord but imperialism and control.

NOTES

1. Translation by J. A. Wilson, *Ancient Near Eastern Texts Relating to the Old Testament*, 3d ed., ed. J. B. Pritchard, (Princeton, N.J.: Princeton University Press, 1969), pp. 445–46.
2. Ibid., pp. 19–20
3. Ibid., pp. 20–21

SUPPLEMENTARY READINGS

Adams, R. M. 1974. "Anthropological perspectives on ancient trade." *Current Anthropology* 15, pp. 239–58.

Brinkman, J. A. 1980. "Kassiten." *Reallexcion der Assyriologie* 5, pp. 464–73.

————. 1976. *A Political History of Post-Kassite Babylonia*. Analecta Orientalia 43. Rome: Pontifical Biblical Institute.

Bryce, T. R. 1985. "A Suggested Sequence of Historical Developments in Anatolia during the Assyrian Colony Period." *Altorientalische Forschungen* 12, pp. 259–68.

Dever, W. G. 1985. "Relations between Syria-Palestine and Egypt in the Hyksos period." In *Palestine in the Bronze and Iron Ages: Papers in Honour of Olga Tufnell*, ed. J. Tubb, pp. 69–87. Occasional Publication 11. London: Institute of Archaeology, University of London.

Edwards, I. E. S.; C. J. Gadd; N. G. L. Hammond; and E. Sollberger., eds. 1973. History of the Middle East and Aegean Region, c. 1800–1380 B.C. *The Cambridge Ancient History*, vol. 2, part 1. Cambridge: Cambridge University Press.

————. 1975. History of the Middle East and Aegean Region, c. 1380–1000 B.C. *The Cambridge Ancient History*, vol. 2, part 2. Cambridge: Cambridge University Press.

Gelb, I. J. 1961. "The Early History of the West Semitic Peoples." *Journal of Cuneiform Studies* 15, pp. 27–47.

Goedicke, H., ed. 1985. *Perspectives on the Battle of Kadesh*. Baltimore, Md.: Halgo.

Gurney, O. R. 1975. *The Hittites*. Harmondsworth, U.K.: Penguin Books.

Kemp, B. J. 1984, 1985. *Amarna Reports*. Vols. 1 & 2. Occasional Publications 1 & 2. London: Egypt Exploration Society.

————. 1977. "The City of El-Amarna as a Source for the Study of Urban Society in Ancient Egypt." *World Archaeology* 9, pp. 123–39.

Kitchen, K. A. 1983. *Pharaoh Triumphant: The Life and Times of Ramesses II, King of Egypt*. Leiden: Brill.

Laroche, M. E., ed 1978. *Actes de la 24e Rencontre Assyriologique Internationale, Paris 1977: Les Hurrites*. Revue Hittite et Asianique 36. Paris. (Several articles are in English.)

Larsen, M. T. 1976. *The Old Assyrian City-State and Its Colonies*. Mesopotamia: Copenhagen Studies in Assyriology 4. Copenhagen: Akademisk Forlag.

Liverani, M. 1979. "Three Amarna Essays." *Materials from the Ancient Near East* 1, pp. 73–106. Malibu, Calif.: Undena.

Macqueen, J. G. 1986. *The Hittites and Their Contemporaries in Asia Minor*. Ancient Peoples and Places 83 (2d revised edition). London: Thames and Hudson.

Morrison, M. A., and D. I. Owen, eds. 1981. *Studies on the Civilization and Culture of Nuzi and the Hurrians in Honor of E. R. Lacheman.* Vol. 1. Winona Lake, Ind.: American Schools of Oriental Research/ Eisenbrauns.

Oates, D. 1968. *Studies in the Ancient History of Northern Iraq.* London: Oxford University Press.

Oates, J. 1986. *Babylon.* Rev. ed. Ancient People and Places 94. London: Thames and Hudson.

O'Conner, D. 1983. "New Kingdom and Third Intermediate Period, 1552–664 B.C." In *Ancient Egypt: A Social History.* B. G. Trigger, B. J. Kemp, D. O'Conner, and A. B. Lloyd, pp. 183–278. Cambridge: Cambridge University Press.

Oppenheim, A. L. 1967. *Letters from Mesopotamia.* Chicago: University of Chicago Press.

Redford, D. B. 1984. *Akhenaten: The Heretic King.* Princeton, N.J.: Princeton University Press.

Ruffle, J. 1977. *The Egyptians.* Ithaca, N.Y.: Cornell University Press.

Sandars, N. K. 1978. *The Sea Peoples: Warriors of the Ancient Mediterranean.* London: Thames and Hudson.

Silver, M. 1985. *Economic Structures of the Ancient Near East.* Beckenham, Kent, U.K.: Croom Helm.

————. 1983. "Karl Polanyi and Markets in the Ancient Near East: The Challenge of the Evidence." *Journal of Economic History* 43, pp. 795–829.

Van Seters, J. 1966. *The Hyksos: A New Investigation.* New Haven, Conn.: Yale University Press.

Veenhof, K. R. 1972. *Aspects of Old Assyrian Trade and Its Terminology.* Studia et Documenta ad Iura Orientis Antiqui Pertinentia 10. Leiden: Brill.

Weinstein, J. 1981. "The Egyptian Empire in Palestine: A Reassessment." *Bulletin of American Schools of Oriental Research* 241, pp. 1–28.

Wertime, T., and J. D. Muhly, eds. 1981. *The Coming of the Age of Iron.* New Haven, Conn.: Yale University Press.

Wiseman, D. J., ed. 1973. *Peoples of Old Testament Times.* Oxford: Society for Old Testament Study.

Yoffee, N. 1977. *The Economic Role of the Crown in the Old Babylonian Period.* Bibliotheca Mesopotamica 5. Malibu, Calif.: Undena.

V

THE FIRST
MILLENNIUM B.C.:
THE PASSAGE TO
EMPIRE

Severe disruptions to interregional trade—especially the trade in metals—accompanied the end of the Bronze Age and stimulated a very significant technological development: the coming of the Age of Iron. Shortages in copper and tin, notably the latter, made it impossible to produce bronze on any but the most limited scale. Confronted with these shortages, the metalsmiths of the late second millennium B.C.—as well as the polities or individuals who supported them—had to find an alternative source of metal. Iron deposits existed in diverse regions of ancient western Asia and the Mediterranean. But heretofore, iron had been regarded only as a curiosity, an exotic metal used mainly in ceremonial weapons and jewelery. The socioeconomic collapse that occurred between about 1250 B.C. and 1150 B.C. altered this situation permanently.

The first steps toward the widespread use of iron as a utilitarian, "working" metal—as opposed to its ornamental usage—occurred already during the twelfth century B.C. in the eastern Mediterranean lands of Cyprus, Israel, and Jordan. On present evidence, the island of Cyprus seems to have been an innovator in the production and use of iron tools, implements, and weapons. This precocity probably stemmed partially from Cyprus's millennium-long tradition of economic dependence on metals (and thus a "cultural disposition" to metallurgical innovation) and partially from its rapid revitalization after the turmoil that accompanied the end of the Bronze Age. Once the techniques of **carburization** (the prolonged heating of an iron object in close contact with charcoal) and **quenching** (rapid cooling of carburized iron to strengthen it) had been learned, iron became a metal superior to bronze in hardness and durability. Carburized iron, in fact, is nothing less than steel. Because iron ore was widely available, the production and use of iron not only spread rapidly, it did so at far less cost than bronze ever had. The coming of the Age of Iron represents a high point in the technological processes that had begun hundreds of thousands of years earlier in the Paleolithic, when early hunters and gatherers first began to fashion tools of stone.

In political terms, the first millennium B.C. witnessed another dramatic change: the advent of full-blown imperialism. Ancient western Asia had already fostered supranational political systems built around a city-state or nation-state, notably the Akkadian state under Sargon and Naramsin, the Babylonian under Ḥammurapi, and the Egyptian New Kingdom. Genuine imperialism, however, presupposes expansion, domination, and the exploitation of one system by another, enforcing a constant shift of wealth from periphery to center.

The trend in Mesopotamian history toward complexity and direct, centralized rule culminated under the Assyrians in the first millennium B.C. The Assyrians were the first to build an imperialistic system with the necessary transportation and communication apparatus to collect taxes and tribute, move large armies, and deport masses of people over long distances. The Assyrian empire almost parasitically drained wealth from its periphery by imposing taxes and exacting tribute. Although Assyria's ultimate successor, the Persian empire, functioned (at least ideologically) as a commonwealth of its individual parts, tribute and goods poured into Persia's heartland from provinces near and far, just as they did in the era of Assyrian rule.

Imperialism's effect on the Near East's two most ancient states was dramatic and permanent: Babylonia briefly followed in Assyria's footsteps before becoming, like Egypt, one more victim of imperialism. In the west, the commercial networks of the Phoenician port cities achieved an unprecedented economic hegemony in the Mediterranean. Israel eventually succumbed to imperialistic expansion, but the monotheistic worship Israel engendered slowly shed political fetters and ultimately came to exercise a dominant worldwide influence.

MESOPOTAMIA: ASSYRIA'S MIGHT AND BABYLONIA'S PLIGHT

After the collapse of the Kassite and Middle Assyrian states, Babylonia sank into political and cultural oblivion. Intruding Semitic-speaking tribes, Aramaean and Chaldean, wreaked political havoc in ancient western Asia until about 1000 B.C., when they finally consolidated themselves into a number of settled tribal states in Syria and Babylonia. Chaldean monarchs (the Neo-Babylonian Dynasty) later consolidated the Babylonian south and ruled precariously between the downfall of the Assyrian and the rise of the Persian empire. Attempts to reestablish political and economic hegemony over the known world succeeded initially but soon faltered and—in the midst of a religious crisis— failed.

The Rise of Assyria: Power, Propaganda, and Prestige

Assyrian domination during the eleventh and tenth centuries B.C. was limited to the heartland of Assyria, a 100- by 50-mile area bordered by the cities of Assur, Arrapha, Arbela, and Nineveh. Assyria had become ineffective in trade and reduced in territory and was exhausted by centuries of struggle for independence. The open terrain of the Assyrian heartland, lacking the sort of geographic features that might be used for defensive purposes, exposed Assyria to seminomadic intrusion or hostile attack. Perhaps it was precisely because of these factors that Assyria could still muster well-trained warriors and boast an unbroken dynastic line. Appearances to the contrary, Assyria

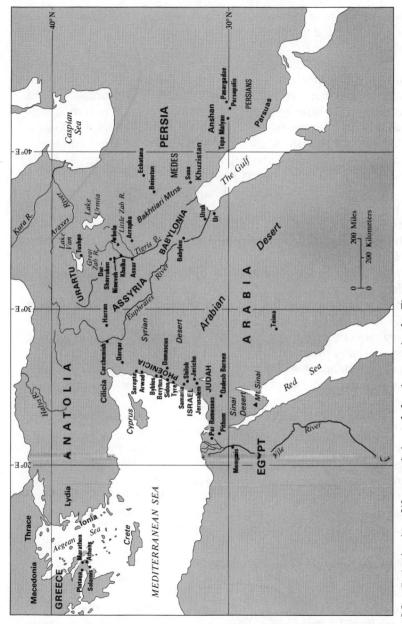

Map 5–1 Ancient Western Asia and the Aegean in the First Millennium B.C.: Sites and Geographic Features

remained a solid and well-balanced nation. That strength and balance soon led to unprecedented political power and territorial expansion.

By the ninth century B.C., more stable conditions (especially among the Aramaean tribes) opened the way to renewed Assyrian expansion westward. Adad-Nirari II (911–891 B.C.) led Assyria's first offensive military campaigns in over two centuries. He and his successors Assurnaṣirpal II (883–859 B.C.) and Shalmaneser III (858–824 B.C.) pushed Assyrian dominion westward as far as the Mediterranean, north and east into Anatolia and Iran, and south toward Babylonia.

Assyria's first independent capital city, Assur, on the right bank of the Tigris, lay open to the western steppe and thus to seminomadic intrusion. That vulnerability and other considerations prompted Assurnaṣirpal II to move the capital to *Khalku* (Nimrud), about 40 miles (64 kilometers) to the north. Protected by the Tigris to the west and the upper Zab River to the south, *Khalku*'s strategic position was enhanced with a massive rectangular wall punctuated by watchtowers. To protect the town still further and to provide water to the surrounding plain, a canal was dug from the River Zab to *Khalku*. A ziqqurat, several temples, and the royal palace stood on a low hill in the southwest corner. (Shalmaneser III later added the imperial arsenal, which housed barracks, workshops, storerooms, and another royal palace.)

Assurnaṣirpal celebrated the completion of the main palace in 879 B.C. with an enormous banquet attended by the entire population of the town—63,000 people, including 47,000 workers transported from conquered territories. The stela commemorating this event, which even includes the menu, records that the feast lasted ten days. Remnants of bronze and ivory tribute still survive from this first attempt to house the new imperial Assyrian state and its dynasty in splendor.

Continued Assyrian annexations and deportations (see also page 225) prompted the western states to form defensive coalitions during the reign of Shalmaneser III. One such coalition, encompassing the region from Cilicia in the north to Israel in the south, confronted Assyria's army at Qarqar on the Orontes River in 853 B.C. Assyrian losses and abandonment of the cam-

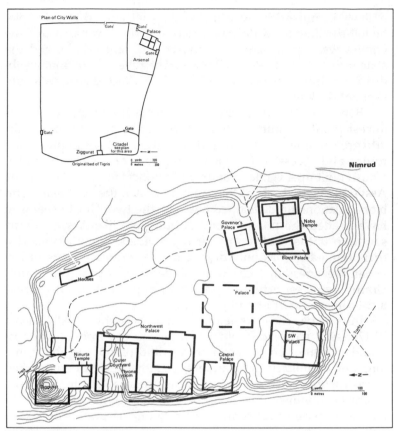

Plan of City Walls

Gate   Gate
Palace

Gate
Arsenal

Gate   Gate

Ziggurat   Citadel
see plan
for this area

Original bed of Tigris

Nimrud

Govenor's
Palace   Nabu
Temple

Burnt Palace

Houses

'Palace'

Northwest
Palace   SW
Palace

Ninurta
Temple   Central
Palace
Outer
Courtyard
Throne
room

Ziggurat

(The Robert Harding Picture Library)

Plan and layout of Assurnaṣirpal's Nimrud (Khalku).

paign cast serious doubt on Shalmaneser's claims of a great victory.

Shalmaneser's long reign ended in an uprising by the Assyrian rural nobility and free citizens against high court officials, the king, and the powerful provincial governors to whom the king had entrusted recently conquered lands. The rebels demanded a thoroughgoing reform of the Assyrian state: power accorded to high officials should be limited; land tenure and authority should be more evenly distributed; and the king himself should be an administrative and political leader, not just a military commander. Even if Shalmaneser agreed in principle, he felt the time for widespread reform had not yet arrived—the empire was still a fledgling—and accordingly he plunged the state into a four-year-long civil war. The rebels were finally subdued, but unrest persisted and certainly affected Assyria's subsequent decline.

Between 825 and 750 B.C. the Neo-Assyrian state sank to its lowest point. Simultaneously Assyria's northern neighbor Urartu grew in military stature and gained control of essential trade routes and access to the metal resources of eastern Anatolia. Urartu built up a viable military and political force much like the Assyrians were doing at the same time. A rather peculiar, symbiotic relationship developed between the two: Urartu seems to have needed the pressure of a strong state like Assyria on its southern border to keep its deeply divided, mountainous districts unified. It was only during the seventy-five years of Assyrian weakness that Urartu expanded west of the Euphrates. Urartu's greatest extent of power, during the seventh century B.C., coincided with that of Assyria.

In Assyria, meanwhile, revolution brought Tiglath-Pileser III (746–727 B.C.), probably a usurper, to the throne. The real founder of the Neo-Assyrian empire and one of the ablest in a long line of military commanders, Tiglath-Pileser III engineered a striking reversal in Assyria's decline. Internally he inaugurated extensive administrative reforms designed to humble the nobility and impose direct centralized rule on the provinces. Externally he defeated Urartu and established Assyrian control over the west. Tiglath-Pileser III also campaigned victoriously against Aramaeans in Babylonia and the Medes in northwest Iran. Systematic terrorization and mass deportation accompanied Tiglath-Pileser's campaign of expansion and reorganization.

The god Assur: A theology of holy war

In many respects, all wars in Mesopotamia since the time of the Early Dynastic Sumerians had been holy wars: city-state residents believed that their respective gods were pitted against each other and that divine favor followed victory. The Assyrians, however, claimed divine sanction for all their territorial ambitions. The god Assur issued a single command to his earthly representative, the Assyrian king: enlarge the frontiers of Assyria. The dynamism of the Assyrian empire was founded on a virtual theology of holy war, the dominant theme of which was the god Assur's claim of universal rule. As Assur was supreme in the Assyrian pantheon, so the Assyrian king held sway over all other earthly rulers. Assyrian inscriptions attribute to divine intervention the capitulation or death of enemy kings and the payment of tribute. If military campaigns may be considered as crusades, the resultant booty and tribute represented tokens of submission to the supreme deity of Assyria.

The concept of holy war was an extreme, pervasive, and successful component of Assyria's imperial ideology. The Assyrian people, the core of the empire's military machine, had to be convinced—as fully as the ruling class—that imperial expansion was desirable and justified; they were subjected to constant propaganda.

In order to splinter fidelity to local gods and traditions and at the same time to uproot provincial political sentiment, the Assyrians adopted the ruthless practice of mass deportation. Whole towns or districts were emptied of their inhabitants and replaced by other displaced peoples from distant reaches of the empire. Although these mass deportations at first seem politically motivated, eventually they may have addressed economic needs, to allay labor shortages on imperial agricultural estates. In the end, the deportation policy failed to integrate into the Assyrian scheme of things those who endured it. Rather it came to stand for just one more dose of the systematic terrorization—an early form of psychological warfare—that promoted a growing fear and contempt for the Assyrian military machine.

The key instrument of Assyria's remarkable expansion was its army, the most powerful and sophisticated the world had yet seen. Assyrian military engineers built bridges, tunnels, moats, and efficient siege weapons (towers and earthworks) capable of penetrating even the most strongly fortified towns. New and improved iron arms and weapons—swords, shields, and helmets; long lances and heavy bows—gave the Assyrian army an overwhelming military advantage. Although little is known of its actual size, organization, and tactical methods, the army boasted unparalleled infantry (slingers, bowmen, and lancers), cavalry, and chariotry. The army's leaders formed a rich, powerful class in Assyrian society. They shared with the king booty taken in battle and often received large estates of agricultural land as a reward for prowess, valor, and victory. State-of-the-art weapons, engineering skills, and a frightening reputation for macabre punishments made the Assyrian empire a mighty military polity.

Neo-Assyrian administration and economy

To ensure centralization of power and smooth operation of the empire, Tiglath-Pileser III sought to end the conflict between noble and royal interests. Men who enjoyed independent power bases by virtue of aristocratic lineage or large private landholdings had to be checked or eliminated. Tiglath-Pileser reorganized large provinces into much smaller units to prevent rebellion against their governors. His reforms also extended the scope of direct provincial rule and created new provinces beyond the former borders of the Assyrian state. Lands that could not be incorporated as provinces, usually for reasons of distance, were placed under supervision of an Assyrian overseer. The new governors were granted broad powers, but their authority was intentionally circumscribed by the small size of their domains and by constant government meddling in their affairs. Thus Tiglath-Pileser drastically increased the power of the king at the expense of the nobility. In place of an army conscripted annually from peasants and slaves, a permanent army levied from conquered territories was formed. A rapid and efficent system of communication developed between center and periphery.

The Assyrian empire was a broad-based, finely tuned military and administrative machine, whose smooth operation ensured a continual flow of taxes, tribute, and goods from periphery to center. Assyrian officials and tax collectors directed most economic activity. Although commerce must have thrived, few surviving Assyrian texts mention trade; as in the Old Assyrian period, commerce may well have been in the hands of private entrepreneurs.

The system of trade seems to have been one in which independent middlemen conducted commerce in the frontier zones at the edges of Assyrian-controlled area. Arab tribesmen dominated overland trade within the western desert. The Phoenicians, conversely, were specialists in maritime trade, and at least one Phoenician port city, Arwad, contained a *kārum*, or merchant community.

As in the Akkadian, Old Babylonian, and Kassite eras, private landholding existed under the Assyrian regime, but it was virtually the exclusive domain of high officers of state or members of the royal family. Private land was cultivated by freemen or slaves bound to the great estates. Tiglath-Pileser had successfully restructured the Assyrian empire into a highly centralized, economically efficient monarchy not unlike the Akkadian and Ur III states but with much larger territorial holdings. Admittedly ruthless, Tiglath-Pileser was, nonetheless, an able and intelligent ruler who took the necessary military and administrative steps to bring prosperity and power to the Assyrian state.

The Sargonids: Expansion and downfall

Under Sargon II (721–705 B.C.) and his successors Sennacherib, Esarhaddon, and Assurbanipal—known collectively as the Sargonids—Assyria systematically conquered and annexed one western Asiatic kingdom after another. The Sargonid empire came to embrace nearly the entire civilized world: Syria, Phoenicia, Israel, Urartu, and Babylonia all fell to Assyrian armies. Esarhaddon even successfully invaded Egypt, the first time any Near Eastern power controlled—even if peripherally—both the Tigris-Euphrates and Nile River valleys. Assurbanipal, however, promptly lost his hold over Egypt while suppressing a revolution in Babylonia. The Sargonids enlarged the Assyrian state to unprecedented size and raised Assyrian civilization to its zenith. As overlords of most of the Near East, they had access to the Mediterranean in the northwest and the Gulf in the south; they controlled river trade as well as overland passages and mountain passes.

Immediately upon ascending the throne, Sargon II built a new capital city *Dūr Sharrukēn* (fortress of Sargon), modern Khorsabad. This northernmost of Assyria's capitals commanded the main pass from the mountains to the north and probably served to fend off any threat of invasion by northern tribes.

Never an important center of communications, its sudden rise and decline evidently reflect only the anxieties and perhaps the whims of one king.

On Sargon's death, his son Sennacherib again moved the capital, this time to Nineveh. Located in the center of a rich agricultural plain between *Khalku* and *Dūr-Sharrukēn*, Nineveh had formerly served as a royal residence. Enlarged from a circumference of 2 to nearly 8 miles (approximately 3–13 kilometers), fortified, and embellished, Nineveh became the central city of the Assyrian empire at its apex. Sennacherib built a magnificent palace there, purportedly adorned with copper pillars resting on bronze lions, accompanied by protective monsters of silver, copper, and stone. Military scenes adorned huge limestone slabs lining the walls. A great park and garden, watered by a remarkable aqueduct, surrounded the palace compound.

Nineveh stood as a symbol of Assyrian power, prestige, and wealth—a capital city representative of the vast empire it controlled. Built with the returns of ruthless and bloody campaigns and decorated with scenes that proudly depicted Assyrian terror and might, Nineveh was the last and most splendid of Assyria's capitals. It housed the final three monarchs of the Assyrian empire: Sennacherib, Esarhaddon, and Assurbanipal.

The Sargonids lived prosperously, supplied with raw materials and luxury goods by their subjects, vassals, and allies. Had they not pursued such an oppressive foreign policy, they might have lived peacefully as well. Economic as well as political imperialists, the Assyrians took much and gave little in return. Subject states were probably made destitute and frequently rebelled; they were urged on by such antagonists as Egypt. Assyria's energy and resources were drained by repeated struggles to contain Babylonia and by far-flung campaigns against Egypt and the perennially rebellious regions of western Iran.

About 660 B.C., just when total victory (save for Egypt) seemed assured, the Assyrian empire began to crumble. Textual sources dry up, and a coherent account of the declining years is difficult to provide. Assurbanipal's death in 627 B.C. touched off a struggle for the throne, followed by a series of revolts and secessions. The Assyrians' policies of terror and deportation and the havoc their army wrought had earned them a legacy of hatred.

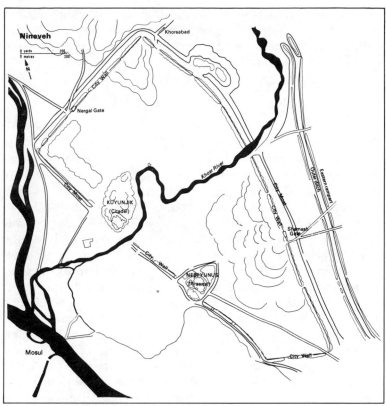

(The Robert Harding Picture Library)
Area plan of Sennacherib's Nineveh.

Within a decade, Chaldean-controlled Babylonia was on the offensive against Assyria. Iran had also been a constant trouble spot for the Assyrian dynasts, and now the Indo-European–speaking Median tribes of western Iran joined with the Babylonians to invade Assyria. In 612 B.C., joint Babylonian and Median forces devastated Nineveh. Sporadic resistance continued for a few years, but the Assyrian empire vanished quickly, its cities sacked and pillaged, its people reduced to slavery. The last remnants of the Assyrian state were stamped out in battles at Harran on the Balikh River in 609 B.C. and at Carchemish on the Euphrates in 605 B.C. The Medes temporarily withdrew behind the Zagros curtain and turned their attention to Armenia and the rest of Asia Minor, while the Neo-Babylonian kings inherited the Assyrian empire. Within twenty years of Assurbanipal's death, the largest and most powerful empire the world had yet known was no more.

The Neo-Babylonian (Chaldean) Dynasty: Potentates and Priests

The Neo-Babylonian dynasty (626–539 B.C.), the eleventh and last dynasty centered on the old capital city of Babylon, bequeathed to posterity an abundance of cuneiform sources: royal inscriptions, chronicles, poetic accounts, and numerous contracts and administrative documents. The Neo-Babylonian period witnessed a major religious revival. Temples again became significant economic and social institutions, and architectural efforts took precedence over military adventures. Most kings invested considerable time, energy, and wealth in restoring sanctuaries and constructing or elaborating defensive works.

The Neo-Babylonian rulers sought to emulate and build upon the inheritance of their Old Babylonian predecessors. Nebuchadrezzar, most powerful of these dynasts, magnificently restored the capital city of Babylon and attempted, with some success, to pay homage to Babylonian culture and politics of Hammurapi's time. Certain traditional aspects of Babylonian law, literature, and government prevailed throughout much of the Neo-Babylonian era. Even in religious practice, the customary adoration of Marduk predominated until the reign of Nabonidus, last of the Neo-Babylonian rulers. In addition to Marduk's traditional worship, Nabonidus sponsored an astral religion—focused on the moon-god Sin—in which the gods were exalted as omnipotent, unapproachable beings. This stark departure from past traditions brought on vehement protests from Marduk's priesthood. The Chaldean affinity for astronomy may well be related to astral worship and the attempt to calculate the divine will that resided in and propelled the heavenly bodies. Astronomy too was part and parcel of the Old Babylonian past; it is one of ancient Babylonia's most enduring cultural legacies.

Assyria's Chaldean successors: Political history

Even as they imposed themselves on the rest of western Asia, the Assyrians upheld the worship of Babylonian gods and recognized the political rights of Babylonian citizens. Assyria always accorded special status to Babylonian culture. At the same time, they pursued an ongoing effort to contain the troublesome Aramaeans and Chaldeans who had settled in the southernmost alluvium. (The Chaldean and Aramaean tribal groups must have been related somehow, although Babylonian sources make a clear distinction between them.) Assyria's seventy-five–year decline allowed for the intruding Chaldean tribes in the south to eclipse the native rulers. Some Chaldeans clung to seminomadic traditions; others (following old, established patterns) became city dwellers, who possessed large herds of cattle and horses and perhaps controlled the southern trade routes that bore exotic products from the Gulf. They stubbornly maintained tribal practices, even in the administration of the later Neo-Babylonian dynasty.

Between north and south, by the seventh century B.C., an odd and uneasy relationship developed in which Babylonian cultural dominance offset Assyrian military supremacy. Yet rebellion led to Assyrian intervention, and much of Babylonia fell under Assyrian sway until the Chaldean rulers reclaimed the south in 626 B.C. Assyria's fate was sealed in 614 B.C., when the Chaldean Nabopolassar (625–605 B.C.), founder of the Neo-Babylonian dynasty, concluded a treaty with the new Median power in western Iran. Two years later, the resulting coalition devastated Nineveh. The Chaldean kings of Babylonia and the Median kings of Iran had bided their time well: when the opportunity arose, they suddenly and thoroughly destroyed Assyria and became the new masters of ancient western Asia.

By 607 B.C., Nabopolassar had made his son Nebuchadrezzar co-regent, to act for him in both political and military capacities. Nebuchadrezzar engineered the final victory over Assyria at Carchemish in 605 B.C., but his mopping-up campaign was cut short by his father's death in Babylon. Hastening back to the capital,

Nebuchadrezzar claimed the throne. Thus began his illustrious forty-three–year reign (604–562 B.C.).

Nebuchadrezzar waged a long series of campaigns in Syria, evidently to enforce the collection of taxes and tribute and to make insurgent cities toe the line. Twice he besieged Jerusalem when the state of Judah revolted. After the second revolt, Nebuchadrezzar looted Jerusalem, leveled its walls, and burned the palace and temple of Solomon to the ground. Judah was incorporated into a Babylonian province, and the remaining population followed earlier deportees into captivity in Babylonia. (On this, the "Babylonia Captivity" of the Jews described in the Old Testament, see pages 252–54.)

Nebuchadrezzar's death in 562 B.C. was followed by the brief reigns of three insignificant rulers, the last of whom was overthrown after only three months. This rebellion brought to the throne Nabonidus (556–529 B.C.), the last and most enigmatic of the Neo-Babylonian dynasts. Although some aspects of internal politics remained unchanged (Nabonidus made his son Belshazzar coregent, for example), his administrative and religious reforms provoked sharp resentment.

Cuneiform documents from the Neo-Babylonian period indicate that temple authorities enjoyed a great deal of autonomy and owned considerable agricultural land. The palace still had certain privileges in connection with the temple, such as a share in some of its revenues, but its influence was waning. In an attempt to shore up royal prerogatives, Nabonidus appointed royal officers and even installed one of his henchmen as chief administrator of the great landowning temple of Eanna at Uruk. This official exercised control over all of the temple's estates, workers, land use, canal rights, transportation, use and redistribution of agricultural products, and record-keeping. Thus the palace came to control a greater share of the temple revenues.

Despite the agricultural wealth of its temples, the Neo-Babylonian empire suffered severe economic strains. The ambitious military and building campaigns of Nabopolassar and Nebuchadrezzar had taken their toll, and important trade routes to the north and northeast of Babylonia fell under Median control. Economic texts bear witness to severe inflation—prices rose by 50 percent between 560 and 550 B.C.; to make matters worse, famine and plague dogged Babylonia. Nabonidus attributed the famine to the impiety of the Babylonian people and thus placed the issue in a religious framework. Economic disaster, coupled with unpopular religious and administrative reforms, probably provoked the severe crisis that broke out in Nabonidus's seventh year, 549 B.C.

Leaving Belshazzar in charge in Babylon, Nabonidus led his troops through Syria and Lebanon to the Arabian plateau, where he settled at the oasis-and-market city of Teima. Economic problems surely precipitated Nabonidus's departure, but the religious controversy may have been more critical. Whatever the purpose of his stay in Arabia, Nabonidus bore the brunt of hostile propaganda spread by the priesthood of Marduk.

Arabia was of considerable economic value to Babylonia: from Damascus in the north, Egypt in the west, Sheba in the south, and the Gulf in the east, trade routes converged at Teima, a natural entrepôt for Arabian trade. By controlling the commercial traffic that passed through Teima, Nabonidus might have been able to offer some relief from the famine that raged in Babylonia. Such a motivation, however, cannot be verified from the surviving documentary evidence. And even if true, the move to Teima was never understood in such terms by the Babylonian populace.

Nebuchadrezzar's Babylon: Architectural wonder of antiquity

Although Nebuchadrezzar's military campaigns in Palestine were immortalized in the Bible, and his abilities as statesman were publicly remembered by later generations of Babylonians, his stature as ambitious builder also deserves special notice. His unrivaled building and restoration activities draped in imperial splendor the old capital of Babylon, last stronghold of the ancient Semitic world.

The stately and celebrated capital described by the Greek historian Herodotus was chiefly the work of Nebuchadrezzar and his architects. Excavations by a German archaeological team between 1899 and 1917 provide most of our information about ancient Babylon; since 1958, Iraqi archaeologists have conducted further investigations and begun restorations. The ruins of imperial Babylon extend over about 2,000 acres (800 hectares). The city proper, roughly square in plan, covers about 500 acres (200 hectares) and is bisected by the Euphrates.

Nabopolassar and Nebuchadrezzar erected thick inner and outer walls protected by moats and reinforced by towers to strengthen the defenses of Babylon. The space between these walls was filled with rubble and may have served as a roadway, which Herodotus described as wide enough for a four-horse chariot to turn around in; it would also have allowed for the rapid deployment of troops from one part of the city to another.

The elaborately defended inner city's eight gates controlled access to the royal palace, Marduk's temple complex, other religious structures, and private houses. The most elaborate and best-preserved gate was dedicated to Ishtar; its 36-foot–high (11 meters) walls still stand. The front wall and passageway were splendidly ornamented with deep blue-glazed bricks featuring molded figures of bulls and dragons executed in yellow and white. The Processional Way leading to the Ishtar Gate had high defensive walls whose blue-enameled bricks bore molded lions in white, red, and yellow.

Paved with large limestone slabs bordered by other slabs of white-veined red breccia, the Processional Way flanked Nebuchadrezzar's Southern Palace. This resplendent structure boasted five courtyards surrounded by offices, royal apartments, and reception rooms. In the northeast corner of the palace, the excavators discovered an underground crypt containing numerous vaulted rooms. A three-shafted well in one of the cellars seems to have been some sort of hydraulic lifting system; this unusual installation may well have served as the understructure and water source of the Hanging Gardens of Babylon. (One recent hypothesis, however, suggests that the gardens were located on the "Western Outwork" between the Southern Palace and the Euphrates.)

About ⁶⁄₁₀ mile (1 kilometer) farther south, the Processional Way approached the main temple complex of ancient Babylon, the dwelling place of Marduk. In the middle of a vast open space surrounded by a buttressed wall stood the ziqqurat—the famed Tower of Babel; only its foundations, about 300 feet square, still survive. South of the ziqqurat, on the other side of the Proces-

Ishtar Gate, Babylon: Reconstruction in the Pergamon Museum, (East) Berlin.

Ishtar Gate, Babylon: Western Wall of "Gate Room" that leads through inner part of town wall.

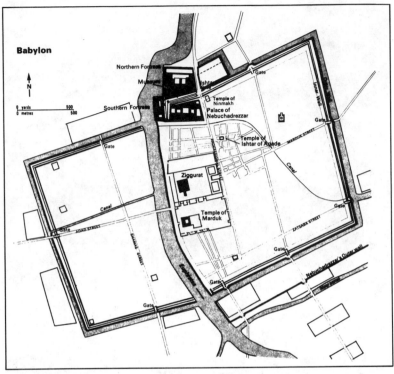

(The Robert Harding Picture Library)

Reconstructed layout of Nebuchadrezzar's Babylon during the Neo-Babylonian period, about 500 B.C.

sional Way, which made a right-angle turn west at this point, lay the Esagila, Marduk's main temple. All previous kings of Babylon had elaborated this temple, which Nebuchadrezzar rebuilt and adorned anew. Even Herodotus described the splendor of what he called the "Lower Temple," with its golden statue of Marduk.

Neo-Babylonian culture: Astronomy and religion

The reign of the best-known early Chaldean king Nabonassar (747–734 B.C.) is noted for its precise recording of historical events and accurate astronomical observations. The Greeks later recognized Nabonassar's era as pivotal in the development of science, and the Greek word *Chaldean* came to mean astronomer. The astronomical omen tablet series *MUL.APIN*, dating from about 700 B.C. but based on earlier material, classified all known fixed stars into three parallel "paths." Thus it records the movements of the moon and the planets.

This series and other early recorded efforts of Babylonian astronomy were somewhat superficial. But after about 700 B.C., systematic observation of the sky generated data that were ultimately calculated accurately enough to predict solstices, equinoxes, eclipses, and other planetary phenomena. The *MUL.APIN* text also made reference to a zodiacal belt within which lay fifteen zodiacal constellations, or signs of the zodiac. The names of some of these constellations remain in use today: the Bull, the Twins, the Lion, the Scorpion, and the Archer.

Chaldean astronomers also sorted out an elaborate system of keeping time. A mathematical system (sexagesimal) based on the number 60 led ultimately to the division of hours and minutes still in use today. Since each Babylonian month began with the sighting of the new crescent moon, it was essential to be able to predict accurately the date of the new moon. The astronomers of the third and second centuries B.C. therefore composed *ephemerides,* which calculated and predicted new moons, eclipses, and other planetary and lunar movements. Accompanying documents called "procedure texts" outlined the rules for such calculations. The methods Babylonian astronomers developed to calculate the movements of the moon are ranked by modern scholars as among the highest achievements of ancient science.

Religion almost certainly supplied the motivating force behind Babylonian astronomy. The heavens were mapped and ephemerides composed in order to elicit divine intentions. By the reign of Nabonidus, worship focused on astral deities, especially the moon-god Sin, the sun-god Shamash, and the Venus-star Ishtar. Nabonidus's mother had been a priestess in the temple of Sin in Harran, the Assyrian center of moon worship; perhaps this lay behind Nabonidus's peculiar reverence for the moon-god. Nabonidus continued to pay respect to Babylon's chief god Marduk, but his unorthodoxy was extremely unpopular with Marduk's conservative priesthood: their comfortable economic situation was in jeopardy. In the eyes of the priesthood, Nabonidus had become a religious fanatic who blasphemed Marduk and worshiped a foreign deity.

The astral religion Nabonidus propagated dehumanized the gods and made them more inaccessible to the Babylonian populace; only scientific astronomers could determine divine intention. Despair of knowing the divine plan may have encouraged submission to it and promoted an attitude of piety heretofore unknown in Mesopotamian religion. Anonymous hymns as well as royal prayers address these astral deities humbly and penitentially. Still, however, Chaldean prayers invoke the gods to grant long life, abundant offspring, and a comfortable living. Stirrings of a spiritual consciousness may have been present, but they had little effect on morality and material pursuits.

The fall of Babylon

The priesthood of Marduk rigidly determined to restore the material wealth of its temples; its blind hatred was aimed maliciously and effectively at Nabonidus. During the latter's ten-year absence at Teima, political developments in Iran brought Cyrus the Great to the Persian throne and thus to the forefront of world politics. Cyrus proceeded to conquer all of Asia Minor, which meant that the Babylonian kingdom was surrounded from the Mediterranean Sea to the Gulf. According to the Greek historian Xenophon, Cyrus had tried to conclude a treaty with the Arabs, perhaps intending to attack Babylonia from the west. Nabonidus's move to Teima would certainly have thwarted such a plan.

Persian propaganda accompanied Cyrus's military campaigns in Babylonia. The priests of Marduk in effect served, as a Persian "fifth column" within Babylon: entrenched in this veritable holy city, they induced its population to extend a welcome hand to the Persian conquerors. Cyrus's growing reputation for tolerance, together with well-aimed monetary persuasion, secured the unopposed entry of his army into Babylon in 539 B.C. Nabonidus was captured in retreat and met an unknown fate, exile or death. Cyrus appointed a Persian governor but left Babylon's religious institutions and civil administration intact. Thus the Babylonians, like the Assyrians before them, ceased to exist as a great power. Semitic dominance—rule by Akkadians, Amorites, Babylonians, Assyrians, Chaldeans, and Aramaeans—had come to an end. The victorious entry of the Indo-European Persians into Babylon represents a decisive turn in the course of ancient Near Eastern history: the center had fallen, the periphery emerged triumphant.

EGYPT: VICTIM OF IMPERIALISM

After the demise of the New Kingdom, Egypt gave up any pretense of foreign dominion. The small local states of Syria and Palestine became independent, and Assyria's plan for imperial expansion began to unfold. The era of Egyptian military campaigns in ancient western Asia was over. Political interference, intrigue, and armed raids by Egypt's neighbors became commonplace, and the pharaohs began to rely heavily on foreign mercenaries. Gradually the mighty kingdom that had ruled the East became no more than a pawn in the imperial strategies of Assyria, Babylonia, Persia, and Greece.

How had mighty Egypt fallen so low? The causes are manifold: internal political and religious upheavals, economic chaos, external interference. Pharaonic power declined as powerful priesthoods asserted themselves in the political arena; the Egyptian state no longer had a clear, centralized focus. The movements of the Sea Peoples, although checked at Egypt's gates, were emblematic of the total disruption of international commerce that had fattened the coffers of all eastern Mediterranean lands, including Egypt. This lucrative economic outlet was permanently blocked. And once the Sea Peoples had pierced—however ineffectively—the armor that had long shielded Egypt from foreign meddling, a devastating and unending penetration of Libyans, Ethiopians, Assyrians, Persians, and Greeks permanently subjected Egypt to the vagaries and consequences of imperial expansion.

The Tale of Wen-Amon: Egypt in Decline

The story of Wen-Amon vividly illustrates the decline of Egyptian prestige. Although scholars still dispute the date of its composition, the events it recounts indisputably took place during the Twentieth Dynasty (in the eleventh century B.C.). Wen-Amon, an official of the temple of Amon-Re at Thebes, sailed to Byblos in Phoenicia to buy cedar for a ceremonial boat. Unescorted and lacking sufficient funds, Wen-Amon had to arrange his own transportation. To make matters worse, the crew of his ship made off with his gold and silver, leaving him penniless and without identification. Such straitened circumstances were symptomatic of decline: under the imperial system of New Kingdom Egypt, a wealthy Wen-Amon would have traveled in splendor to his Phoenician destination.

Once in Byblos, Wen-Amon's lack of funds and credentials precluded even a visit with the prince of Byblos. When Wen-Amon finally won an audience, the prince insulted him and refused to release any cedar without immediate payment. This ultimatum for cash-on-delivery underscores yet again Egypt's plight: economic credibility had evaporated along with political stability. The Byblian ruler praised Amon as the universal god and acknowledged the Phoenician debt to Egyptian civilization but continued to berate and demean the destitute Wen-Amon. Defending himself against these rebukes, Wen-Amon finally convinced the ruler of Byblos to send his secretary to Egypt for prepayment; the secretary soon returned with a shipload of Egyptian goods. Shortly thereafter, Wen-Amon had to flee hostile Palestinian ships newly arrived at Byblos. The papyrus breaks off at the point of Wen-Amon's arrival in Cyprus: the hapless Wen-Amon's destiny still hangs in the balance.

This tale is a candid acknowledgement of Egypt's lost glory, a loss sharpened by the fact that such humiliation could occur in Byblos. Ever since Middle Kingdom times, Egyptians had been honored at Byblos; the father of the prince who insulted Wen-Amon had been eager to do business with representatives of Amon-Re. The rudeness of the prince of Byblos anticipates the words of Sennacherib's Assyrian commander, who was to taunt Jerusalem's defenders around three centuries later:

> "We know you trust on the staff of that broken reed, Egypt, which pricks and pierces the hand of the man who leans on it. That is what Pharaoh, king of Egypt, is like to all who rely on him" (2 Kings 18:21).

The unity and glory of the land of the Nile were shattered. Egypt became a dependency of imperial powers intent on ruling the world.

Twenty-first through Thirty-first Dynasties: Egypt in Vassalage

Imperialism as a worldview had long since faded from Egyptian politics. Political patterns during the first millennium B.C. show repeated alternation of native Egyptian and foreign rule: the Twenty-first and the Twenty-third Dynasties were Egyptian in origin, the Twenty-second and the Twenty-fourth Libyan, and the Twenty-fifth Ethiopian. But by the seventh century B.C., encroachment by efficient, imperially minded Assyrian forces severely limited Egyptian response. A temporary respite during the Twenty-sixth Dynasty (sixth century B.C.) enabled the Egyptians once again to benefit from Mediterranean commerce.

During the reign of the Twenty-sixth Dynasty pharaoh Necho II (610–595 B.C.), the Egyptian army marched victoriously through Palestine and Syria in support of the Assyrians, who meanwhile fought a losing battle against the Babylonians and Medes. The Egyptians also suffered in this Assyrian defeat and returned home with political visions narrowed. Necho thereafter concentrated on developing Egyptian commerce. During this time, colonies of Greek and Ionian (east Greek) merchants settled in the **Delta**, and Ionian mercenaries composed pharaoh's bodyguard. Necho's sponsorship of a Phoenician voyage to circumnavigate Africa was probably carried out successfully, and a canal linking the Nile with the Red Sea was begun but not completed.

Toward the end of the sixth century B.C., the Persian ruler Cambyses II (son and successor of Cyrus the Great) entered Egypt, proclaimed himself pharaoh, and founded the Twenty-seventh Dynasty (525–404 B.C.). Commercial contacts were severed. Aside from a brief period of independence, Egypt became a province in the vast Persian empire. Some Persian rulers took an active interest in Egyptian civilization. Darius I, for example, built temples, codified Egytian law, and ordered completion of the commercially important canal between the Nile and the Red Sea begun by Necho II. Others, like Xerxes, never visited Egypt and took no interest in building or maintaining temples there.

Egypt's final interlude of freedom (404–343 B.C.) followed revolts in the Delta against the Persians by "native" Libyan princes of the Twenty-eighth through the Thirtieth Dynasties. In 343 B.C., the Persians under Artaxerxes III briefly regained control of Egypt. The Persian Thirty-first Dynasty (343–332 B.C.), the last dynasty recorded by Manetho, brought disaster to Egypt. Temple treasuries were looted, sacred books destroyed, and city walls razed in a determined effort to discourage rebellion in Egypt. But the end of Persian rule was already in sight.

In 332 B.C., Alexander the Great of Macedon marched into Egypt. Persian sway passed unopposed to the Greeks under Alexander and, finally, to his successors. The Persian governor relinquished his authority without a struggle, and Alexander was proclaimed pharaoh at Memphis. Ancient Egypt was a changed land. By 321 B.C., Egypt had become the exclusive domain of Alexander's general Ptolemy, whose successors (including Cleopatra) ruled Egypt until it became part of the Roman empire.

The native history of ancient Egypt effectively ends at this point, as first Greek and then Roman administration regulated the land. No doubt Egyptian farmers continued to follow their rustic ways, speak the Egyptian language, and worship ancient Egyptian gods. Greek and Latin-speaking "pharaohs" adopted a suitably native pose to forestall dissent among peasants as well as priesthoods, but the patterns of intervention that riddled Egyptian politics throughout the first millennium B.C. now set the standard: the voice of ancient Egypt was silenced forever by the peal of imperialism.

SYRIA–PALESTINE: MERCHANTS AND MONOTHEISTS

Throughout antiquity, the **Levant** repeatedly fell prey to the political and military ambitions of more powerful neighboring lands. Syria-Palestine represented an economic and political prize. Every northern and eastern power that arose in the ancient Near East tried to penetrate and occupy Syria. Egypt's imperial designs left their mark on much of the Levant throughout the second millennium B.C. But only in the first millennium B.C. did the empires of Assyria and Babylonia and, later, Persia succeed in extending their sway as far south as Palestine.

Syria-Palestine's pivotal geographic location made turbulent change almost routine in all spheres of life: economic, political, demographic, and spiritual. Recurrent international hostilities created an atmosphere of political and economic insecurity in the Levant, which in turn led to repeated disputes among local states. In Phoenicia, this situation ultimately resulted in the establishment of a number of wealthy, independent ports of trade that supplied the inland empires and the entire Mediterranean trading network with raw materials and luxury manufactured products.

In Israel, an active participant in this vast commercial system during the reigns of David and Solomon, very different developments took place. Earlier the hardships of enslavement, escape from Egypt, and conquest and settlement of a new land had engendered the founding of a new nation and the worship of a single deity. While the Phoenicians established economic hegemony in the Mediterranean, the Hebrews laid the foundations of a religious dominion that crystallized in quite another form 1,500 years later when the emperors of Rome adopted Christianity and forcibly spread the worship of a single god.

The Phoenicians: Purveyors of the Mediterranean

The Phoenicians' homeland was a long, narrow strip of land along the Levantine coast, with fixed western and eastern borders (the Mediterranean Sea and the Lebanon Mountains) and with flexible northern and southern limits. Phoenicia's maximum north-south extension was about 500 miles (800 kilometers)—that is, the entire eastern Mediterranean seaboard. Its minimum length was less than 200 miles (320 kilometers), centered roughly on Byblos, and approximated modern Lebanon in size.

The history of Phoenicia is the history of its coastal towns: Arwad, Byblos, Berytus (Beirut), Sarepta, Sidon, and Tyre. Some of the inland region was fertile, but much of it was too mountainous to be more than self-supporting agriculturally. The Phoenicians showed very casual interest in their hinterland: land in itself did not necessarily contribute to successful commercial enterprise or production for exchange, the two mainstays of a trading strategy based on the sea.

Phoenicia's native raw materials included two types of sea snail from which purple dye was extracted, pine and cedar hardwoods, fish, wine, honey, and olives. The availability of hardwood was the essential requirement for shipbuilding and thus for seafaring. Phoenician sailing skills are demonstrated by such feats as the first circumnavigation of Africa about 600 B.C. (according to Herodotos, at the command of pharaoh Necho II); the first known commercial sea voyage to the British isles, under the Carthaginian admiral Himilco, in search of tin, about 450 B.C.; and Hanno's journey from Carthage down the west coast of Africa about 450 B.C.

Phoenicia was never a united geopolitical entity. In fact, the very concept "Phoenicia," as employed by the Greeks and Romans and by modern scholars, reflects neither the Phoenicians' own view of their land nor that of the Israelites, who knew them as Sidonians, Gublites (from Byblos), and Tyrians. The Greek term *Phoenician* refers, culturally and linguistically, to the Canaanite (Amorite) branch of the West Semites. The exact origin and meaning of the term are still argued, but most proposed etymologies—Greek, Hurrian, Hebrew, and Egyptian—derive from the reddish-purple dye for which the Phoenicians were famed in antiquity.

The Phoenician cities' orientation toward the sea is readily apparent in their political history. Strategically situated on an important communication route between powerful inland states, the cities of Phoenicia played a decisive role in transmitting goods from one area to another and enriched themselves in the process. By the end of the second millennium B.C., the Levantine ports of trade were focusing their efforts on transforming raw materials into higher-value products for exchange and on developing the skills and institutions necessary to maintain their growing commercial activities.

The rise of Assyria during the first half of the first millennium B.C. may have facilitated, if not accelerated, traditional commercial relations and localized specialization while creating new opportunities and new trade networks. The tribute imposed by the Assyrians may even have encouraged trade. Phoenician cities increasingly and narrowly devoted their attention to the production and distribution of luxury goods: fine dyed linen, tapestries, glass and faience, metalwork and ivorywork, wines, spices, and incense. The commodities available at Phoenician ports became so specialized that the Assyrians granted these cities commercial advantages and military protection. In order to force the redistribution of trade to Assyria, Assyrian foreign policy usually aimed at control over its trading partners; yet the Phoenicians remained virtually autonomous.

After Tiglath-Pileser III incorporated the Syro-Palestinian states into the Assyrian empire late in the eighth century B.C., the Phoenicians' former role as suppliers of manufactured goods to ruling elites gave way to the much more vital task of supplying raw materials. Subsequent high demand for such goods throughout the regional trading system may have prompted Phoenician expansion around the Mediterranean—to Cyprus, Italy, Sardinia, Corsica, Malta, parts of southern France and Spain, the Balearic islands, and North Africa. To characterize the Phoenicians as mere middlemen is inadequate and misleading. They were also excellent craftsmen and manufacturers, and their role as intermediaries in the westward transmission of the alphabet and of Hurro-Hittite literature was central (see pages 196–98). Phoenician seamanship, furthermore, opened up the Mediterranean to shipping and commerce on an unprecedented scale.

Phoenician commercial ventures in the Mediterranean may well have paved the way for the Greeks. Eventually Phoenician and Greek trading enterprises overlapped, at least in the central Mediterranean. The Phoenicians had set out to create support stations for their trade routes; in the end, they established colonies across North Africa and in the western Mediterranean (i.e., Carthage). The Greeks, by contrast, began as frank colonizers and sought new homes abroad to alleviate overpopulation and to escape political conflict at home.

The Hebrews: From Tent to Temple

From seminomadic tribes to national state, from the Ark of the Covenant to Solomon's temple, from the Creation of the universe to the development of monotheism, the Bible is indisputably the fullest account of Hebrew history. It records the Hebrews' traditional rendition of their own history as the unfolding of the relationship between Yahweh, god of Israel, and his Chosen People. The authors of the Bible wove the Hebrews' historical experience into a literary work celebrating their nation and its faith.

The Hebrew Bible has three main parts: (1) the Torah, or Law of Moses, as it is articulated in the Pentateuch (the first five books of the Bible); (2) the Prophets, consisting of the "historical" books of the earlier prophets (Joshua, Judges, Kings, and Chronicles) and the books of the later prophets (Isaiah, Jeremiah, Ezekiel, and the twelve "minor prophets"); and (3) the Writings, or Scriptures, some composed over generations (Psalms, Proverbs) and others of later origin (the books of Job and Ecclesiastes, the Song of Songs).

The origins of the Old Testament are manifold and complex. Although much biblical poetry and philosophy is unique, the Bible's debt to neighboring peoples is unquestionable: its myths are based on Mesopotamian originals (for example, the Flood story), its proverbs and psalms compiled from Egyptian collections, and its poetry adapted from Ugaritic forerunners. The authors of the Old Testament grafted earlier writings on cosmology, history, and law onto the prophetic writings, psalms, proverbs, and other "wisdom literature" to produce a remarkable work of literature and ethics.

Although very little of the Bible can be considered primary historical evidence (contemporary with the events it describes), its testimony is often the only source available. Just as historians use the epic of Gilgamesh to help reconstruct events in the Sumerian Early Dynastic period, and the propagandistic pseudoautobiography of Sinuhe to understand developments in Middle Kingdom Egypt, the Bible—subjected to the same rigorous standards—helps to elucidate the history of the Israelite nation. The chief problem the Bible poses for the modern historian arises from its religious focus: secular events are often skimped and religious occurrences magnified. Historians must also keep in mind that the Bible was compiled several generations after the episodes it recounts and drew on a variety of oral traditions and earlier literary sources.

The Israelites attached great importance to the deeply rooted belief that their various tribes shared a common ancestry; this belief justified the founding of a nation. Consequently the biblical tradition assumed its final form only when disparate traditions had been thoroughly absorbed, interwoven, and infused with new meaning. Though the Bible is, above all, a religious and moral work, its prescriptions, prophecies, and teachings were woven into an historical narrative. Hebrew religion was thus firmly rooted in history rather than myth.

The Old Testament and Hebrew history

The Old Testament presents a general historical outline from patriarchal origins to the period of the reformulation of Judaism under the Second Commonwealth. The more "historical" books of the Bible—Genesis, Exodus, Leviticus, Numbers, Joshua, Judges, Samuel, Kings, Chronicles—follow the Hebrews' own reconstruction of their past.

Beginning with **cosmogonic** traditions in Genesis, the Bible bridges the long span between Creation and the era of the patriarchs with a series of ancient tales and genealogies. The stories of Adam and Eve, Noah and the Flood, and the like—events beyond the confines of absolute time—may be regarded as the mythic and moral prelude to Hebrew history. The history of the Hebrews begins in Genesis with a description of the wanderings of Semitic-speaking, seminomadic, patriarchally organized tribes. These migrations, which actually lasted for centuries, were telescoped for narrative purposes into three generations, those of the patriarchs Abraham, Isaac, and Jacob. The patriarchs are presented as essential to the divine scheme, which ordained that they establish the nation of Israel, be prolific in their seed, and ensure the perpetual inheritance of the land. Most scholars regard the patriarchal narratives as a literary account of West Semitic seminomadic migrations, in particular those of the Amorites or Aramaeans.

Having moved into Canaan, some of the Hebrews subsequently migrated into Egypt to escape famine. During their sojourn in the land of Goshen—the northeastern Delta—the Hebrews were enslaved to build the cities of Pithom and Rameses. This is the first point in the Biblical narrative where it is possible, though not acceptable to some scholars, to synchronize Israelite history with primary archaeological and documentary evidence from Egypt. Some authorities equate the biblical Hebrews who lived in Goshen under Egyptian domination with the historical Ḥapiru, employed by the thirteenth century B.C. pharaoh Rameses II on his building projects in the eastern Delta (see page 181).

The Old Testament interprets the Hebrews' Exodus from Egypt and the subsequent wanderings in the Sinai desert as part of a divine plan. In fact, the Hebrews' transformation from seminomadism to nationhood may have revolved around the religious metamorphosis symbolized by Yahweh's revelation to Moses on Mt. Sinai.

Perhaps as early as the patriarchal period and certainly by the time of the Exodus, the Hebrews revered one god. Initially, however, they probably practiced not monotheism but monolatry: worship of a single god without denying the existence or power of others. Yahweh may originally have been a local god, worshiped at Mt. Sinai before Moses made him the supreme deity of the Hebrews. Through Moses, Yahweh made a covenant with the Hebrew people: in return for their exclusive worship and loyalty, the Hebrews would become the "Chosen People." Once the elders and the people agreed to this contractual relationship, Yahweh gave Moses stone tablets inscribed with the Ten Commandments—the moral responsibilities imposed on the Israelites by the Covenant.

Gradually the guiding spirit of the Hebrew tribes became the focus of the Israelite state. (The ethnic term *Hebrew* may now be replaced with *Israelite*, which designates a people united both spiritually and politically under the god with whom they made a covenant.) From an oasis in the northeastern Sinai, Kadesh-Barnea (modern Tell Qudeirat), the Hebrews embarked on the conquest of their "Promised Land." What later commentators described as a unified Israelite conquest must in actuality have been a complex, drawn-out military and migratory adventure.

Archaeological excavations have verified that numerous sites throughout Canaan were violently destroyed in the late thirteenth and early twelfth centuries B.C. These sites were resettled, and previously unsettled sites in the hill country of Palestine were colonized, both by people with an impoverished material culture—

indisputably Israelite. These destructions and (re)settlements lasted for generations; some Canaanite enclaves survived only to be conquered over the course of the next two centuries. Historical and archaeological interpretation of this period is complicated by the bewildering ethnic disruptions and displacements that carried Philistines—a branch of the Sea Peoples—to the southern coastal plain of Palestine and Aramaeans to regions just north of Palestine.

By the time the Hebrews entered Palestine, they consisted of twelve tribes. Neither racial nor national entities, these tribes were united in their covenant with Yahweh. Patriarchally organized, they recognized no central authority. The geographic focus of the confederation of tribes was a shrine at Shiloh in the hill country that contained the tablets of the Ten Commandments and housed the Ark of the Covenant—a box borne along on a wagon and believed to hold Yahweh's throne. The tribes, represented by their leaders, gathered at Shiloh to worship and renew their allegiance to Yahweh and to resolve conflicts.

Settlement in Palestine initiated a very gradual shift from a seminomadic to an agricultural mode of life. A shortage of arable land and pressure from other tribes and hostile neighbors led to repeated tribal and subtribal movement. Only slowly did wandering shepherds become settled farmers and craftsmen. Although the tribe remained the foremost social and political unit, permanent settlement changed social patterns.

Time and again the Israelite people fell into worshiping other deities, in particular the agricultural or fertility gods of the Canaanites and later the imperial deities of the Assyrians. The bargain struck while wandering in the desert wilderness proved hard to keep once the Israelites were settled and prosperous in Palestine. Yet the Covenant served as a binding force in Israelite history, fostering and nourishing allegiance to Yahweh. In order to maintain that allegiance, the Israelites had to develop and shape their concept of Yahweh—a stormy, impassioned, martial deity. Religious ceremony became more elaborate and formal, influenced by borrowings from Canaanite ritual: among the numerous rites, Yahweh's worship entailed the bloody sacrifice of beasts and concomitant libations of wine.

The most fundamental change was in leadership. A new kind of leader, the Judge, arose during the period of settlement to confront the external military threats Israel faced. In the troubled times between about 1200 and 1050 B.C., the people of Israel experienced a growing desire to stabilize and perpetuate leadership, and the Judges were charismatic leaders well suited to fill that need.

Eventually the elders of the tribes offered kingship to the Judge Gideon. When Gideon refused the offer, the people of Israel forced Samuel, last of the Judges, to anoint their first king, Saul. Saul's reign (about 1020–1000 B.C.) was a period of transition between tribal Judges and national monarchs. During the political crisis that followed the death of Saul and his sons in battle with the Philistines, David (a member of the tribe of Judah who had distinguished himself in Saul's court before falling from favor) was eventually accepted as king of a nation uniting the southern tribes of Judah and the northern tribes of Israel.

Shortly after his reign began, about 1000 B.C., David wrested the city of Jerusalem from a group the Bible calls the Jebusites. As a neutral area that belonged to no particular tribe, Jerusalem could serve as a unifying bond between north and south. Jerusalem became David's city—the capital of his kingdom, the estate of the Davidic dynasty, and the emblem of his pan-tribal status as king of Judah and Israel. Ministers and warriors alike converged on the city. The Ark of the Covenant, the symbol of tribal unity, was brought from Shiloh. Henceforth Jerusalem was to be both the political and religious center of the land.

King David liberated the country from the Philistines and conquered extensive surrounding areas; eventually his rule extended as far as Syria in the north and the Gulf of Aqaba in the south. Control of a major inland trade route and a close alliance with the Phoenician port of Tyre expanded the new kingdom's economic horizons. David introduced social and administrative changes that diminished the power and status of the elders and the old tribal institutions; henceforth a class of royal servants administered the new state.

In a bitter struggle for the succession, David supported Solomon (the son of his favorite wife Bathsheba), who eventually succeeded to the throne. Solomon's long reign (about 965–928 B.C.) brought the unified states of Israel and Judah new wealth and a number of political and commercial advantages. A series of treaties and political marriages cemented relations with neighboring kings, basically for economic reasons. Trade opened up throughout the eastern Mediterranean and as far afield as East Africa. Iron tools and implements, agricultural surpluses, and energetic building activity, especially in Jerusalem, also spelled economic progress.

By the time of Solomon, however, social stratification had isolated rich from poor in Israelite society. The Covenant ideal gave way under new sedentary social and economic pressures. The demands of state building projects—foremost among them the temple and palace in Jerusalem—and the provisioning of the royal court and army induced Solomon to institute forced labor and taxes, from which Judah (the royal district) may have been exempt. Although the Israelite people continued to reject secular domination of religious institutions, palace and temple began to struggle for control of the elaborate religious machinery. The burden of taxes, hatred of forced labor, the growing wealth of the court and its ministers, and possibly favoritism toward Judah all widened the gap between the populace and the newly wealthy nobility. This polarization led to political and economic crisis late in Solomon's reign and to open conflict between north and south after his death.

The House of David had failed to erase either the vestiges of tribal particularism or deep-rooted differences between northern and southern tribes. Yet the century of united monarchy was the strongest and most successful period in Israelite history. From this time forward, the kingdoms of Israel and Judah developed separately. Occasionally linked by treaties or royal marriages, they were sometimes allied, sometimes in opposition. Infighting between the two states disrupted trade, and the country slowly deteriorated. Social divisions also deepened: small farmers, artisans, and tradesmen resented urban and monarchic institutions, and the prophets championed their position.

Prophetic pleas for national unity and moral rectitude assumed much sharper focus after Sargon II incorporated the state of Israel into the Assyrian empire in 721 B.C. Hezekiah, king of Judah (715–687 B.C.), based his rule on anti-Assyrian policies and religious reform (the prophet Isaiah was graciously invited to his court). By the end of the century, Josiah (640–609 B.C.) was able to declare Judah's political independence from Assyria.

Nonetheless, other foreign powers—first Egypt, then Babylonia—claimed Assyria's position. Nebuchadrezzar crushed revolts in Jerusalem in 598 and 587 B.C., totally destroyed the city,
and exiled its citizens. The reign of David's house had come to
an end. The prophets Jeremiah and Ezekiel helped to keep the
faith alive among the exiles in Babylonia. Although Jeremiah
was forced to flee into Egypt, Ezekiel exhorted his companions
in exile to prepare for the return to Jerusalem and the restoration
of Solomon's temple. His cries were vindicated when Cyrus the
Great assumed control of Babylon: 40,000 Israelites left Babylon
under Zerubabel in 538 B.C. to return to Jerusalem and rebuild
their hallowed city.

Hebrew religion and the prophets

In the greater political scheme of ancient western Asiatic history,
the Hebrews' impact was minimal. The evolution of their ancient
faith, however, and the biblical account of it were extraordinarily
momentous accomplishments, central to the foundations of
western culture. By about 500 B.C., Judaism's basic tenets were
set and practiced. In turn, Judaism served as the source of two
other major world religions: Christianity and Islam.

The death of Solomon and the division of the Israelite monarchy dealt a severe blow to the ancient Hebrew religion. The
prophets struggled to keep alive the worship of Yahweh, and
all espoused the same message: if the Chosen People would keep
the Covenant, and render to Yahweh the service due him, they
would be linked to and forever protected by Yahweh.

The prophets of Israel were entirely different from the divination priests and fortune-tellers of other ancient Near Eastern
cultures. Originally teachers, the prophets eventually became
political reformers, counterbalancing royal and priestly power.
Between the ninth and fifth centuries B.C., prophets urged kings,
priests, and commoners alike to keep the Covenant and to worship the one true God. All who remained steadfast in worship
and adhered to the Law would be entitled to the same justice
in the eyes of Yahweh: there would be no distinction between
the rights and privileges of rich and poor. The prophets of Israel
were critics of contemporary mores, not soothsayers of future
events. Always in the background, however, was the prophetic

promise that if the Israelites purged themselves and kept their agreement with Yahweh, they would be forgiven and ultimately survive the depradations of their oppressors.

In the ninth century B.C., the prophet Elijah railed against worship of Phoenician gods and royal infringements on popular rights. The exploitation of peasants by nobles in the eighth century B.C. brought on a wave of popular protest led by the prophets Amos, Hosea, and Isaiah. Amos threatened divine retribution for those who took advantage of the poor. Amos and Isaiah of Judah both condemned the people and the state of Israel for failure to keep the Covenant; in so doing, they integrated the divine into the course of Israelite history.

Prophetic influence waned in the seventh century B.C., perhaps partially the result of Sargon II's defeat of Israel in 721 B.C. In the southern kingdom of Judah, King Josiah (attempting to avert a similar fate) instituted radical reforms in 621 B.C. A book of the Torah, probably Deuteronomy, was discovered in the temple. When that Law was read to the people, one and all swore to renew the Covenant. Foreign cults were banished, their priests executed and false shrines destroyed. Monotheism was made compulsory, and worship of Yahweh was confined to the temple in Jerusalem.

Nonetheless, the great prophet Jeremiah warned that it was already too late, that Babylonia would act as God's agent to punish Judah for its previous sins. Nebuchadrezzar's destruction of Jerusalem fulfilled Jeremiah's prophecy and resulted in the forced exile of its citizens. Jeremiah, whose message focused on personal ethics instead of the temple cult, counseled the exiles to make the best of their stay in Babylonia. During the exile, the prophets Ezekiel and the so-called "second Isaiah" preached Jeremiah's message about the individual's relationship with God and ceaselessly reminded the Israelites that they were the Chosen People, that God would be forgiving, and that they must preserve their hope for restoration of the temple and an eventual golden age.

The release from captivity came from an unexpected quarter. The Persian ruler Cyrus (the Great) freed 40,000 exiles, who returned to Jerusalem to establish a new order (see pages 257–58). Despite obstacles, the new temple was completed in 515 B.C. Strengthened by the hardships of the exile and the cultural vestiges of the pre-exilic period, the returnees inaugurated a new, theocratic state. The constitution of the new theocracy was the Torah, introduced to the people by the priest Ezra as a guide to the conduct of everyday life. The promulgation of this law about 400 B.C. was the beginning of the formulation of the Old Testament. By about 100 A.D., the Old Testament had assumed approximately the form in which we know it today. The people who accepted the Torah and worshiped in the reconstructed temple in Jerusalem became uncompromising monotheists, dedicated to the ritual and ethical purity prescribed in priestly and prophetic writings.

This new ritual and ethical purity of the Jews tended to isolate them culturally: they had decisively rejected the polytheistic paganism of the ancient Near East for the worship of a unique and ethical god. The Jewish community was reorganized, essentially around the Torah. Judaism allowed a new, individual freedom of worship but at the same time prescribed a rigid code regulating daily life and behavior. Jews were specifically obligated to avoid marriage with foreigners, to avoid work on the Sabbath, to let land lie fallow, and to forgo debts every seventh year, to remit an annual tax for maintenance of the sanctuary, and to see that all cultic demands (firstfruits of the harvest, tithes, and the like) were regularly met. The people adopted this code as the constitution of their community and as a solemn renewal of their Covenant with Yahweh.

Judaism made stern demands on individuals by regulating behavior in intricate detail, but every Jew had recourse to a just and forgiving God. Judaism was clear and pragmatic; mysticism entered into it only in small measure. Through Judaism and its offshoots, the religious views of the ancient Hebrews still remain prominent the world over.

PERSIA: THE MARCH OF IMPERIALISM

Babylonia had successfully assimilated many foreign regimes over the millennia. When Cyrus the Great of Persia entered Babylon in 539 B.C., however, new religious and cultural forces were at work, imperialism was the political mode, and the outcome was to be decisively different.

The Mesopotamian concept of universal monarchy—"the King of the Four Quarters of the Universe"—that had first emerged under the Sumerians in the third millennium B.C. took on triumphant reality under the Persians. Rejecting wanton destruction and humiliating subjection, the Persians instead embraced imperialism's static dimensions: peace, harmony, and benevolent rule. Stabilizing and enlarging on the erratic unity established by the Assyrians, Persia led the ancient Near East to the maximum extent of its political magnitude and power. The geographic limits that had previously demarcated ancient western Asia and partially determined its independent history were obliterated: roads opened up to Europe in one direction and India in the other. Only the west remained outside this fusion, and there the long-raging discord of war set the stage for a decisive clash. All the while, the history of ancient western Asia and Egypt drew inexorably to a close.

Emergence of Empire under the Achaemenids

The Medes and Persians, related Indo-European–speaking tribes that arrived on the Iranian plateau from the east, had a long history of interaction, both peaceful and hostile, with the Mesopotamian world. Sometime during the eighth century B.C., the Medes established a capital at Ecbatana (modern Hamadan) in west-central Iran on the mountainous eastern fringes of Babylonia. The Persians settled farther south, on the edge of the Bakhtiari Mountains, in a region known in antiquity as Anshan, centered on Tepe Malyan. This area eventually came to be called Parsuas, after the Persian tribes; the modern Iranian province of Fars preserves the name. There, in the seventh century B.C., a leader named Achaemenes established the Persian, or Achaemenid, dynasty.

Late in the same century, the Median king Cyaxares (in Persian, Huvakshatra), who had helped Nabopolassar destroy Assyria, subjugated the Persians. In the first half of the sixth century B.C., the last of the Median rulers, Astyages (Ishtuwegu), arranged for his daughter to marry the Persian dynast Cambyses I, perhaps in recognition of the Persians' rising political strength. The fruit of this marriage was Cyrus, a great soldier and conqueror who was to be the instrument of the Medes's ultimate defeat. Encouraged by the Neo-Babylonian king Nabonidus, Cyrus conspired with the Median army in revolt against his grandfather Astyages, who capitulated without a struggle. In 559 B.C., Cyrus was welcomed in Ecbatana as the ruler of a united Persia. Cyrus went on to penetrate India, conquer Anatolia, and occupy Babylonia and all its territories as far as the frontier of Egypt. So began the greatest of all the eastern empires.

Killed on a distant battlefield in 530 B.C., Cyrus was succeeded by his son Cambyses II (529–522 B.C.). Cambyses promptly conquered Egypt, the last and most independent of the ancient Near Eastern powers. Although he treated political disobedience harshly, he perpetuated the enlightened, benevolent policies practiced by his father. Egyptian evidence, for example, contradicts Herodotus's assertion that Cambyses ridiculed Egyptian religion.

On his way home from Egypt in 522 B.C., having just received news of a domestic revolt, Cambyses died. His successor Darius I (522–486 B.C.), the scion of another branch of the Achaemenid dynasty, successfully overcame revolts in all quarters (including Babylonia) and within two years restored peace. Darius's achievement is commemorated in an inscription carved high on the walls of a pass in northwestern Iran; this Bisutun Inscription, written in three languages (Old Persian, Elamite, and Akkadian), later became the key to the modern decipherment of the cuneiform script.

Darius extended Persian control as far as India in the east and the Balkan peninsula and Black Sea region in the west. The western frontiers of the empire, however, were to prove a chronic problem for the Achaemenids. Nonetheless, these wide-ranging expeditions demonstrate the offensive capacity of a state with unprecedentedly extended boundaries.

Imperial administration and administrative centers

Their seminomadic pursuits still fresh in mind, the early Median and Persian conquerors found themselves literally "between tent and palace," newcomers in an old world. That Cyrus the Great readily adopted whatever he needed from his Assyrian and Babylonian predecessors is apparent in his unparalleled conquests and his construction of an opulent royal residence at Pasargadae. Cyrus inherited not only Babylon's imperial power but also its ambitions and its splendor.

The new Persian administration, which retained most local officials, proved highly acceptable to conquered peoples. Cyrus claimed to offer peace and friendship to all defeated peoples, and he enlisted the support of local gods to uphold his regime. Though the Persian kings adopted a policy of minimal interference, they were warriors nonetheless. When resisted, they conquered violently and with vengeance. Yet conflict and conquest are presented only in the vaguest terms, and seldom overplayed in Persian royal inscriptions. Persian documents contain none of the graphic accounts characteristic of the Assyrian royal annals and little of the bombastic boasting typical of the Egyptian pharaonic records.

The immense empire the Persians molded from widely divergent peoples and cultures could not have lasted without a reformulation of social and political reality, through which old and new could be reconciled, conflicts minimized, and unification fostered. This reformulation seems to have been Cyrus the Great's most extraordinary achievement. Cyrus always presented himself as the legitimate successor of local dynasties, embraced and elected by the local deities. Marduk, he claimed, became his "friend and companion" in the appropriation of Babylon. Cyrus respected and adapted himself to local traditions. Existing institutions were incorporated without modification into the new political framework. Expediency and propaganda must have played a part, but leniency and coexistence were nonetheless promoted to an unprecedented degree.

Unusually tolerant in religious matters, Cyrus was well disposed toward the Jews whom Nebuchadrezzar had exiled to Babylonia. On assuming control of Babylon in his second year, Cyrus permitted 40,000 Israelites to return home and issued an edict reestablishing the temple at Jerusalem. The Jews had only to recognize the overlordship of Cyrus, which even their prophets encouraged them to do. The Old Testament calls Cyrus the "annointed" and "beloved" of Yahweh, god of Israel (Second Isaiah).

In the conquered provinces, or *satrapies*, Cyrus retained local officials but installed Persian governors called **satraps**. The power of the satraps was held in check by the appointment of other officials directly answerable to the king. Tax collectors restricted the satraps's opportunities to embezzle imperial funds, and garrison commanders prevented the satraps from deploying imperial troops in rebellion against the king.

To facilitate rule in their expansive realm, Persian dynasts utilized as regional capitals such cities as Ecbatana, Susa, and Babylon. Nonetheless, Pasargadae under Cyrus and Persepolis under Darius and his successors were the focal, orthodox centers of Persian pomp and power. Formal and functional differences distinguish the two cities.

Cyrus's palaces at Pasargadae—in a fertile plain about 30 miles (50 kilometers) north of Persepolis—borrowed freely from the architectural styles of the lands he conquered: Median columned halls, Lydian masonry techniques, and perhaps Babylonian sculpture, the whole overlaid with a Persian veneer. Scattered over ¾ square mile (2 square kilometers) were a fortified quarter, a square stone shrine, and two palaces with columned halls, porticoes, and the corner towers representative of Persian architecture. The totality was a somewhat undigested agglomeration, a royal residence and gardens apropos of a king recently risen from tribal obscurity.

Cyrus's tomb—about .6 mile (1 kilometer) southwest of the palaces—is set on a six-step platform not unlike a miniature Mesopotamian ziqqurat. The tomb chamber itself is a simple gabled hut, a suitable resting place for the unpretentious Persian dynast who so rapidly and unexpectedly realized universal power and became master of the world.

By contrast, Persepolis (begun under Darius I and elaborated by his successors) became the showplace of a world empire, secure in its power and splendor. If Pasargadae's experimental eclecticism had promised a new style, Persepolis fulfilled that promise by transforming formerly ominous images of power and kingship into a new ideology of "commonwealth" that faithfully expressed the historical reality of Achaemenid rule.

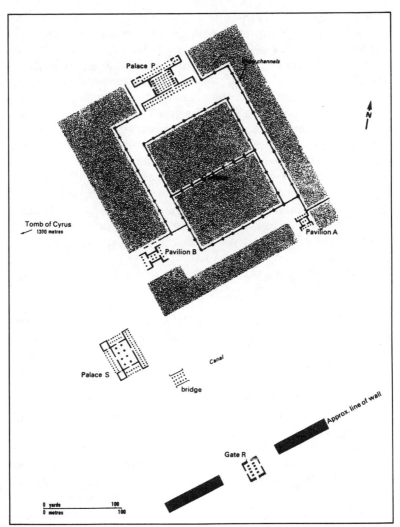

Labels within the plan:
Palace P.
channels
N
Tomb of Cyrus
1300 metres
Pavilion A
Pavilion B
Palace S
Canal
bridge
Approx. line of wall
Gate R
0 yards 100
0 metres 100

(The Robert Harding Picture Library)

Plan of Cyrus the Great's palace complex at Pasargadae.

The ceremonial city of Persepolis stood on a huge stone terrace-platform approximately 40 feet (12 meters) high. Over a dozen structures arose there over a period of sixty years. Entered at the northwest through a gatehouse whose doors were supported by stone bulls, this platform supported a maze of columned buildings, including two huge halls, the Apadana and the Hall of 100 Columns, as well as a harem, a treasury, and three palaces. Columned halls and porticoes abounded. The relief sculptures on the staircase approaching the Apadana, Persepolis's largest building, depicted representatives from throughout the empire bearing gifts and rare animals to the king.

Since these parading sculptures are often presumed to represent the elaborate New Year ceremonial, Persepolis has come to be regarded as the great New Year's center of the Achaemenid empire. Yet surely other significant moments in royal life—coronations, audiences, burials—would have been celebrated at Persepolis, and the site may better be regarded as a rich and eloquent monument to Persian kingship and imperialism. The art and architecture of Persepolis expressed in stone the empire's eclecticism. Its imperial style made use of Near Eastern, Egyptian, Greek, and native Iranian artistic and building conventions. The entirety was Iranian and imperial; the parts were integrated symbols of what has aptly been called the Achaemenid commonwealth.

In addition to inspiring and initiating construction at Persepolis, Darius also built and carefully maintained a complex system of roads, notably the famous Royal Road from Susa in present-day Khuzistan (southwestern Iran) to Sardis and Ephesos in western Anatolia. Almost 1,700 miles (2,700 kilometers) long, with over 100 post stations, the Royal Road fostered the economic life of the empire and facilitated swift commercial and military movement. The political and economic stability of Darius's reign permitted the expansion of commerce, facilitated by the introduction of coinage. The common currency for trade and banking was the gold *daric*, worth twenty shekels of silver (about ⅓ to ½ pound).

Darius is also credited with reorganizing the imperial administration. He ensured the loyalty of his satraps by appointing members of his own family and those of friends; other important nobles served the king as a council of advisors. Darius periodically dispatched royal officials to the satrapies, and questioned them and other returning travelers about the loyalty of his subordinates.

Darius was an innovative ruler, deeply concerned with imperial power and ideology. During his reign, he designed and

(J. Powell, Photographer)

General view of Persepolis. (Darius I, Xerxes, Artaxerxes I).

at least partially built Persepolis, extended and quickened communications through imperial highway construction, and reorganized efficiently the entire administrative and economic system of the state. Commerce thrived and expanded, and a common law was imposed on all conquered peoples. Even in the religious realm, evidence points to a solemn, devout Darius. For all of Cyrus the Great's unusual qualities and the opportunity he would have had to absorb the faith of Zoroaster, the core of Persian religion, Darius was the dynast who emerged as a deeply committed Zoroastrian.

Zoroastrianism: Persian religion

> Ahuramazda is a great god . . .
> he it is who had created heaven and earth,
> who had created men . . .
> who has granted dominion to the king Darius
> over this wide territory which includes many nations . . .
> on this side the sea,
> on the other side the desert.[1]

Thus Darius acknowledged receipt of power from Ahura-Mazda, greatest divinity of the Persian religion. With that power,

Darius gained unity for the empire as well as endurance for his own rule. In a cosmos divided, Ahura-Mazda—represented as a winged disc—reigned in the heavens and protected with his outstretched wings the earth and its Achaemenid ruler. As Ahura-Mazda's viceroy, the Persian king would enjoy a prosperous, beneficial, long-lasting rule. Far more enduring, however, was the influence of ancient Persian religion and its founder Zoroaster (in Persian, Zarathustra).

The roots of Zoroastrianism run deep in time, almost 1,000 years earlier than its namesake and founder, who lived about 600 B.C. Zoroaster's purpose in establishing the religion was twofold: to eliminate traditional superstitions and to institute a more ethical and spiritual worship. The ultimate outcome was a synthesis, a magnetic blend of Persian dualism—good and evil—with Babylonian pessimism and supernaturalism.

Zoroastrianism may be distinguished from earlier religions by its dualistic beliefs and ethical nature. Mesopotamian divinities were generally capable of both good and evil intentions and actions. Not so the two spiritual principles of Persian belief: good (Ahura-Mazda) and evil (Ahriman) dominated the universe. The struggle between these two principles was between thought and passion, truth and treachery, lightness and dark. Ahura-Mazda was incapable of malevolence, Ahriman unsuited to benevolence. Engaged in an otherworldly struggle for universal supremacy, Ahura-Mazda was destined to save the earth from darkness, cast his adversary into the netherworld, and enable mankind to stand for final judgment.

Mankind, itself good and evil, became part of the struggle. People were free to sin or to do good works, but they would be judged according to their actions and rewarded or punished in the hereafter. The Good had to avoid heresy and be kind to animals; a good ruler defended his people as well as his faith and protected and nourished the poor and weak. The Wicked comprised the inequitable ruler or judge, the oppressor of the weak, the neglectful farmer. Older currents guided new waves: the good king of Persian times had the same constraints and aspirations as his Sumero-Babylonian counterparts.

Strict rules, tinged with earlier superstitious practices, guided initiates. Since animals were beneficial to people, their sacrifice was forbidden. Intoxicants were banned. And in order to avoid defiling the sacred elements earth, fire, and water, corpses could not be buried, burned, or drowned. Instead the dead were exposed, to be torn asunder by beasts or birds of prey. Like the belief in good and evil, the practice of exposing the corpse may be traced to the Median priestly class known as the Magi. Although they appear in quite another guise in Christian belief, still the Magi came to Bethlehem as wise and pious men from the mysterious east.

Magic—the word derives from the Magi—and priestcraft came to dominate Persian beliefs. The synthesis of Zoroastrianism and the more superstitious, animistic beliefs of Mesopotamia produced a number of new, mystical religions: Mithraism, Manichaeism, Gnosticism. Mithra, divine viceroy of Ahura-Mazda in his battle against evil, rose gradually from minor deity to become the most widely worshipped of the Persian gods. Zoroastrian rituals may be traced to him, as may two very important Christian beliefs: Sunday as the week's most sacred day and December 25 as the year's most sacred.

Mani, a devout and noble priest from Ecbatana, attempted more serious reform and preached complete human detachment from physical needs and sexual desire. His absolute dualism of good and evil extended even to his believers: the Perfect, who would follow all sanctions, and the Hearers, who could only try. Gnosticism distinguished itself from the others through its mysticism and its belief in an exclusive spiritual knowledge held only by initiates. Zoroastrianism, initially based in the aristocracy, spread with increasing intensity and more popular aspirations through all these Persian-derived mystery religions.

Persia versus Greece: Beginning of the End

In his expeditions to subdue the city-states of mainland Greece, Darius had harnessed the full aggressive capacity of the Persian state. Intending at first only to check the incursions of Scythians (horsemen from the Russian steppes) on the western shores of the Black Sea, Darius conquered large areas of the north Aegean, or Thracian, coast. From those Greeks and from the Ionian Greeks of western Anatolia, Darius demanded heavy tribute. Supported by Athens, the Greek cities, although by no means united, resisted. Darius, finally overextended, had met his match.

Defeated at Marathon in 490 B.C., Darius died soon after and bequeathed to his son Xerxes (485–465 B.C.) the problem of a recalcitrant western frontier. When Xerxes (even less effectively than Darius) turned his attention to Greece, the Greeks repelled a joint Persian land and naval force at Salamis and Platea in 480–479 B.C. Part of the empire nearer home also caused problems; Xerxes dealt harshly with a revolt in Babylon.

Greek sources portray the Persian empire in its last century and a half as wracked by intermittent intrigues, rivalries, and assassinations incited by the death of the ruling monarch and conflict over the accession of a new leader. Some dynastic strife surely existed—Babylonian documents report two concurrent kings ruling in different places—but it is unclear how severely court intrigue affected the welfare of the empire.

Under Xerxes' successor Artaxerxes I (464–424 B.C.), endless strife mellowed into cultural interaction between Greeks and Persians. Greek merchants, mercenaries, and historians, most notably Herodotus, traveled widely in the east, familiarizing themselves with the area's history, religions, and science.

Persia's next two rulers, Darius II (423–405 B.C.) and Artaxerxes II (404–358 B.C.), and their satraps acted to solve the Greek problem by pitting opposing Greek cities against each other and by bribing Greek politicians. Artaxerxes reaped the fruits of this policy when war-weary Greece accepted his proclamation of peace in Greece and his dominion over all Greeks living in Asia Minor. No such success ensued in the empire's other trouble spot, Egypt, now in a state of nearly continual rebellion. Artaxerxes III (357–337 B.C.) had to contend with the greatest threat to Persian power since the time of Cambyses' death: revolts by western satraps, Phoenicians and Egyptians, all of which were crushed. (It is noteworthy that old foes had become new allies: one of the king's top generals was a Greek mercenary).

Artaxerxes watched with concern as the kingdom of Macedon, north of Greece, extended its influence over the entire Balkan peninsula under its able king Philip II. Artaxerxes' death, probably the result of court intrigue, was untimely for the empire, and the reign of his successor Arses (338–336 B.C.) was short and troubled. To thwart the continued growth of Macedonian power, the Persian satrap in northwest Asia Minor sent mercenaries into Europe. Philip retaliated by sending his own troops into Asia Minor.

The last of the Achaemenids, Darius III (Codomannus, 334–330 B.C.), might have saved his empire had he not come up against a military genius: Philip's son Alexander, who ascended the throne of Macedon after his father's assassination. Alexander, who at least in the company of Greeks espoused the pan-Hellenic ideal of a united Greece and who campaigned under the banner of Greek liberation from Persian domination, decisively defeated the Persians in Anatolia, Phoenicia, and Egypt before he turned his attention to the heartland of Persia.

Once Mesopotamia and Iran were securely in his grasp, Alexander embarked on a long campaign to the eastern limits of the settled world. As he was preparing to bear down on India, his troops balked. Eventually he resigned himself to their wishes and turned south, triumphantly marching along the Indus River valley in modern-day Pakistan to the coast of the Indian Ocean where he built a fleet to sail westward. By spring of 323 B.C., Alexander had returned to Babylon, where in June he fell ill (perhaps from malaria) and died at the age of thirty-three.

The Persian empire had fostered a synthesis of all Near Eastern cultures: Mesopotamian, Egyptian, Syro-Palestinian, Anatolian, and Persian itself. Imperialism, an excellent system of roads, communication, and commerce, and a monumental, eclectic architecture were its immediate legacy to the conquering Macedonians. Even the Romans eventually came to emulate the world empire of the Achaemenid dynasts. The just governance inspired by Ahura-Mazda, however, conditioned and guided all these secular elements. Divinely inspired authority, another relict of the Mesopotamian past, bolstered Persian rule just as it continues today to sustain and rationalize political dominion.

NOTE

1. Quotation from R. Ghirshman, *Iran* (Harmondsworth, U.K.: Penguin Books, Ltd., 1949), p. 155.

SUPPLEMENTARY READINGS

Bierbrier, M. L. 1975. *The Late New Kingdom in Eqypt (c. 1300–664 B.C.): A Genealogical and Chronological Investigation.* Liverpool Monographs in Archaeology and Oriental Studies. Warminster: Aris & Phillips.

Dever, W. G. 1982. "Retrospects and Prospects in Biblical and Syro-Palestinian Archaeology." *Biblical Archaeologist* 45, pp. 103–108.

Edey, M. A. 1974. *The Sea Traders.* Emergence of Man Series. New York: Time-Life Books.

Edwards, I. E. S.; C. J. Gadd; N. G. L. Hammond; and E. Sollberger, eds. 1982. The Prehistory of the Balkans; The Middle East and the Aegean World, Tenth to Eighth Centuries B.C. *Cambridge Ancient History,* Vol. 3., part 1. Cambridge: Cambridge University Press.

Kempinski, A., and M. Avi-Yonah. 1979. *Syria-Palestine II: From the Middle Bronze Age to the End of the Classical World (2200 B.C.–324 A.D.).* Basel, Switzerland: Nagel.

Kitchen, K. A. 1986. *The Third Intermediate Period in Egypt (1100–650 B.C.).* Rev. ed.

Moorey, P. R. S. 1976. *Biblical Lands.* Making of the Past Series. Oxford: Phaidon Press.

Muhly, J. D. 1985. "Phoenicia and the Phoenicians." In Biblical Archaeology Today. *Proceedings of the International Congress on Biblical Archaeology,* pp. 177–91. Jerusalem: Israel Exploration Society, Israel Academy of Sciences, ASOR.

Oded, B. 1979. *Mass Deportations and Deportees in the Neo-Assyrian Empire.* Wiesbaden: Harrassowitz.

Root, M. C. 1979. *The King and Kingship in Achaemenid Art.* Acta Iranica 19. Textes et Memoires 9. Leiden: Brill.

Silver, M. 1983. *Prophets and Markets: The Political Economy of Ancient Israel.* Boston: Kluwer-Nijhoff.

Stronach, D. 1978. *Pasargadae: A Report on Excavations Conducted by the British Institute of Persian Studies from 1961 to 1963.* London: Oxford University Press.

Wertime, T., and J. D. Muhly, eds. 1980. *The Coming of the Age of Iron.* New Haven, Conn.: Yale University Press.

Wiseman, D. J., ed. 1973. *Peoples of Old Testament Times*. Oxford: Society for Old Testament Study. (Contains papers on the Hebrews, Egyptians, Aramaeans, Assyrians, Babylonians and Chaldeans, Phoenicians, and Persians.)

Zimansky, P. E. 1985. *Ecology and Empire: The Structure of the Urartian State*. Studies in Ancient Oriental Civilization 41. Chicago: University of Chicago Press.

VI

EPILOGUE: VESTIGES OF ANCIENT WESTERN ASIA AND EGYPT

The chronological gap that isolates us from the ancient world is also a cultural gap. Any modern assessment of the legacy of the ancient Near East is, like its history, subject to the haphazard survival of artifacts, to cultural and philosophical discontinuities between the two ages, and to the inability of modern scholars in a time of acute specialization to master all aspects of history and archaeology. Institutions and ideas that were inseparably intertwined in the experience of ancient Near Eastern people are typically treated separately by present-day specialists.

Ancient ideology and technology have reached the modern world through diverse channels. The technique of writing originated in the Near East and with it the very concept of education. Details of ancient Near Eastern myths and literature have become part of our heritage through such media as the Bible and Greek and Roman literature. Mesopotamian scientific and mathematical achievements have been transmitted through the intermediacy of Greece, Rome, Byzantium, and the Arab world. Agricultural practice originated in the Fertile Crescent, and urban living commenced in southern Mesopotamia. Artistic motifs, coinage, medicinal herbs, and even vocabulary words can be traced back to ancient western Asia and Egypt. It is even possible to discuss—debate is probably more accurate—the roots of western thinking in terms of Near Eastern **mythopoeic** (mythmaking) thought.

WRITING AND LITERATURE

The West Semitic alphabet spread throughout the world by way of the Aramaeans, Phoenicians, and Greeks. While the literature of the ancient Near East has had a less pervasive influence, the most influential book in the western world, the Bible, draws liberally on Babylonian, Egyptian, and Ugaritic literature. The Biblical accounts of Creation, the Garden of Eden, and the Flood closely parallel Near Eastern myths. The Book of Job, whose imagery, insight, and philosophy are unsurpassed, shares the theme of the righteous sufferer with a Babylonian treatise known as *Ludlul bēl nemeqi*—"Let me praise the lord of wisdom."

Preoccupation with moral and ethical problems led to the development of a rich genre of "wisdom literature" in Babylonia and Egypt during the second millennium B.C. Numerous dialogues, sometimes called fables, have biblical as well as modern counterparts. The Babylonian Theodicy, a dialogue between a pessimistic sufferer and his friend, has been compared to the biblical book of Ecclesiastes. The desire for immortality that pervades Babylonia's most renowned tale, the epic of Gilgamesh, also influenced biblical thought. Religious beliefs that originated in the east—the vegetation cycle, good and evil—were soon reflected in the west, but the monotheism that evolved in Israel ultimately superseded all others.

It has been suggested that the annals of the Assyrian kings, beginning about 1300 B.C., should be considered the first truly historiographic documents. Alongside basic geographic and tactical information about military campaigns, the Assyrian annals attribute and criticize motives, appraise political events and individuals, and generalize about foreign peoples and their lands. Whether Herodotus's claim to be the "father of history" is thus placed in jeopardy ultimately depends on individual definitions of the writing and meaning of history (see Chapter I).

If speculation still exists about ancient Near Eastern literature's influence on the present, its impact on ancient populations
is no less clear. Since literacy was chiefly restricted to scribes,
some ancient literature may have been composed solely for their
edification. But dialogues may have been publicly performed;
some hymns and epics were recited to music at religious festivals. The *Enūma Elish*, for example, was read aloud at each New
Year's festival. The extent of public participation in such events,
however, remains unknown.

Vocabulary: Ancient Words in Modern Dress

A number of words have been transmitted from ancient Near
Eastern languages to those of modern European languages or
English. The following list, which shows ancient, intermediate,
and English forms, is representative but by no means complete.

English	Intermediate	Ancient Near Eastern
abyss	abussos (Greek)	apsû (Sumero-Akkadian)
alcohol	koḥl (Arabic)	guklu ("antimony") (com-mon Semitic)
alkali	al-qalīy (Arabic)	qalati{qalû ("to roast") (Akkadian)
cane	kanna (Greek)	qanû (common Semitic)
carob	charrouba (Greek)	kharūbu (common Semitic)
chemistry	kimiya (Arabic)	kmt (Egyptian)
chrys- ("gold")	chrusos (Greek)	khurāṣu (Akkadian)
dragoman	targama(Arabic)	targumānu (common Semitic)
ebony	ebenos (Greek)	hebni (Egyptian)
gum	kummi (Greek)	kemai (Egyptian)
horn	cornu (Latin)	qarnu (common Semitic) [fortuitous?]

English	Intermediate	Ancient Near Eastern
jasper	iaspis (Greek)	jashpû (Akkadian)
("poor,	mesquin(French)	mushkēnu (Akkadian)
paltry")	meschino(Italian)	
mina	mina (Greek)	manû (Sumero-Akkadian)
myrrh	murra (Greek)	murru (common Semitic)
naptha	napthos (Greek)	napṭu (Akkadian)
niter, natron	nitron (Greek)	nṭr(y) (Egyptian)
plinth	plinthos (Greek)	libittu {*libintu (Akkadian)
sack	sakkos (Greek)	s/shaqqu (common Semitic)
saffron	zaᶜfaran (Arabic)	azupirānu (Sumero-Akkadian)
shekel	sheqel (Hebrew)	shiqlu{shaqālu ("to weigh, pay out") (Akkadian)
sparrow	ᶜuṣfūr (Arabic) ṣippōr (Hebrew)	ṣibāru (common Semitic)

SCIENCE, PSEUDO-SCIENCE, AND MATH

The Babylonians excelled at astronomy and mathematics. The earliest systematic astronomical observations—of the planet Venus—date from the seventeenth century B.C., the Old Babylonian period. Probably intended to serve as a basis for omens, these so-called Venus tablets were not highly accurate but have some value for determining ancient chronology. Astrological omens based on astronomical observations date from the beginning of the second millennium B.C., and were later grouped in series such as *Enūma Anu Enlil*.

Accurate astronomical observations by the seventh century B.C. led to the development of a more precise calendar. Throughout Babylonian history, the calendar was lunar, making for a year of only 354 days. Once every three years, an extra month had to be inserted to bring the lunar calendar into line with the

solar year. By the eighth century B.C. (757 B.C., under Nabu-
naṣir), a regular intercalation of seven months every nineteen
years had been established. By the fourth century B.C., this intercalation was performed mathematically. This calendar, known
as the Metonic Cycle, served as the basis of the later Jewish and
Christian religious calendars.

While the aims and methods of the astronomers were gen-
uinely scientific, their computations were also instrumental in
the invention of the zodiac and horoscopic astrology. Initially,
astrological omens were interpreted as referring only to the future of the country and its ruler. The transition to horoscopic
astrology necessitated a technique whereby celestial phenomena
could be related to single individuals. That technique was the
zodiac. By the fifth century B.C., the zodiacal belt had been
divided into twelve zodiacal signs of 30 degrees each; this reformulation arose from the schematic year of twelve thirty-day
months used in the seventh century B.C. *MUL.APIN* text. The
Hellenistic Greeks were once credited with developing horoscopic astrology. However, the earliest known Greek horoscope
dates only from 62 B.C., whereas the first known Babylonian
example was cast for a child born April 29, 410 B.C. At least four
other examples date from the third century B.C.

The paucity of surviving mathematical texts obscures the
Babylonians' truly remarkable mathematical achievements.
Mathematical calculation was well advanced by the Old Babylonian period (about 1800–1600 B.C.). Tablets from that era em-
ploy multiplication; division; calculation of squares, cubes, square
roots and cube roots; cubic equations; reciprocals; and the like.
Algebraic and geometric problem texts frequently addressed such
practical matters as engineering and surveying. The Pythagorean
theorem was in regular use in Babylonia 1,000 years before Pythagoras. Babylonian mathematics employed a system of notation based on the number 60. The "load" (that is, whatever could
be carried by man or donkey) was the standard unit of measurement; it was also divided and subdivided by units of 60.
Grain, the original measure of weight and value, was replaced
by silver no later than the third millennium B.C.

The most striking innovation of the Babylonian numerical
system was its positional notation. The size of a number was

initially indicated by the size of its pictographic sign, but place-value notation had come into common use by the nineteenth century B.C. In our modern place-value system, derived from the Babylonian system through Hindu-Arabic intermediaries, the numbers 17 and 71 indicate the differing value of 7 by means of its position relative to the other integer. In the Babylonian system, 𝐓◁ indicates 70 (𝐓 = 60), and ◁𝐓 indicates 11 (𝐓 = 1); in both cases, ◁ stands for 10. The sign for zero was probably invented later, during the Persian period (perhaps in India).

While the division of the hour into minutes originated in Babylonia, the division of the day into hours reflects both Babylonian and Egyptian influence. Babylonian days consisted of twelve "double hours" (*bēru*), each of which contained sixty "double minutes." The Egyptians, meanwhile, divided the period from sunrise to sunset into twelve unequal parts—unequal since the length of the "hours" depended on the season of the year. Babylonian astronomers then divided the entire day and night into six parts of equal and constant length for computational and observational purposes. Adopting this subdivision of day and night into equal parts, Hellenistic astronomers divided the twelve double hours into twenty-four units. This division was comparable to that of the Egyptians, except that each unit now had equal length. Thus the twenty-four–hour day came into being.

Astrology, certain mathematical computations, and even the subdivision of the hour and day are all by-products of the science of astronomy. Probably Babylonia's most direct legacy, astronomy is the only branch of ancient science to have survived the collapse of the Roman empire.

MUSIC AND ART

It has recently become clear that modern music theory also has roots in ancient Mesopotamia. Seven seven-tone and eight-tone musical scales, including our standard modern major scale, were in use as early as the Old Babylonian period (about 1800 B.C.). Knowledge of music theory and practice spread to the Levant and to ancient Greece by the first millennium B.C. Pythagoras probably did, as he asserts, learn his math and music in the Near East. This ancient music was probably heterophonic and harmonic; it was used for nearly a hundred different categories of compositions, but the style in which it was performed remains unknown. Although wind and percussion instruments existed, stringed instruments were the most highly developed. Harps appear in pictorial evidence dating from the end of the fourth millennium B.C.; lyres appeared early in the third millennium B.C. and lutes by the end of the third millennium B.C. All these instruments continued to evolve and spread throughout the ancient world.

In the area of architecture, the classic Ionic column, the standard form of which developed during the Classical Greek period, originated in the early reed structures of southernmost Mesopotamia. This deep-fluted column with its volute (scroll-like) capital may be traced to a bundle of tall reeds tied together in a loop at the top and used as a building post; the Marsh Arabs of southern Iraq still use such "columns" today. Some early Muslim minarets, such as the mosque of Samarra in Iraq, are thought to be based on the ziqqurat, albeit with a circular rather than square plan. Spiral towers of this type spread from the Islamic world to China, where they were further elaborated between the eleventh and thirteenth centuries A.D. (see figure on p. 276). Besides the crescent and the cross, the foremost symbol that has survived from the ancient world is that of intertwined serpents. In Mesopotamia, the rod with intertwined serpents was the distinguishing mark of Ningizidda, son of the god Ninazu (Lord Doctor). Today it universally betokens the healing professions, particularly pharmacy.

MEDICINE AND TECHNOLOGY

Numerous medical texts survive from the library of Assurbanipal at Nineveh, the last Assyrian capital, and related texts exist from much earlier periods. There are two main classes of such texts: descriptions of symptoms and lists of remedies. A pharmacopoeia from the Ur III period is the earliest known medical text. Since illness was often thought to result from divine intervention or demonic possession, patients could be treated either to heal the symptoms or to expel the malefactor.

(From H. and R. Leacroft, *The Buildings of Ancient Mesopotamia, Leicester,* 1974)

In a modern Marsh Arab village, the mudjhif *(guesthouse) exhibits the "column" of reed bundles so similar to an Ionic (Classical Greek) column.*

A text from the Neo-Assyrian period lists the names of certain plants, the diseases for which they were prescribed, and methods of administration. By far the largest group of medical texts is a first millennium compilation of forty tablets entitled *enūma āshipu* (if an exorcist . . .) after its opening lines. This reference book restricts itself almost exclusively to the patient's behavior and appearance; only the badly damaged fourth section mentions treatment. Medical texts written in the style of omen texts, with "if-then" clauses, refer to the physician (*asû*) instead of the exorcist (*āshipu*) and accompany descriptions of specific symptoms with detailed instructions on appropriate medications. A wide range of medicinal herbs and minerals was available to the Babylonian *asû*.

Babylonian medical texts demonstrate extensive knowledge of herbal medicine, including several drugs of known medicinal value. In ancient Egypt and possibly in Mesopotamia, for example, a cure was known for the skin disorder vitiligo. The plant-derived cure, transmitted to some north African tribes, was not rediscovered by modern medicine until 1947. Medical texts written in cuneiform indicate that a wide variety of diseases, including contagious types, were known and treated.

Clinical examinations were performed, but anatomical and physiological knowledge appears to have been rudimentary. As the Code of Ḫammurapi testifies, some surgery was performed;

TURRIS BABEL

(Courtesy of the Behmann Archive, Inc.)

*Medieval conception of Tower of Babel, depicting a ziqqurat of spiral
construction (after a copper engraving of the seventeenth century).*

surgeons seem to have been adept at setting broken bones. Mesopotamian physicians never enjoyed the fame of their Egyptian counterparts, perhaps partly because the penalty for surgical error in Babylonia was mutilation or death. One can only lament the disappearance of the Babylonian system for the payment of medical fees: the charge varied with the patient's social status.

Technology

Modern knowledge of Babylonian technology derives chiefly from archaeological remains and from cuneiform vocabulary lists focusing on minerals, chemical substances, and technical matters. Rarely are technical knowledge or technological practices spelled out: they may have been well-kept secrets or else such common knowledge as not to warrant documentation. Formulas and recipes for making glass, glazes, perfume, and bronze have survived; but even in these instances, the precise technology is seldom revealed, and modern attempts to recreate the processes often fail. Babylonian chemists' familiarity with acids, sodas and silicates, lime, and even metals and metallic oxides made possible such industries as leather tanning, wool dyeing, and the production of soap, glazes, frits, and glass. Technological development is attested by archaeological finds of crucibles, filtering apparatuses, distillation and extraction equipment, drip bottles, mortars and pestles, mills, and strainers.

The wool industry—spinning, fulling, weaving—was already well developed in the prehistoric era. Even earlier, ceramic and metallurgical industries had begun to evolve. The very earliest attempts to make pottery succeeded by about 8000 B.C. at Mureybet in northern Syria, but Mesopotamian potters only began producing a variety of ceramics in the sixth millennium B.C. The potter's wheel was invented no later than 4000 B.C.

Metal objects were often recycled, and thus little evidence remains to interpret earlier metallurgical developments. Copper in its natural state (called native copper) was used by 7000 B.C. Within 1,000 years, the first smelting operations were conducted; there is evidence for casting by 4000 B.C. By the beginning of the historical period, about 3000 B.C., coppersmiths smelted refined copper ores with arsenic or tin to form true bronze: thus began the Bronze Age. For analogous reasons, the first millennium B.C.—when iron was first used extensively—is called the Iron Age.

THE INTELLECTUAL ADVENTURE

By the time classical Greek civilization began to flourish, the ancient Near East had already accumulated 2,500 years of history. The complex socioeconomic, cultural, and political systems of ancient western Asia constituted an immense bloc whose profound influence on the succeeding Greek civilization is well recognized but imperfectly understood.

The people of the ancient Near East regarded the universe as animate, imbued with intelligence and will. Some modern commentators regard such a **mythopoeic** conception of the universe as nonrational, incapable of distinguishing between science and myth. Others cite ancient achievements in astronomy, medicine, and mathematics as clear evidence of the capacity for sophisticated scientific thought. In any case, the writings of Plato demonstrate forcefully that Greek thought did not abandon myth and fantasy. Instead, rational reflection on the universe continued to develop alongside mythological perspectives. Greek thought achieved its distinction and independence by delineating the principles of intellectual order, being and becoming, in the universe and by developing the disciplines of logic and epistemology—the study of the origins, nature, methods, and limits of knowledge.

No deep philosophical divide separated east and west. The Greeks freely borrowed elements of Near Eastern culture and thought—the alphabet, mathematics and music, anthropomorphic deities—but did not bind themselves to forms crystallized by millennia-old traditions. New, Greek outlooks on the universe took their place beside old, mythical, Near Eastern concepts. Supplementing old with new, myth with logic, the Greeks achieved a novel philosophical genius. "The Wonder that was Greece" can be fully appreciated only by recognizing that it was built on the cultures of ancient western Asia and Egypt.

SUPPLEMENTARY READINGS

Bowen, J. 1972. *A History of Western Education.* Vol. 1: *The Ancient World, Orient and Mediterranean, 2000 B.C.–A.D. 1054.* London: Methuen.

Hodson, F. R., ed. 1974. *The Place of Astronomy in the Ancient World.* London: Oxford University Press.

Mitchell, T. C., ed. 1974. *Music and Civilization.* British Museum Yearbook 4. London: British Museum.

Moscati, S. 1962. *The Face of the Ancient Orient.* Garden City, N. Y.: Doubleday Publishing.

Naveh, J. 1982. *Early History of the Alphabet: An Introduction to West Semitic Epigraphy and Paleography.* Jerusalem: Magnes Press, Hebrew University.

Neugebauer, O. 1957. *The Exact Sciences in Antiquity.* 2 ed. Providence, R.I.: Brown University Press.

―――――. 1975. *A History of Ancient Mathematical Astronomy.* 3 vols. Studies in the History of Mathematics and Physical Sciences I. Berlin: Springer Verlag.

GLOSSARY

Absolute dating   Precise dating in terms of calendar years (e.g., 910 B.C., A.D. 1986).

Acrophonic   The arrangement of words, word-signs, or syllables according to their initial sound or sign.

Alluvial plain   Relatively flat tract of land where (usually) fertile soil has been deposited by a river.

Bronze   Alloy of copper and tin, typically consisting of nine parts copper to one part tin.

C–14 dating   See **Radiocarbon dating**.

Calibration/Calibration curves   A correction process conducted on radiocarbon dates to adjust them to calendar years, utilizing dates obtained from counting (annual) tree rings from dead timber, and represented graphically in the form of a curve. Most published radiocarbon dates are uncalibrated and are therefore "raw" dates in radiocarbon years.

Carburization   Process of heating bloomery iron (relatively pure iron with bits of slag) in direct contact with charcoal. Carbon is then absorbed into the iron, and areas where they combine are converted into steel.

Cartouche   Oval or oblong figure that encloses Egyptian hieroglyphs expressing royal or divine names and titles.

Cataract   Waterfall or rapids on a river that make navigation

difficult but not impossible.
There are six cataracts on the
River Nile.

Chalcolithic   Translates as
"copper-stone." Period
associated with the widespread
use of copper for tools and
weapons, in conjuction with
stone tools and weapons.

Copper ingots   Smelted/melted
copper cast in a mold. During
the Bronze Age, ingots were
often cast in the shape termed
"oxhide."

Corvée   Unpaid work done in
lieu of rental payments, taxes, or
other services owed.

Cosmogonic   Concerning the
theory of the origin of the
universe. The Genesis tradition
holds that all real beginnings
issued from divine commands
and acts.

Culture (archaeological)
Common and recurrent
assemblages of artifacts in space
and time.

Culture (general)   The totality
of human activity—behavioral
patterns, beliefs, arts,
institutions—common to a group
of individuals. Culture is
transmitted by learning, not by
genetic inheritance.

Cuneiform   System of writing
developed in southern
Mesopotamia that used "wedge-
shaped" signs impressed into
clay or clay tablets.

Cylinder seal   Small stone or
metal cylinder carved with
various designs or inscriptions
and rolled over wet clay to leave
an impression. Cylinder seals

were often used to indicate
ownership.

Delta   Lower Egypt, where the
Nile River splits into a number of
tributaries before reaching the
Mediterranean Sea; so called
from the delta-shaped (from the
Greek letter Δ) alluvial plain that
contains the river's tributaries
and its deposited soils.

Dendrochronology   Dating
dead timber by counting the
annual growth rings of the tree.

Desiccation   In arable land, the
drying-up process due to low
rainfall and/or the overuse of
resources by people and
animals.

Divination   Various methods
employed to forecast events
distant in space and time.

Domestication   The taming and
breeding of plants or animals for
human use. Most plants and
animals used in modern
agriculture have been
domesticated.

Ecology   A system of
relationships between organisms
and their environment.

Extispicy   A form of divination
that examines the entrails of
animals to forecast events.

Food production   Cultivation of
crops and breeding of animals to
provide food for human use.

Galena   The principal ore of
lead (often used by the
Egyptians as makeup).

Gloss   Brief explanatory word, note, or translation of a difficult or technical expression, usually in the margin of a text. In cuneiform texts, especially the Amarna letters, the *Gloss* is indicated by a marker and is in the form of a "Canaanite" word that defines or clarifies the preceding Akkadian word.

Gulf   The body of water between the eastern Arabian Peninsula and Iran.

Hepatoscopy   A form of divination that examines an animal's liver to forecast events.

Hieroglyphic   System of writing developed in ancient Egypt that uses pictures and abstract symbols to represent words and speech.

Historical period   Period of time characterized by the use of written documents. Cultural and historical interpretation is based on analyses of both written records and material remains.

Homo sapiens sapiens
Translates as "wise, wise man." The most recent (modern) genus of "man," whose earliest known appearance in the archaeological record is about 40,000–50,000 years ago.

Hydraulic civilizations   A culture or nation that utilizes irrigation for agriculture (e.g., ancient Egypt, Mesopotamia, India, China, or the Helmund River valley in eastern Iran).

Isohyet   In this book, the 8-inch (200 millimeter) minimum

annual rainfall line that demarcates the area where agriculture supported by rainfall is possible.

Jezirah   Area between upper reaches of the Tigris and Euphrates rivers in modern Iraq and Syria. It is the Arabic term for island.

Kārum   Akkadian word for the merchant's (commercial) area in a city or town.

Lapis lazuli   A semiprecious, deep-blue stone found in the Old World only in Afghanistan.

The Levant   The seaboard and hinterland of the eastern Mediterranean; synonymous in this book with the area of Syria-Palestine. From old French *levant* (rising)—said of the sun.

Limmu   Lists of Assyrian officials whose terms lasted for a single year; the Assyrians kept track of time by *limmu* years.

Malachite   Copper carbonate, green to black in color, chiefly used as a source for metallic copper but also as (highly polished) stone ornaments or, when powdered, as eye makeup.

Millennium   Period of 1,000 years.

Mudbricks   Mud shaped into various brick forms, usually sun-dried but occasionally kiln fired. Used for building in areas where timber and stone are scarce.

Mythopoeic "Mythmaking" thought. A term used by some scholars to distinguish between ancient Near Eastern thought processes and the more "logical" or rational thought that characterized classical (Greek-Roman) civilizations.

Neolithic Translates as "new stone." The period associated with the beginnings of agriculture and typified by the extensive use of stone tools and implements.

Nome Administrative district in pharaonic Egypt, headed by a **nomarch**. There were twenty nomes in Lower Egypt and twenty-two in Upper Egypt.

Obelisk Tall, four-sided stone pillar, often decorated with inscriptions and reliefs; commonly used in ancient Egypt.

Obsidian Extremely hard and sharp, dark, glass-like volcanic stone used for making tools or weapons.

Palaeography Study of ancient scripts and writing systems.

Palaeolithic Translates as "old stone." Period associated with the emergence of stone-tool–using Homo sapiens, beginning about 700,000 years ago and lasting until about 20,000–10,000 years ago. The period between about 20,000 and 10,000 years B.P. (before the present) is variously called Epipaleolithic or Mesolithic.

Palestine. Seaboard and hinterland of the southeastern Mediterranean Sea. Named after the Philistines, a group of the "Sea Peoples" who settled in this area in the twelfth century B.C.

Pastoralists Persons involved in animal husbandry. Sheep or goat herders who often live off their animals' products and whose living habits are largely nomadic but occasionally supplemented by crop planting at a base point.

Philologist Person who studies ancient languages and literatures.

Phonetic elements Sounds of speech, often represented by a set of distinct symbols, each of which denotes a single sound.

Pictographic writing A system of writing (like ancient Egyptian) that uses pictures to represent words, sounds, and ideas.

Prehistoric period Period of time wherein writing was not used. Cultural interpretation is based solely on analyses of material remains (e.g., stone, bone, architecture, and art).

Pyramid Massive stone monument with rectangular base and four triangular faces culminating in a single apex; burial place for Egyptian pharoahs.

Quenching Plunging hot metal (e.g., iron) into cold water or other medium for rapid cooling. Most commonly used in the process of making steel.

Radiocarbon dating   Method of obtaining "raw" (approximate) dates by counting the rate of decay of radioactive carbon isotopes (^{14}C) in samples of charcoal or other organic matter such as shell, teeth, or bone. The time *limit* for radiocarbon dating—using a particle accelerator—is currently about 100,000 years.

Rainfed agriculture   Agriculture that relies on regular rainfall as the principal source of water. Such agriculture can only be undertaken in temperate zones where the average annual rainfall exceeds 8 inches (200 millimeters).

Relative dating   A date expressed in relation to a known sequence of artifacts or cultures. The date may be earlier or later than, or contemporary with, a known sequence or event, but it usually cannot be expressed in exact calendar years.

Salinization   A process whereby the amount of salt minerals or alkali in the soil builds up and renders the soil unsuitable for agriculture. Salinization is often the result of extensive irrigation in areas with a high salt water table.

Satrap   Ruler or governor of an administrative district or province (**Satrapy**) in the Achaemenid (Persian) empire.

Seminomadism   See **Pastoralists**.

Scribe   Public official responsible for letter writing, record-keeping, and accounts.

Scribes were among the very few literate persons in ancient Near Eastern society.

Steppe   Semiarid plain, often covered with seasonal grasses in springtime after winter's rains; the steppe in western Asia is often heavily utilized by pastoralists with their herds.

Stratification   Accumulated sequences (strata) of occupational debris that typify archaeological sites.

Tell   A mound that results from repeated construction, occupation, and destruction on the same site over an extended period of time. The layers that represent these various activities are said to be stratified, one under (or over) the other.

Unilinear   Development in a single progression ("one line"), usually referring to a presumed sequence of cultural developments.

Vizier   Prime minister of Egypt responsible for administration of the land; in power, second only to the pharaoh.

Wadi   (Arabic) Dried-up river bed, gully, or valley that remains dry except during the rainy season.

Ziggurat   Mesopotamian step-tower of successively receding stories, with a shrine dedicated to a specific divinity at the top.

INDEX

i

A Note on the Type

The text of this book was set in 10/12 Palatino using a film version of the face designed by Hermann Zapf that was first released in 1950 by Germany's Stempel Foundry. The face is named after Giovanni Battista Palatino, a famous penman of the 16th century. In its calligraphic quality, Palatino is reminiscent of the Italian Renaissance type designs, yet with its wide, open letters and unique proportions it still retains a modern feel. Palatino is considered one of the most important faces from one of Europe's most influential type designers.

Composed by Carlisle Communications, Ltd., Dubuque, Iowa

Printed and bound by R. R. Donnelley & Sons Company, Crawfordsville, Indiana